General Subject-Indexes
Since 1548

PUBLICATIONS OF THE A. S. W. ROSENBACH
FELLOWSHIP IN BIBLIOGRAPHY

General Subject-Indexes Since 1548

By Archer Taylor

Philadelphia

University of Pennsylvania Press

7508
Printed in the United States of America

For
Hasseltine

Preface

THIS HISTORICAL AND CRITICAL ACCOUNT OF GENERAL SUB-ject-indexes is concerned with those in Latin and vernacular European languages in so far as they have come to my attention. I do not include those written in other languages and mention only rarely those compiled in medieval and earlier times. The terms "general subject-index" and "subject-index" refer to classified or alphabetical lists of references to books and articles. The emphasis is on the adjective "general" because the works under consideration are encyclopedic in scope. I will identify subject-indexes limited to a single field and its sub-divisions (for example, folklore, geography, or medicine), to writings of a particular kind such as dissertations, journal articles, government publications, or bibliographies, and to publications belonging to a particular period or country and refer to them for special purposes.

A subject-index resembles many other kinds of reference works, especially an encyclopedia, but differs from each of them in significant ways.[1] Bibliographers have not recog-

[1] I hope to discuss these reference works on another occasion.

nized the general subject-index as a category of bibliography and have, except in bibliographies of bibliographies, mentioned few of the works here discussed. It is a reference work primarily useful to a scholar with historical interests. The latest examples with an emphasis on currently useful titles have a general utility for immediately practical purposes but usually cannot compete with the subject catalogue of a large library.

These subject-indexes are discussed with reference to their place in an historical development and to their contemporary and modern value. The historical orientation is developed by references to the life, training, and interests of the compiler and by comparisons with earlier and later works of the same kind. I have tried to indicate briefly their accuracy, completeness, and convenience with adequate supporting evidence. The older and less familiar indexes are more fully described than modern ones, and indexes which are still useful have been more generously considered than those of little value. Except for those generally known and easily available, the individual indexes have been illustrated with enough quotations for the reader to form an independent judgment concerning their style, their intrinsic merits, and their possible usefulness today. In order to make a comparative appraisal, I have chosen articles on Astronomy, Bibliography, English history, and Medicine, with supplementary remarks as to their special weakness or strength in other fields. These four subjects seem most likely to indicate adequately the quality of the bibliographer's work and at the same time to have some contemporary scholarly value. The history of astronomy and of medicine are now of great interest to specialists. In the other two fields, the competence of the bibliographer will soon be evident as he deals with bibliography which he should know well or with English history which he usually knows only from reference books.

Subject-indexes exist in Arabic, Chinese, and other languages with which I am not acquainted. As far as I can see, knowledge of them has come late to the western world, and they have not had a discernible influence. George Sarton seems to be one of the few western scholars to cite them in a general work. For example, he remarks, "I must say here, once for all, that anyone undertaking to study the history of science and civilization in the second half of the tenth century, from whatsoever angle, must begin by consulting 'The Keys of the Sciences,' the letters of the 'Brethren of Purity,' and the 'Fihrist.'" The *Kitāb al-fihrist* or, more usually, the *Fihrist* (index), completed in A.D. 987 by Mohammad b. Ishaq an-Nadīm (al-Warraq), the son of a Baghdad bookseller, has been described as "an index of the books of all nations on every branch of knowledge with biographical particulars concerning their authors and compilers, since the beginning of every science that has been invented down to the present epoch." [2]

[2] Christopher Dawson, *The Making of Europe*, London, 1932, pp. 163–164. On the *Fihrist* see George Sarton, *Introduction to the history of science* (3 vols. in 5), Baltimore, 1927–48, I, 648, 662; G. Brockelmann, *Geschichte der arabischen Literatur* (2nd ed., 2 vols. and 2 vols. supplement), Leiden, 1944–1949, I, 153; Supplement I, pp. 226–227. It was not the first Arabic work of its kind; see Julius Lippert, "Ibn al-Kufî, ein Vorgänger Nadîms," *Wiener Zeitschrift für Kunde des Morgenlandes*, XI (1897), 147–155. For two recent examples of the use of the *Fihrist* by western scholars see Ben Edwin Perry, *Fabula*, III, 1959, pp. 5–27; H. G. Farmer, "Tenth century Arabic books on music: as contained in 'Kitāb al-Fihrist' of Abu'l-Faraj Muhammad ibn al-Nadīm," *Annual of Leeds University Oriental Society*, II, 1959–1961, which I have not seen.

I have not seen another work cited as a subject-index, and it appears to be an interesting example of lexicographical method rather than bibliography. This is Ali ibn Isma'il ibn Sidah, called Ibn Sidah (d. 1066), *Al-mukhassas fi al-lughah* (roughly equivalent to *The realm of language*, ed. Muhammad Mahmud al-Shin-Kite

Many books cited in this study have been forgotten, and many are difficult to locate, even in large libraries. Therefore I have been generous with quotations and with citing locations of the volumes. Examples of bibliographical style have been quoted in the original, especially when my intention is to illustrate the compiler's technique. In such quotations, I have not ordinarily tried to identify or control his references, except when there is a question of his accuracy. I have usually translated or paraphrased a bibliographer's comment. Bibliographical details have often been incorporated in the text because they are significant in the context. In an historical and critical account of a bibliography, the title, date and place of publication, and the number of references given are pertinent matters for the reader. The title and especially the subtitle of older bibliographies often tell the compiler's purpose. The date of publication suggests the historical background. The place of publication may imply the scholarly milieu. The number of volumes and pages and the number of references cited are guides to the size of the bibliography and are likely to indicate its importance. Books cited by short titles and books cited with only a date of publication have been quoted frequently and will be cited with additional bibliographical details in the bibliographies at the end of the study. I have tried to be precise in reference to pages, generous in the quantity and quality of quotations, and exhaustive in the index. For the purposes of this study it

and others, 17 pts., Bulak, 1898-1903), an encyclopedic dictionary arranged according to subjects. See Brockelmann, *Geschichte*, I, 376 and especially Supplement I, 542, n. 1, citing western parallels and discussing the problems of its arrangement. It may serve here as an example of the difficulty of identifying these works. I am particularly indebted to Professor Donald B. Sands and Dean Joseph A. Devenny, S. J., of Boston College for information about this book.

has seemed unnecessary to describe the arrangement of these subject indexes beyond the terms "classified" and "alphabetical." In other words, I have attempted to write a history of indexes rather than a history of cataloguing. At the end of the last century A. G. S. Josephson wrote "The crowning point of our work, that makes it the necessary servant of all sciences, and that renders it a science itself, is the 'subject bibliography.' " [3] This study intends to be an historical description of one variety of subject bibliography.

This study goes beyond the usual practice in citing examples of how subject-indexes have been or might be used. In my opinion, writers about reference books have too often assumed that readers can use them readily. The examples serve two purposes: they characterize a particular subject-index and they show both its value and the value of subject-indexes generally. A student of chemistry or of law perceives at once the usefulness of a reference to a carbon compound or to a legal decision. The usefulness of general subject-indexes seems to be less readily appreciated. Perhaps the difficulty of getting from a specific question to a category is a handicap, such as moving from a question about William Caxton to the heading, Printing. In choosing examples I have sought for the concrete and practical and for variety, while avoiding the obvious and banal.

The compiler of a bibliography is a self-effacing man with a desire to serve the common welfare who deserves to be judged in a kindly spirit. The compiler of a general subject-index has undertaken a task exceeding any man's strength and resources and can justly claim our sympathetic understanding. It is shooting fish in a rain-barrel to

[3] *The Library Journal*, XIX (1894), 227.

point out his deficiencies. Anyone with special knowledge
of a field or with access to great libraries or abundant
resources can easily find a stick with which to beat a dog.
I have tried to avoid such sport. I have tried to point out
a compiler's merits as generously as I could and to explain
his deficiencies. My intention is to write a historical and
interpretative study that is incidentally useful as a practical guide to subject-indexes.

Titles are cited in italics, but otherwise in a style generally similar to library practice. The first word after "or"
or "sive" in a sub-title is capitalized. In Latin titles the
use of *i* and *j* or *u* and *v* is standardized. In German titles
the ordinary rules for capitalization are followed. Books
cited with a date but without a place of publication are
listed in a bibliography at the end of this study. Others
are cited in full, when they are mentioned. References to
headings in subject-indexes are indicated by the use of
capitals without quotation marks: Anatomy, Giant, or
Zoology signifies an article identified by these words. In
citing headings in alphabetical subject-indexes, page or
column references have usually been dispensed with unless the extent of the article is significant.

The subject of this book was briefly discussed in lectures for the A. S. W. Rosenbach Foundation of the University of Pennsylvania in April, 1961. I am indebted to
the Foundation for this opportunity to organize my ideas
once more and for printing this substantially enlarged
version of the lectures. Early in his life Mr. Rosenbach
compiled a bibliography of some 14,000 items dealing
with English authors and throughout his life he was keenly
interested in bibliography and its problems. In a general
way, therefore, this book continues studies to which he
gave much time and thought.

It is pleasant to recall and thank once more the many persons and institutions that have aided me in this work. Without generous assistance it could never have been completed. A fellowship of the John Simon Guggenheim Memorial Foundation made it possible for me to continue and enlarge my collections in European libraries. Friends in the University of Pennsylvania Library have given me practical help and good counsel, notably Dr. Rudolf Hirsch, who read the manuscript closely and made invaluable suggestions for its improvement, and Mr. Jesse C. Mills. I owe much to Bibliotheksrat Dr. Johannes Widmann, Universitätsbibliothek, Tübingen; Dr. Rudolf Blum, Deutsche Bücherei, Frankfurt a.M.; Dr. Erik Dal, Kongelige Bibliotek, Copenhagen; Dr. Anna Birgitta Rooth, her husband Dr. Gösta Rooth, and Dr. Jan-Öjvind Swahn, all of the University of Lund, Sweden. Professor Vittorio Santoli, University of Florence, enlisted Professor Cesare Segré, University of Milan, in discovering for me the long-overlooked second edition of Fabianus Justinianus, *Index universalis alphabeticus.* My friend Lucien Gerschel has searched Parisian libraries for me with a skill and success that awaken my admiration. I am peculiarly grateful to him because he undertook the task when circumstances made it difficult for him to give time to it. In this country Professors Donald B. Sands, Boston College; Professor Donald F. Bond, University of Chicago; Dr. R. H. Rouse, Cornell University; Professors Hugh Dick and B. M. Woodbridge, Jr., University of California; Professor William A. Jackson, Harvard University; Professor Francis Very, Northwestern University; the staff of the University of California Library; and especially Dr. Stanley Pargellis, Mrs. Mabel Erler, and Mr. James M. Wells of the Newberry Library, Chicago, have helped me.

Contents

16 CONTENTS

General Subject-Indexes
Since 1548

1

The Nature and Arrangement of Subject-Indexes

THE NATURE OF SUBJECT-INDEXES

AGAIN AND AGAIN MEN HAVE CONCEIVED THE BOLD IDEA OF
a subject-index embracing all knowledge and have endeavored to execute it. A list of all that has been written
on all subjects would be obviously useful and its compilation has at times seemed possible. The history and criticism of such endeavors are the subjects of this study. The
idea is allied to efforts to classify knowledge, but makers
of subject-indexes have ordinarily learned little from them.
The classifications contain few references to books, and
makers of subject-indexes have preferred their own plans
of arrangement. The schemes for arranging books in libraries also classify and organize information, but they
are largely independent of philosophical classifications
of knowledge. The practical exemplifications of these
schemes in library catalogues are subject-indexes of a sort,

but being limited to the books owned by a single man or institution, they have been generally recognized as an independent variety of bibliography. A few examples of library catalogues will be discussed in this study for special reasons. Neither the theoretical classifications of knowledge nor the practical classifications of books have had much influence on the development of subject-indexes. Their characteristics and histories are extremely interesting, but can be best studied in other connections.

Subject-indexes are reference works that collect bibliographical references and arrange them in various ways. They do not contain discussions of the subjects listed or, if they do, the remarks go little further than definitions. Some subject-indexes have a universal scope or deal with subjects grouped together as "philosophy" in its former meaning of all learning other than theology, law, and medicine. This meaning we still have in the academic title "doctor of philosophy." Books of this sort will be discussed in this study.

The restriction of "philosophy" to more or less its modern sense occurred in the latter half of the seventeenth century and needs more discussion than would be appropriate here. Since this study is concerned with general subject-indexes and does not deal with indexes of particular disciplines, it will include seventeenth-century bibliographies of philosophy and pass over those published in the eighteenth century and later. Paulus Bolduanus, *Bibliotheca philosophica* (1616) will be commented on at length and Burkhard Gotthelf Struve, *Bibliotheca philosophica* (Jena, 1704) will not be mentioned again. The meanings of "philosophy" illustrate a serious and unavoidable difficulty in the use of subject-indexes. This word and many other words used as headings in subject-indexes have altered their meanings in the course of time and thus created difficulties for one in finding quickly and easily the information one wants. Such difficulties annoyed men three centuries ago (although they did not often comment on them) and it will annoy a modern user. J. F. Reimmann, an early eighteenth-century bibliographer, offers a good example of this situation in his comment on Ambrosius Rhodius, *Mathematicarum disciplinarum encyclopediae* (Wittenberg, 1611. Not seen).[1] He condemns Rhodius for including judicial astrology, chiromancy, and metoscopy among the mathematical sciences. Whatever we may now think of this classification, men in 1611 regarded these subjects as mathematical in nature. Rhodius was employing a classification that was soon to become obsolete, but we must be familiar with it, if we are to consult the encyclopedic and bibliographical works of his day with any ease. We are likely to agree with Reimmann in his objections to Rhodius's categories, but we would not agree with him in rejecting "mimi ridicula spectacula" as a subject not related to comedy and tragedy.

Bibliographers have recognized the subject-indexes of the three major disciplines of theology, law, and medicine and the subject-indexes of special fields like art, Buddhism, economics, electricity, or zoology as a variety of bibliography. In large and carefully made reference works such subject-indexes will usually be identified as a separate category. They will be mentioned only incidentally in this study. Bibliographers do not, however, recognize general subject-indexes as a category of bibliography. Julius Petzholdt, Theodore Besterman, and Mlle Louise-Noëlle

---

[1] *Bibliotheca historiae literariae* (Hildesheim, 1743), pp. 314–315. The title of Rhodius's book is an early instance of the word "encyclopedia."

Malclès, who can properly be called our best authorities, cite general subject-indexes among bibliographical dictionaries, bibliographies of bibliographies (to which subject-indexes are closely allied), guides to reference works, and the like. Nor are general subject-indexes brought together in one place on library shelves. They may be found with books of ana, books on the theory of knowledge, reference books, and in still other places. Although the authors intended them to serve general needs, they often fail to get on the shelves of a reference room.

During the last four centuries a few dozen general subject-indexes have been planned or compiled. With the passage of time those that were published have become rare books known to few and used by even fewer scholars. Reasons for this neglect are not difficult to find. With occasional exceptions they have not been recognized for what they are. Many have been published by firms that could not give them wide circulation and thus ensure their appreciation and use. If one can draw an inference from their infrequent occurrence in the antiquarian trade, the editions have been small. The neglect of subject-indexes —here, as always, I refer to works of general scope—arose also from their frequently unsatisfactory quality. Men who had neither the training and ability necessary for the task nor the resources to execute it have all too often undertaken it. These men were very likely not to be in the main stream of bibliographical studies and rarely informed themselves sufficiently about what had already been done. They failed to enlarge upon the good qualities or to avoid the faults of their predecessors. It is not surprising that critics have spoken harshly about their labors and that scholars have neglected their books. I have not refrained on occasion from defending men whose enthusiasm carried them further than a cautious man with adequate preparation and resources might have gone. Perhaps the chief reason for the failure to appreciate and use general subject-indexes is the fact that they offer to do more than can be humanly performed and therefore disappoint their users. Their universal scope means that any reader will find that subjects with which he has a special familiarity have been incompletely and unsatisfactorily treated. A generation ago H. G. Wells, *An outline of history* had a similar fate. Readers found it stimulating and informative in every field but the one in which they had a special competence. So it has been with general subject-indexes. Few have been often consulted even two generations after their publication, and none has been kept up to date by revision and supplements. Subject-indexes of less than general scope where a long process of selection and improvement has been operative have had a happier fate, but with them we are only incidentally concerned.

THE ARRANGEMENT OF SUBJECT-INDEXES

Men have chosen three ways to arrange the headings of a subject-index: (1) a classification according to an essential and widely used text that embraced all knowledge, (2) a logical organization with a place for every subject, and (3) an alphabetical listing of headings. This might be either a single alphabet that included all headings or four alphabets, one each for theology, law, medicine, and philosophy.

Subject-indexes have developed historically in the sequence just described, their materials being arranged according to an accepted standard work, in a logical scheme, and in an alphabetical order. An example will show the characteristics of these three methods as well as suggest their advantages and disadvantages. In the *Household Tales* (*Kinder- und Hausmärchen*) the Brothers Grimm offered a generous sampling of the best and most popular German folktales. Since they attached comparative notes to the collection, scholars found it convenient to refer to them. In 1857, after Wilhelm's death, Jacob Grimm enlarged these notes into a survey of folktales generally. For more than half a century the third volume of the *Household Tales* was virtually an encyclopedia of the folktale. It lacked adequate indexes and did not include many tales unknown in Germany, but it was the foundation of comparative study and has remained so in an enlarged edition in five volumes by Johannes Bolte and Georg Polívka (Leipzig, 1912–1932). Almost immediately after the publication of the volume of 1857 scholars proposed systematic classifications to replace the haphazard order of the *Household Tales*. These were tentative and incomplete until Antti Aarne published a classification of thousands of tales collected in Finland. This has been accepted as standard and is still used. Finally, Henning Fredrik Feilberg (1831–1921), who was born and reared in Copenhagen and spent his life in a Jutland parish, made an alphabetical list. It came about in a curious way. He found the local dialect so different from his own that he began making a dictionary.[2] In it he included references to traditional materials of all kinds without regard to the countries where they had been collected. The article "Ring" is typical of his method. After commenting on dialectical matters, he gave references to the use of a ring as a symbol of engagement or marriage, mentioned the medieval story of

---

[2] *Bidrag til en ordbog over jyske almuesmål* (4 vols., and suppl., Copenhagen, 1886–1914).

a young man who slipped a ring on a statue's finger and found himself married to it and the classical story of Polycrates's ring that was recovered from a fish, and concluded with references to magic rings, superstitions and customs concerning rings, and riddles about rings. In brief, Feilberg has given us a subject-index of folklore generally, and incidentally of folktales. These three methods of arrangement—notes on a familiar text, a logical system, and an alphabetical order—have been employed in the same historical sequence in the subject-indexes discussed in this study.

In any subject-index the headings necessarily have a more or less abstract quality. In a classified subject-index the defects of this quality are increased by the fact that the compiler employs a classification that does not arise directly from the materials. He has fitted references into categories and has not made categories to include references. The user must repeat the process of abstraction that the compiler employed to go from a question to the place where information will be found. It is obvious that the more direct the passage from the question to the answer the more convenient the reference book will be. In subject-indexes generally we see the victory of an alphabetical arrangement in the making. After a century and a half Robert Watt's *Bibliotheca britannica* with an alphabetical arrangement has come into its own and is justly appreciated. Courtney's *Register of national bibliography*, which was made two generations ago, owes its popularity to an alphabetical arrangement, although complicated by the use of four alphabets. The subject-indexes of the British Museum and the London Library confirm the trend. The failure of Hirshberg's *Subject Guide* and Murphey's *How and where to find it* does not arise from their arrangement but from defects that will be discussed.

In a lecture given fifty years ago (Nov. 30, 1911) before the Bibliographical Society, G. K. Fortescue pointed out some disadvantages of a classified arrangement. His experience of thirty years in indexing the 262,651 titles in the first five volumes of the British Museum *Subject-index* led him to say:

The compiler of a scientific class catalogue begins by taking a number of sweeping class headings such as Theology, History, Sociology, Belles Lettres, and so forth. He then proceeds to divide and sub-divide and classify and specify until he imagines he has arrived at something approximating to a correct classification of human knowledge. Having accomplished this more or less impossible task, he endeavors to force his books into one or the other of the hundreds or thousands of classes and sub-classes he has formed to receive them; his work is in vain, the books will not fit into his pigeon-holes, and the result is inevitable failure.[3]

His criticism is not entirely fair, for he does not refer here to the use of cross-references and he does refer to them in the discussion of an alphabetical arrangement. Brunet might also have given cross-references. Fortescue illustrates the difficulties that arise by an example:

[In] the best of Class-Catalogues, Brunet's Table Méthodique, the searcher will be compelled to grope his way through the main heading Sciences and Arts until he arrives at the sub-heading Medical Science.

At the end of this heading he will find a sub-sub-heading entitled Veterinary Science where he will find one-half of his subject, viz., books on the anatomy, physiology and history of the Horse. For the other half he will have to turn to quite another sub-heading of the main heading Sciences and Arts, namely, Gymnastic Exercises, when [where?] he will discover the literature of horsemanship.

[3] See *Transactions of the Bibliographical Society*, XII (1911–1913, pub. 1914), 4.

A LOOK BACK

In the Middle Ages and the early Renaissance a scholar could consult many conveniently arranged books for information about subject matter. They were not listed then as reference works nor have they been brought together under this heading since then, except in the most general fashion. Perhaps the most significant remark to be made about them as a group is that they were not sharply differentiated and do not fall easily into modern categories. A dictionary of words contained information about proper names and was likely to include and identify proverbs and ideas generally. A dictionary of proverbs, quotations, and sententious remarks did not separate them into these categories and might contain narrative materials or textual criticism. An index of themes served as sculptor, artist, or writer of emblems and could suggest illustrations of general ideas. A collection of stories yielded ideas and instances pertinent to widely different kinds of subjects: avarice, good faith, officials, tyrants, and marriage. Conrad Gesner looked upon Aesop's Fables as a treatise on ethics. Renaissance readers of collections of stories often found them classified according to subjects. The variety and nature of these books were familiar knowledge to a Renaissance scholar. He knew them from daily use and did not need to have the purposes they served named and pointed out in the way I have tried to point them out. It was enough to call one of these books "a work indispensable to teachers, preachers, and writers" (opus docentibus, concionantibus, ac scriptoribus pernecessarium).

2

Subject-Indexes Based
on the Bible

THE ARRANGEMENT OF INFORMATION ACCORDING TO A
familiar text—and for most purposes according to the
Bible—has been in use for a long time. It is still employed
in indexing legal knowledge according to codes. When
scholarship was largely theological in character and derived its final authority from the Bible, an index of this
sort was a convenient guide to subject matter. The discussion might concern economics or politics, but could
be easily classified according to a Biblical text. Antonio's
aphorism in *The Merchant of Venice*, "The Devil can cite
Scripture for his purpose," which is now virtually prover-
bial in the sense that good can be perverted to evil ends,
suggests that pertinent remarks on any subject can be
found in the Bible [1] and that consequently the Bible offers

[1] The idea was formulated in various ways at the time; see Morris
P. Tilley, *A Dictionary of the Proverbs in England in the Sixteenth
and Seventeenth Centuries* (Ann Arbor, 1950), D230.

nd his many successors. I shall mention here only
printed example and three characteristic English
s of indexes to sermons and other comments on
texts.

g the many titles cited by Walch a very rare and
tive *Bibliotheca* by Jacob Zannachius is the first
publication dealing with sermons and commen-
ccording to the order of the Biblical texts.[6] Petz-
omments (p. 499) briefly on it, and in a surpris-
nd manner. Besterman (*Beginnings*, pp. 27, 71–72)
it only on this authority. I have used a copy in
al Library at Copenhagen and a microfilm in the
rry Library. It has the instructive title: *Bibliotheca*
ica, sive Catalogus tam auctorum qui in Sacros
s Libros veteris et novi Testamenti in hunc usque
scripserunt, quam materiarum, quarum autores
tant, non solum ex Bibliotheca Gesneriana, quae
583. prodiit, verum etiam ex catalogis nundinan-
rancofurdensium, qui ab anno 1583. in lucem pro-
, collectus, & plus septuaginta autoribus recenti-
lurimum auctus, ut vice supplementi haberi possit:
n commune Christianorum commodum divulgatus.
ulum non bibliothecis tantum publicis privatisve
tuendis necessarium, sed & studiosis sacrae theolog-
pietatis ad studio melius formanda maxime utilissi-
& pernecessarium (Mulhouse, 1591, Ll. 20). The
s and interesting points concern the sources and the
sted use of the book. Zannachius has gathered refer-
from Josias Simler's edition of Gesner's *Bibliotheca*
ore correctly, his edition of an epitome of that work,
he Frankfurt fair catalogues since 1583. He has added

alch, IV, 370 cites editions of 1606 and 1608 unknown to
oldt and Besterman.

a handy frame of reference for materials that needs to be
classified.[2] The citing of Biblical texts to justify slavery or
the use of wine is too familiar to call for more than mention. We know well enough these uses of Scripture, but it
needs to be stressed that the texts are a way into the
thought of an earlier age. Both Catholic and Protestant
handbooks are guides on this way.

For those who knew the Bible well and were in the
habit of quoting it as a final authority—and in the Middle
Ages and even the Renaissance what scholar did not?—a
classification of subjects according to the Bible was natural
and convenient. Theology was a science and indeed the
queen of the sciences. Consequently everything that might
be an occasion for scholarly discussion could be stated in
theological terms or had Biblical connections of some sort
and could be referred to a Biblical text. Theology and
philosophy remained closely related for a long time and
have not yet completely lost contact. Although a philosopher might think in Aristotelian terms, he could readily
enlarge his argument and make it more forceful by an
appropriate Biblical citation. A jurist might arrange his

[2] Should a man write on habit (we might call his work a study
in psychology or ethics), Jer. 13: 23 gave him a text and his remarks
could be classified accordingly. In a letter of July 13, 1950, Ronald
H. Bainton of the Yale Divinity School kindly cites some Biblical
texts that served as guides to important subjects: Deut. 13, Titus
3:10, Luke 14:23 justified the persecution of heretics; Matt. 13:30,
Acts 5:34, and 2 Tim. 3:12 the claim to liberty. Gen. 1:22 and 2:18,
Eph. 5:32, and I Cor. 7:9 gave counsel about marriage. Gen. 4:19
justified bigamy and Mark 10:4 and Matt. 19:9 divorce. The condemnation of usury followed from Deut. 23:19–20 and Levit. 25:36.
Theories about property rested on Matt. 19:21, Acts 4:34 and 5:4.
Negro segregation had a basis in Acts 17:26. A wide range of
theories about government derived authority from such texts as
Judges 3:16 (the right to revolt); Ps. 82; Mark 12:17 (Matt. 21:41
and Luke 20:25); Romans 13. I Peter 2:17 and 2 Kings 2:17 were
a basis for the notion of government as a compact.

professional studies according to a code and at the same time show the social and theological bearing of his comment and decisions by a Biblical reference. A medical student, who looked to Hippocrates and Galen, could naturally find less for such purposes in the Bible. For the disciplines of theology, law, and philosophy an index of Biblical commonplaces yielded useful materials.

It is no longer easy for us to bring subjects into theological categories and find an appropriate Biblical text to classify them. We can proceed as a medieval or Renaissance scholar did and consult a concordance in search of it. The concordance should be in Latin, since the works to which it leads will also be in Latin.[3] It is difficult to proceed in this fashion because one probably does not have in mind the special Latin words needed in order to use the index easily. The bibliographies will not be helpful with cross-references. It is best to start with a book of Biblical commonplaces, that is to say, a handbook or dictionary of the most familiar ideas with references to pertinent Biblical texts. One can begin with sixteenth- or seventeenth-century compilations[4] or, perhaps more conveniently to-

[3] A suitable book for this purpose is Guilelmus Allotus (William Allot, d. 1590), *Thesaurus Bibliorum, omnem utriusque vitae antidotum secundum utriusque instrumenti veritatem & historiam . . . complectens* (Antwerp, 1577, 1581, 1590). The title suggests its intended use and the editions its success.

[4] See, for example, such an elaborate work as Johannes Binchius, *Mellifici theologici . . .* pars I [-V] (Amsterdam, 1658) with a good index of catchwords or works of more limited scope like [John Hart], *The Fort Royal of the Scriptures, or the Vade mecum concordance presenting unto the world an hundred heads of Scripture, most of them common placed for publique use. Wherein all (especially the weaker sort of Christians) may suddenly command most of all the rarities in the Book of God,* by an Admirer of the Word (Edinburgh, 1649. See Wing, H 950–953, citing five editions. Not seen) or [John Locke], *A common-place book to the Holy Bible; or, the Scriptures sufficiency practically demonstrated. Wherein whatsoever is con-*

---

day, with modern works li
bibliographica. Holy Scrip
Joy, *Harper's topical conco*
A route into these and c
through the name of an aut
the subject in question. Thi
in the case of guides to serr
on Biblical texts because th
authors. Their compilers fou
materials according to the B

There is a bibliography of
Johann Georg Walch (1693
ica selecta.[5] In this classical
eenth-century German biblic
ward to medieval, Reformatio
works of this kind and forwar
studies. He begins with a nir
and makes abundant and int

---

tain'd in Scripture, respecting doct
duced to the proper head; weighty
difficult texts illustrated, and explai
don, 1697. Pp. [xvi], 310, [x]. See
mark that the philosopher John Loc
was reprinted from the fifth Londor
He gave thought to its making; see
viz. . . . VI. His new method of
originally in French, and now tra
1706). On the meaning and use of
"Topos und commonplace" in Gerha
eds., *Strena Anglica* (Halle, 1956),
Marie Lechner, O. S. U., *Renaissa*
places; an historical investigation of t
used in all argumentation and persuas
the educational and literary traditioi
teenth centuries (New York, [1962]. P

[5] 4 vols.; Jena, 1757–1765; see Petz
See Caput VIII, Sectio vii (IV, 369–
turae sacrae." Walch is more a guide
sermons.

---

on him
the first
example
Biblical

Amon
unattra
separat
taries a
holdt c
ingly ki
can cit
the Ro
Newbe
theolog
Biblici
annum
non ex
anno 1
arum f
dierunt
oribus
atque i
Opusc
institi
iae &
mum
curiou
sugge
ences
or, m
and t

[6] W
Petzh

more than seventy authors that he turned up. His procedure suggests how scholars worked in 1591 and how they would have rejoiced in a subject-index to the *Bibliotheca* in addition to Gesner's *Partitiones*. Zannachius says that his work will be valuable for the common welfare and is needed by public and private libraries. Later authors of such theological works will not make such generous claims.

For our purposes an English work—John Wilkins, *Ecclesiastes: or, A discourse concerning the gift of preaching, as it falls under the rules of art* (London, 1646).[7]—is more significant and a better example than Zannachius's *Bibliotheca*. It contains (pp. 58–105) a very condensed bibliography of commentators on Biblical texts with marginal references to bibliographies of bibliographies of commentators. The works cited seem to be chiefly exegetical in quality. It also contains (pp. 113–115) a very interesting brief section dealing with books of commonplaces (see below). There is finally a subject-bibliography (pp. 176–322) in an order too difficult to describe. In this there are occasional citations of sermons, but the emphasis is on treatises and chapters in more or less encyclopedic theological works. The subjects are homiletic in character and may interest a student of Courtesy books and the contemporary Manner of life.

This description of Bishop Wilkins's handy bibliography probably gives an adequate idea of seventeenth-century aids for preachers. At that time such aids had some wider usefulness in obvious directions, but they are now rarely consulted. The standard authority was William Crowe, *The catalogue of our English writers on the Old and New*

---

[7] See Wing, W 2195. I use the seventh ed. (London, 1693, Pp. [xii], 328, [xiii]). This and other later editions contain additions in square brackets, but I cannot say when they were first made.

Testament (2d impression; London, 1668. See Wing, C7376) with an estimated ten thousand titles (see WBB, col. 441). It was the result of a long development lasting over more than two generations and such librarians of the Bodleian as Thomas James and James Verneuil shared in it.[8] It is significant that men of the seventeenth century chose to revise and elaborate this bibliography and did not deal similarly with more general subject-indexes.

A somewhat similar book, but not strictly limited to sermons was published only a century ago, and more recent examples can be turned up. It is enough to comment on the second volume of James Darling (1797–1862), *Cyclopaedia bibliographica* (1854, 1859). It may seem strange that a London bookseller should undertake a task of this sort, but publishers and booksellers have shown a liking for general bibliographies throughout the history of subject-indexes. Darling's first volume is a biobibliographical account limited almost exclusively to theologians. While it may prove handy for references to British theologians, its value is somewhat doubtful. Five years after its appearance he published a second volume with the subtitle *Subjects: Holy Scriptures.* It was clearly foreseen in the making of the first volume. He intended to proceed in this fashion in other fields of bibliography but gave no precise idea of his whole plan. Probably the next pair of volumes was to deal with literature.

The second volume (pp. xi, cols. 1907) contains some introductory and general bibliography (cols. 1–143). On

---

[8] James's Bodleian *Catalogus* of 1605 contained such a list (pp. 163–179) and [John Verneuil] revised it in *Catalogus interpretum S. Scripturae, iuxta numerum ordinem, quo extant in Bibliotheca Bodleiana. Olim a D. Jamesio in usum theologorum concinnatus, nunc vero altera fere parte auctior redditus* (Oxford, 1635. STC, 14448).

this follows a list of commentators on the books of the Bible (cols. 143–1786). Some foreign theologians are named, but Darling gives no adequate account of them. Such value as his list may have consists in his survey of what was written and preached in England. He begins with commentators of Genesis as a whole (cols. 143–149), proceeds to those who wrote on the first chapter (cols. 149–154), and then to those who wrote on the first verse (cols. 154–155) and goes through the whole Bible in this fashion. The writings on individual verses are usually sermons. Darling makes the book accessible to those who are not familiar with Biblical texts by an index (cols. 1901–1907 in triple columns) of "some chief topics." Typical topics are proper names (Aaron, Abel, Abigail), familiar incidents (the barren Fig-tree; Blind men, the two, healed; Blind man of Bethsaida); Parables (grouped under this heading); theological subjects (Apostolical benediction, Atonement of Christ, Baptism); and a few subjects of wider interest: Almsgiving; Ambition; Animals, Humanity to; Benevolence; Charity schools; Geology of the Creation). Darling does not often perceive that the laity might consult his book and does not index texts quoted as authorities in the discussion of slavery, the divine rights of kings, or divorce.[9]

A LOOK BACK

One can properly ask how useful were these subject indexes arranged according to Biblical texts. In the sixteenth and seventeenth centuries their number indicates that they were often used and the fact confirms the claims made on their title pages. When the books they cited be-

[9] For ways to discover such texts see above.

came difficult to find—and this happened quickly with sermons published as pamphlets—the indexes had little value. My copy of Darling's modern index was once in a church library and was discarded with few signs of use. The difficulties in using these indexes will no doubt deter modern scholars from consulting them freely, and their utility is limited to rather few subjects. Nevertheless, there is perhaps no easier place to find materials for the study, at least for its theological aspect, of the controversy about the Origin of the world as narrated in Genesis; see Darling, cols. 149–151 with many references to efforts to reconcile geological observations and the Bible. The preacher's emphasis on dogmas and supporting texts as well as the hortatory and homiletic temper of his sermons limit the amount of information to be obtained. One would probably not learn much about existing Superstitions from Darling's references under Acts 17:22 (col. 1710, with a cross-reference to "Sermons on present Errors and Vices," in the Author Index, col. 170). These indexes will be most useful for subjects usually dealt with in the pulpit and will only reluctantly yield information about other subjects. Darling's *Cyclopaedia* does not tell us much about superstitions, nor does Lynn Thorndike, *History of magic and experimental science,* because the authors are not sympathetic to the study of them. When they do touch on them, the references will often concern unexpected and therefore valuable sources.[10]

[10] An example is a valuable note on Dwarfs and Giants in George Sarton, *Introduction to the history of science* (3 vols. in 5; Baltimore, 1927–1948), III, ii, 1227–1228. This will be useful to many others than the student of the history of science.

3

Classified Subject-Indexes in the Sixteenth Century

THE CLASSIFICATION OF ALL KNOWLEDGE WITH CITATIONS OF
pertinent scholarly writings seemed a feasible enterprise
to Renaissance men.[1] For them the task was larger than
we might conceive it to be, for they included classical and
medieval works that we would omit without a second
thought. They named Euclid as a geometrician and Julius
Caesar as a historian of Gaul and cited their works. We
would restrict our choice of authors and titles to more
nearly contemporary times. The tremendous scope of the
task did not prevent Conrad Gesner (1516–1565) from
accomplishing it. Other men made plans for similar general subject-indexes and collected materials, but failed for
one reason or another to finish what they had begun.

[1] Medieval and Renaissance encyclopedias do not give much
bibliographical information and will therefore not be included in
this study.

Subject-indexes cannot be exhaustive and will vary from
instance to instance in the extent and nature of their choice
of titles. After Gesner no one had regarded classical and
Biblical authorities as calling for mention in subject-indexes. Few writers of subject-indexes after Gesner will
cite works in manuscript, but on this point practice varies.
The older writers of subject-indexes did not, as many recent writers do, intend to offer an account of the best
books, the best recent books, or the books chiefly in a
single language that deal with the subjects they list. Such
intentional selectivity does not appear in bibliographical
history before the nineteenth century.[2]

CONRAD GESNER, *PANDECTAE* (1548) AND *PARTITIONES* (1549)

The first volume (1545) of Gesner's enormous *Bibliotheca universalis* is a comprehensive international bi-

[2] The "Cent Buffets," an appendix to François Grudé de la Croix
du Maine, *Bibliothèque françoise* (Paris, 1584), is not a subject-
index, although occasionally it is cited as one. It is, as James M.
Wells tells me, a curious system of classification. La Croix du Maine
suggested putting a hundred books in each of one hundred bookcases and thus achieving an easily mastered accumulation of all
knowledge, but he cited neither authors nor titles. The system falls
down because there are actually 107 categories. The seven major
divisions—theology, arts and sciences, the description of the universe, matters concerning man, heraldry and genealogy, works of
God (metallurgy, birds and beasts, etc.), memoirs (literature, bibliography, foreign languages, illustrated books, etc.)—are explained in
various epistles. A handsome plate shows one of the bookcases. This
is comparable in some ways to Christofle de Savigny, *Tableaux*
(Paris, 1619. Pp. 37. First published in 1587), that Petzholdt mentions briefly (p. 23) in an account of systems of classification. He
does not know La Croix du Maine. One can also call it a plan for a
collection of best books. In general, both schemes of classification
and lists of best books will not be discussed in this study. An early
and influential example of a scheme of classification is Ramon Lull,
Arbor scientiae. There was an illustrated edition of this work, even
in the sixteenth century (Lyons, 1515. Ll. 224).

ographical dictionary. With it we shall be concerned only incidentally. The second and third volumes, entitled *Pandectae* and *Partitiones* respectively, are subject-indexes. There are cross references from them to the first volume implied in the mention of proper names, but Gesner made no attempt to excerpt it completely for his indexes. A great merit of the indexes is found in the large number of small headings employed, but these are not readily discovered, as we shall see.

According to Gesner's plan, the *Pandectae* consisted of twenty-one chapters or books. He calls them libri, and I shall adopt his term. He finished and published nineteen libri in 1548; the twenty-first liber dealing with theology was separately published in 1549 as the *Partitiones*. The twentieth liber dealing with medicine was never published. He did not explain this omission.

I shall describe the *Pandectae* first. After a brief table of contents that gives no more than the titles of the twenty-one libri, Gesner promises to publish the two lacking libri and a supplement of additions to the biographical dictionary. This supplement was published in 1555. He concludes these prefatory remarks with these verses:

Emptor et liber
Dic quid habes artis? Multos ego multa per annos
Ex scriptis legi variis, multa otia rupi,
Ingeniis iuvenum minus ut labor arduus esset.
Nam quaecunque libet verbis tractare disertis,
Quicquid habeant artes, mundus, natura, Deusque,
Materies cunctis hinc multa & pulchra petetur.

The last two lines are no overstatement of the contents of Gesner's subject-indexes.

In seven closely printed folio pages Gesner tells the purpose of the *Pandectae* and explains how to use it. Then follows a dedication of the first liber [3] to his publisher, Christian Froschauer, with a list of important works that Froschauer had published. Each of the subsequent libri has a similar dedication, but the list is sometimes lacking as in the case of the dedication of liber V (fol. 73[a] to Robert Estienne). These lists are valuable sources for the history of printing. Gesner concludes the introduction with a detailed analytical table of contents of the first liber. This table of contents is an essential means of locating a desired topic. One must determine in the first or general table of contents (which gives only the titles of libri) the liber in which a desired subject appears and then turn to the analytical table at its beginning and find the right section. This is ordinarily easy to do, but there are divisions within sections and paragraphs within divisions, and neither divisions nor paragraphs are listed in the analytical table.

The fourth liber, "De poetica (Literature)," [4] is a good example of Gesner's methods. The first titulus deals with generalities about literature. It is not easy to see a plan of organization in it, but a final paragraph contains references to definitions of the poetic genres.[5] The second titulus, "De fabulis poeticis, ordine literarum," is an alphabetical list of classical themes used by poets.[6] In a prefatory paragraph he says that he excludes stories of the pagan gods, the moral tales of Aesop, and invented tales, i.e., romances and novels, because the first belong to pagan

[3] Here and elsewhere I shall use Gesner's terms liber and titulus for the sake of easy reference. We might render liber by "chapter" and titulus by "heading."

[4] Fols. 59[b]–72[b].

[5] Fol. 61[a], "Poëtarum & poëmatum differentiae secundum genera quaedam carminum, aut argumentum."

[6] Fols. 61[a]–62[a].

metaphysics and theology, the second to ethics, and the third will find a place after his account of true history. The themes listed have, he comments, no connection with the theological beliefs of those who used them. Their number can be increased by consulting indexes to the classical authors, especially those to the Basel edition of Athenaeus and "icones utriusque Philostrati." [7] There then follows a list of eleven writers on poetic themes, among whom are Philip Melanchthon, "De utilitate fabularum," the last oration in his *Declamationes;* Hyginus, and Fulgentius (who has been edited by Jakob Locher). The failure to mention Torrentinus (see below), a contemporary author of a work of this sort, deserves notice. A paragraph sign indicates a subdivision within this titulus. This contains a special bibliography of Ovid, Metamorphoses, a work with which he promises to deal at length later.[8] The following excerpts (references to sources are omitted and the headings are paraphrased rather than translated) show the nature of this list of themes:

Why Aeolus is king of the winds and what the arrows of Aeolus are; Alcyon (in Lucian), an example of transformation; the allegory of the Chimaera; the Cyclops; Ixion's wheel; the Sirens; Tantalus standing in a swamp, but lacking water.

The third titulus, "De poetis qui Bucolica & Aeglogas scripserunt," begins with definitions.[9] Gesner then cites Aelian's remarks on Bucolic song and an anthology just

[7] The Basel edition of Athenaeus, *Deipnosophistae* was published in 1535. The second reference concerns the Aldine edition (1503) of Lucian's works. It contains "Icones Philostrati" and "Icones Iunioris Philostrati" and other writings. It can be found in Gesner's biobibliographical dictionary, but not easily. This will serve as a sample of the more difficult references to be contended with.

[8] Fol. 61ᵃ. For the second bibliography of Ovid see Titulus V, Pars ii (fol. 64ᵇ).

[9] Fols. 62ᵃ–62ᵇ.

published by Oporinus. He concludes with a list of more
than forty writers from Actius Syncerus to Titus Calphur-
nius Siculus, who have written bucolic poetry and ec-
logues. The very brief fourth titulus deals with Georgics.[10]
The fifth titulus, which deals with poets in general and
chiefly the writers of hexameters, consists of three subdivisions: Greek poets, Latin poets, and modern poets.[11]
The first is divided by center heads into lists of women and
men.[12] After these two alphabetical lists, he adds, in a separate paragraph, the names of some modern writers of
Greek verse.[13] Then alphabetical lists of classical and modern Latin poets follow, the latter concluding with the
names of three vernacular poets, Dante, Petrarch, and
Clément Marot, and the remark that these are only a
sample.[14] He has shown what he can do and will deal
similarly with modern writers, if called upon. Writers of
Comedy, Tragedy, Satire, Lyric poetry, and minor genres
are similarly treated. "Dantis comoediarum liber" (fol.
66[b]) raises the suspicion that Gesner did not always "ver-
ify his references." Now and again solid bibliographical
work beyond these lists appears. For example, an alphabetical review of Authors quoted in the Planudean Anthology.[15] The names of three score modern writers of
Epigrams would be a good start for a literary historian
beginning the study of this Renaissance genre.[16] As was
the Renaissance custom, they are cited in alphabetical

---

[10] Fols. 62[b]–63[a].
[11] Fols. 63[a]–65–63[b].
[12] He adds the names of Roswitha and St. Matilda and says of the
latter, "Mechthildin etiam virginem in Germania scripsisse quaedam
fama est." References to medieval authors, other than theologians
and philosophers, are rare.
[13] Fol. 64[a] (indicated by a paragraph sign without a heading).
[14] Fol. 65[b].
[15] Fols. 71[a]–71[b].
[16] Fols. 72[a]–72[b].

order according to first names. Dates and places of publication are usually lacking; titles are loosely cited and are often lacking.

Throughout the *Pandectae* Gesner follows the same general plan: the first sections of a titulus contain definitions and general discussion, pertinent lists of writers follow in chapters, and special bibliographies may be introduced on occasion. These special bibliographies are not always clearly indicated by typographical devices or at least the devices used (often a paragraph sign) do not catch the eye until one has become familiar with the book. Particularly commendable is the careful use of cross-references. Gesner is compelled to give them according to book and chapter (liber and titulus) and not according to folios, but I have not found him failing to give the promised information. Thus, the previously mentioned references preceding the list of themes appear in their proper places: the stories of pagan gods under pagan metaphysics and theology,[17] the moral tales of Aesop under ethics,[18] and narrative fiction, which he calls "historiae fabulosae," at the end of the section for history (Liber XII, Titulus XIII [fol. 160^b]). In the last of these he names Lucian and Boccaccio, setting them apart from such love stories (*historiae amatoriae*) as the story of Eurialus and Lucretia by Aenas Silvius, the folktale or chapbook of Mélusine, and Boccaccio's Griseldis. Gesner's classification of narrative fiction as a variety of history soon disappears, and later subject-indexes do not often refer to fiction or belles lettres. His classification will suggest once more the difficulty of getting at the contents of older subject-indexes.

Another characteristic of Gesner's bibliographical tech-

---

[17] Liber XV, Titulus v, "Deorum gentilium & daemonum enumeratio particularis ordine literarum" (fols. 249ª–255ᵇ).
[18] Liber XVII, Titulus xxii, Pars 6 (fols. 286ª–286ᵇ).

nique is the utilization of unfilled pages for materials allied to the matter under discussion but inconvenient to classify and not always pertinent to a bibliography. Since these materials are not mentioned in the introductory analyses of the libri, one never knows precisely what to expect. For example, the last titulus of the liber dealing with history contains a list of names for which he could find no convenient place (fols. 161^a–163^b) and a final leaf is filled with a chronological list of Roman kings, consuls, and emperors down to Conrad (d. 919), the last of the Carolingian line (fols. 164^a–164^b).

Liber XIV, "De naturali Philosophia (Natural Philosophy)," is Gesner's subject bibliography of the physical sciences (fols. 181^a–236^b). The running head is "De physicis." The first titulus deals with general concepts and works of general scope and lists Commentators on Aristotle, *De physica* and similar writers (fols. 182^a–183^b). It concludes with collectanea dealing with general philosophical ideas like Necessity, Fortune, and Fate and specifically philosophical ideas like Motion (in the philosophical sense), Place, and Vacuum. The second titulus (fols. 184^a–186^b) deals with the Universe. It contains indexes of pertinent passages in Caelius Rhodiginus, *Lectiones antiquae*, Plutarch, and Plato with a long section devoted to the Heavens and another to the Heavenly bodies. Here, as elsewhere, Gesner relies chiefly on general works and does not list contemporary writings at all fully. This use of encyclopedic books soon ceases to occur in subject-indexes. In this instance it means that his account of Astronomy is brief and uninformative. The third titulus (fols. 186^b–188^a) deals with the Elements (earth, air, fire, and water) and the fourth (fols. 188^a–189^a), which also includes Day and night, with their qualities. The fifth titulus (fols. 189ᵃ–192ᵇ) discusses meteorological phenomena: Rain, Lightning, the Rainbow, the Winds, the Sea, Rivers, and Springs. Tituli VI-VIII contain references to the discussion of inanimate physical objects, especially Stones and Gems, Minerals, and Plants and Trees (fols. 192ᵇ–209ᵃ). In several of these categories Gesner includes glossaries, for example, a list of names of stones and gems from agate to topaz (fols. 193ᵇ–194ᵇ). A few glossaries contain bibliographical references; others give only the German equivalents of Latin terms. The whole leaves a medieval impression and does not suggest clearly the state of contemporary science.

In titulus IX Gesner continues with a discussion of the Soul or man's spirit with regard to the aspects interesting to a natural philosopher and not a theologian.[19] Using Aristotle's *Parva naturalis* as a guide, he comments in the second titulus (fols. 217ᵃ–219ᵇ) on Sleep, Memory, Life, Death, and the Ages of man. He has something to say about Animals and concludes with Magic and physical Marvels, for which he has failed to find a better place.[20] His analysis has a more medieval than modern look, and the bibliographical references are also medieval or, more accurately, to authorities that medieval writers would have cited and to handbooks.

In order to characterize the *Pandectae* more adequately, I cite his account of writers on English history. It appears under the heading "De Anglia & reliquis Oceani insulis" (fols. 234ᵃ–234ᵇ), a classification which shows the classical

[19] See fols. 209ᵃ–217ᵃ. Theological writings on these subjects will be found in the *Partitiones*.

[20] For a better account of physical marvels see, however, Liber XIV, Titulus xi (fols. 219ᵇ–235ᵃ). This analysis made in preparation for his *Historia animalium* (Zurich, 1551–1587) is generous with references to contemporary literature.

and medieval separation of England from the European continent. He cites twenty writers on English and three on Scottish history,—altogether respectable figures for a sixteenth-century bibliographer resident in Zurich and probably little interested in such matters.

A few other subjects that Gesner deals with may be mentioned briefly with special attention to those citing contemporary writings and not merely reference works. The sections devoted to the Ratio studiorum,[21] Logic,[22] Geodetics,[23] and the Turks[24] as well as those on the Senses[25] and the Education of children[26] give perhaps more than other sections do about contemporary ideas and books. As the easy test of excerpting a few pages of his biobibliographical dictionary for subjects and comparing the results with the *Pandectae* shows, Gesner did not use all the information he had in his hands.

Gesner does not cite in a convenient place the sources he used most often. He consults classical Greek and Latin authorities, especially those arranged more or less systematically, those containing a variety of information, and compendia. He often cites Pliny and Dioscorides for scientific subjects and Aulus Gellius for miscellaneous information. He gleans personalia from Valerius Maximus and moral ideas from theological handbooks or such a work as Lucius Domitius Brusonius, *Facetiarum exemplorumque libri VII* (Rome, 1518). He often refers to such encyclopedic compilations as the *Lumen animae* by Michael Fari-

---

[21] See Liber I, Titulus i, Paris 10 (fols. 4^a–5^a).
[22] See Liber II, Titulus iii (fols. 44^a–45^a).
[23] See Liber III, Titulus v (fol. 79^a).
[24] See Liber III, Titulus x (fols. 151^a–151^b).
[25] See Liber XIV, Titulus ix (fols. 211^b–213^b).
[26] See Liber XVI, Titulus xxxi (fol. 296^a) with a cross-reference to Liber XVII, Titulus iv (fols. 305^a–305^b).

nator, a Viennese Carmelite. This alphabetical dictionary of 267 articles deals largely with moral subjects but also includes enough references to science to justify an informative discussion by Lynn Thorndike.[27] He draws much from Raphael Volaterranus, i.e., Raffaele Maffei (1451–1522), *Commentariorum urbanorum libri XXXVIII* (Rome, 1506), a well-organized collection of miscellaneous information that is virtually an encyclopedia. It continued to be reprinted down to 1603. The first twelve books deal with geography, mentioning in the last chapter "Loca nuper reperta (Places recently discovered)" like India, America, and the new Portuguese colonies. The following books discuss such subjects as machines of war, coins, wine, astrology, optics, medicine, music, and the dance. Five libri of commonplaces entitled "Philologia" deal with abstract subjects of moral and philosophical nature. Except for the citation of authorities the *Commentariorum* contains little bibliographical information. Still another work of this sort that Gesner uses is Ludovicus Caelius Rhodiginus (Ludovico Ricchieri, c1450–1525), *Antiquarum lectionum libri XVI* (Venice, 1516). As its title suggests, this has a stronger emphasis on classical learning than the *Commentariorum*. It was subsequently enlarged into the *Lectionum antiquarum libri XXX* (Basel, 1550) by Ludovico's cousin Camillo, who added fourteen books. In its final form it includes cosmology, astrology, mythology, morphology, anatomy, music, and chapters on the Talmud and Cabbala. Gesner adds some references of more recent date to what he took from these sources. He avoids the

[27] It was first published in 1477 and was quickly reprinted. The author's name is disputed. For discussion and criticism see Lynn Thorndike, *History of magic and experimental science* (8 vols.; New York, 1923–1958), III, 546–560; George Sarton, *Introduction to the history of science* (3 vols. in 5; Baltimore, 1927–1947), III, 582–583.

pitfall of writing one more medieval encyclopedia and
shows himself aware of his task of compiling a guide to
information. This cannot always have been an easy distinction for him to make.

Gesner's subject-index to theology entitled *Partitiones*
(1549) is organized like the *Pandectae*. His preface describes the purposes and contents of the book and calls
attention to the chapters of the *Pandectae* that will be particularly useful to a theological student. The preliminary
pages conclude with a detailed table of contents and a
recapitulation of the *Pandectae*. Through this table of
contents one finds access to the *Partitiones* by consulting
the appropriate chapter with its exhaustive prefatory
analysis. The headings of the eight chapters (libri) are:
(1) general works on theology, (2) writers on the Bible
and its several books, (3) metaphysics or the study of in-
corporeal substances (God, Trinity, Christ, the Holy
Ghost, the powers and acts of God, good and evil spirits,
man, man's soul, free-will, and conscience), (4) ethics, (5)
the church, (6) heresy, (7) church history, and (8) varia.
As I have said, these are subdivided. For example, the
subdivisions of the last chapter are (1) general reference
works, e.g., summae, collections of commonplaces, indexes,
and glossaries; (2) collections of questions and disputations, (3) collections of letters, (4) dialogues (a favorite
manner of expository and polemic writing in the Renaissance), (5) literature and plastic art, (6) humorous, sa-
tiric, and other writings. These are subdivided in their
turn. Thus, the subdivisions of the first subdivision are (1)
theology, religion and faith in general, the praise of theology, exhortations to the study of theology, outlines for
a theological student, the difference between theology and
philosophy; (2) books dealing with the whole field of

theology; (3) commentators on Peter Lombard, *Sententiae* (a general treatise on theology); (4) catechisms and creeds. His choice and arrangement of materials varies from instance to instance. He may give a subject-index or he may offer only a list of names. Thus, the third pars of the first chapter of liber I (fols. 4ᵇ–6ᵇ) contains an alphabetical list according to first names of more than a hundred and fifty commentators on Peter Lombard. It also contains— and this is not mentioned in the introductory summary at the beginning of either the liber or the chapter—a table of contents of the Sententiae. Nor is a special bibliography (fol. 7ᵃ) of writers on the Apostles' Creed mentioned in the analysis. Without some experience it may not be easy to find a desired subject quickly, but Gesner has organized his materials competently.

The *Partitiones* is a practical and useful reference work that is all too rarely consulted. Since Gesner was a Protestant in an age and a land that rejected Catholicism, he naturally paid rather little attention to Catholic writings. We must get information about them from other sources. He mentions Catholic hymns only by exception and passes over the German translations of the Bible that preceded Luther's translation. His inclusion of Peter Lombard's *Sententiae* reflects Protestant use of a standard and influential Catholic work.

At the end of the *Partitiones* Gesner added an alphabetical index of headings in both the *Pandectae* and the *Partitiones*. This took the place of a third part that had been in Gesner's plan. It was to have been an alphabetical recapitulation of the headings accompanied by abbreviated titles. In the preface to the *Pandectae* he says that he gave up his intention because he came to believe that an index was unnecessary. This recognition of the fact that a classified subject-index requires an alphabetical index of subjects—and, it may be said, also an alphabetical index of authors—shows Gesner's good understanding of bibliographical necessities. Only a few older bibliographers saw clearly how indispensable such indexes are, and even modern bibliographers have often failed to provide them.

In his pioneer work Gesner does not clearly define his task and includes some materials that had no pertinence to it and some that later bibliographers have excluded. The lack of models to guide him appears in the admission of miscellaneous historical and lexicographical information and some bibliographical notes having only the most general connection with a subject-index. For example, the previously mentioned list of identifications of authors of hymns signed by a pseudonym lies outside the purpose of a subject-index. It is pertinent to a bibliography of hymns, and we may accept it. Quite definitely outside the scope of a subject-index in modern terms are Gesner's various lists of themes. These we should admit only when the references are numerous enough to show that the themes were listed as subjects and are not merely being identified. Gesner's lists of themes are lists of identifications in the incidental references to sources; they are comparable to his lists of technical terms with definitions. A modern bibliographer would not hesitate a moment about excluding both kinds of lists from a subject bibliography. In such regards Gesner's procedure shows the idea of a subject-index in the making.

Conrad Gesner lived in his own age and not in ours nor our modern notion of his age. This is easy to say but less easy to bear in mind in reading and using his subject-index. When we think of the twenty-five years before Gesner's birth in 1516 and the roughly thirty years between it and the publication of the *Pandectae* and the *Partitiones* in

1548 and 1549—that is to say, the two generations from 1490 to 1550—we think of the voyages of discovery made by Columbus, Cabot, the Spanish conquistadores in southern and central America, Mexico, and Florida, and the Portuguese sailing southward to the Cape of Good Hope and eastward to India. To a certain extent Gesner was aware of this enlargement of the known world, but he did not find it as significant or as revolutionary as we do. In his own terms he was aware of advances in physical and natural sciences, but he interpreted them in his own way and looked, quite naturally, backward rather than forward. About the time of the publication of Gesner's subject-indexes Conrad Lycosthenes, Gesner's publisher and the author of an epitome of the *Bibliotheca* (1551), and Pierre Boisteau could compile large dictionaries of the marvelous and fantastic aspects of the physical world seen in a very medieval fashion. Gesner did not—and could not—collect and index scientific materials that are necessarily useful to us. Immediately before Gesner's birth and within his lifetime events greatly altered political and social life. We see them in a perspective that Gesner could not have. Girolamo Savonarola's rabble-raising revolt in Florence does not have for him the importance we attach to it. Gesner perceived the significance of Macchiavelli's *Prince* for developments in political theory but only to a limited extent. We look back to the age of Henry VIII as remarkable for disastrous inflation. Gesner seems unaware of what we call monetary theory. He saw the rapid rise of the Fuggers and the interlocking of politics and business, even international business, and might have compared the fate of the earlier Florentine bankers with the impending financial collapse of the Fuggers. We see similarities in these events and Gesner did not. For the use of Gesner's subject indexes we must turn modern ideas into a form appropriate to Gesner's age. In religious matters Gesner is the child of his age. The term is not meant to be derogatory. Being a good Protestant, Gesner will not pay much attention to Catholic publications and doctrines. A more tolerant time is yet to come. We think of the years from 1490 to 1550 as the age of Erasmus and Rabelais. Such writers are at best mentioned incidentally. The modern writers for whom he finds room are Neo-Latins. Classical Greek and Latin literature are in the center of the stage. All this is said not to condemn Gesner but to guide a modern reader. It is hard to say what Gesner would have thought of Henri Hauser, *La modernité du XVI*^e *siècle* (Paris, 1930). We cannot take ideas from this interesting book to Gesner's subject-index and find at once relevant materials for further investigation. Valuable as the *Pandectae* and *Partitiones* are, they must be read and used in their own terms.

Gesner's *Pandectae* and *Partitiones* are not easy books to use. They are rare and many students will not have enough time to work their way into them. Gesner's Latin and especially his technical bibliographical terminology may halt a hasty reader. Such a reader will not easily understand the typographical arrangement and will find the bibliographical style annoying. These obstacles should not defeat him in finding a way into this storehouse. The *Pandectae* and *Partitiones* are one of the few subject-indexes made by a scholar equal to the task and in the possession of adequate resources.

ROBERT CONSTANTIN, *NOMENCLATOR INSIGNIUM SCRIPTORUM* (1555)

This bibliography (Paris, 1555. Pp. 189, [iii]) is mentioned primarily for the second half of its title: *Indexque totius Bibliothecae atque Pandectarum doctissimi atque ingeniossimi viri C. Gesneri.* This promise of an index to Gesner's work Robert Constantin (d. 1605) [28] did not fulfill. He makes no remark about this failure in his preface. Had he accomplished the task, it is easy to conjecture that the general bibliography of subject matter might have received a solid foundation on which later bibliographers would have built.

The *Nomenclator,* that is to say, a handlist with little or no critical comment, is a classified list of best books. The art of bibliography was still in an early stage when such a list and a subject-index had not been sharply differentiated. Constantin stressed his intention by using "insignium (noteworthy)" [4] in his title: *Nomenclator insignium scriptorum, quorum libri extant vel manuscripti, vel impressi, ex Bibliothecis Galliae, & Angliae.* Although it is not altogether clear what he meant by the phrase "ex Bibliothecis Galliae, & Angliae," it is obvious that he has not differentiated his work entirely from a library catalogue. He indicates what could be found in the French royal library at Fontainebleau—and is therefore a very early bibliographer to cite locations—but I do not find references to other libraries. Since I shall mention lists of best books only rarely, I shall describe this example at some length. It belongs to a genre closely allied to the subject-index, being a classified list, but it is selective rather than inclusive in nature.

The *Nomenclator* lists some two thousand titles (the figure is Besterman's; see WBB, col. 463) arranged alphabetically in such categories as Grammar, History, Poetry

---

[28] The date of Constantin's birth is uncertain and was the subject of dispute in the eighteenth century. He was probably not 103 years old when he died.

(i. e., belles lettres), Rhetoric, Dialectics, Mnemonics, Philosophy (including Physics, Politics, and Economics), Mathematics (including Music, Geography, Astrology, and Divination as well as Arithmetic, Astronomy, and Optics), Theology, the Cabbala, Medicine, Chemistry, the Metals, Law, Technology (including Military science, Architecture, Painting and Sculpture, Agriculture, Hunting, Hawking, and Fishing), Weights and Measures, and "Idyllia" (including treatises on Life at court, Navigation, Cooking, Swimming, and Married Life). A last section entitled "Stromata, Encyclia & Catholica" contains Miscellanies, Encyclopedias, and general works. As the classification suggests, the *Nomenclator* is well worth looking into, for it goes its own way in organization and contents.

The titles cited under the subhead "Encyclia" in the last section will indicate what men living around 1550 regarded as encyclopedias and why such works have not been included in this study. They will also give some notion of Constantin's competence as a bibliographer. Books like Apollodorus, *Bibliotheca* (which was still in manuscript when Constantin wrote) contain little bibliographical information. Here he has cited a classical Greek book in manuscript. Later bibliographers will not ordinarily cite either classical Greek books or manuscripts. He continues in a roughly chronological order with Pliny, Gesner, Christopher Mylaeus (the author of a universal history); Georgius Valla (the *De expetendis et fugiendis rebus* [1501] is intended); Henricus [Cornelius] Agrippa, who wrote an essay on encyclia; Joachim Ringelberg and Johannes Ludovicus Vives, who wrote general treatises on education and how to study; Pico della Mirandola (he seems to be named for the variety of subjects mentioned in his writings); Johannes Ravisius, i.e., Jean Ravisius Tixier, who wrote an index of poetical themes (see below);

Caelius Rhodiginus, who wrote a book that might now be called an encyclopedia (see above); Cassiodorus, and Martinus Capella, whose writings were more or less medieval encyclopedias; Polydore Virgil, who is named for his *De rerum inventoribus;* Raffaele Volaterranus, i.e., Raffaele Maffei of Volaterra, the author of a book like that by Caelius Rhodiginus; Ramon Lull, a medieval Catalan philosopher and another author of books having an encyclopedic quality; and finally Sextus Empiricus and Symphorien Champier, whose writings on medicine had some encyclopedic qualities (the first deals with the practice of medicine and the second is a bibliography). This list gives one a favorable impression of Constantin's knowledge and bibliographical ability. The comments are mine and show that he did not include titles foreign to the category of "encyclia." He has arranged them in a very rough chronological order and has set apart the medical works at the end.

Constantin shows unusual bibliographical skill for the middle of the sixteenth century. He gives a location for books at Fontainebleau, marks additions to Gesner's bibliography by an asterisk, and indicates Greek books by "g" with a tilde and works in manuscript by "m" with a tilde. Like bibliographers of his day, he does not often give the date or place of publication. Almost the only instance of critical comment is found (p. 95) in the following entry (paraphrased):

Roger Bacon on magic. Many [of his writings] are still extant and are read and put into practice with great disgrace to the name of a Christian, for they ought to be destroyed at once as material that contains only the cult of demons. As a matter of fact, I am saying this publicly to everyone, but [also] privately to some Englishmen, who (I know) are preserving the manuscripts. I shall say no more.

Constantin's modest *Nomenclator* is what he intended it to be—a brief classified list of good books. At times it shows his special interests more than such a work should. For example, he devotes 10 of his 189 leaves to an account of the Cabbala and works about it, 3 to writings on judicial Astrology, 3 to Divination, and 5 to Alchemy. The *Nomenclator* will reward study for its own sake but we need not linger over it.

Constantin, a professor of medicine at the university of Caen in Normandy, was quite capable of making a good bibliography. His training in Hebrew, Greek, and Latin qualified him to teach belles lettres at his alma mater. Gesner, who was a competent judge, praised his knowledge of languages, history, plants, and medicine. Josias Simler called him a man of profound erudition. Joseph Scaliger, whose bile was easily stirred, thought less well of him, perhaps because Constantin had used the notes of one of Scaliger's critics. A century and a half later Jean Le Clerc declared that Constantin's Greek dictionary was better than Estienne's. Had Constantin delayed a few years in writing the *Nomenclator*, he might have improved it, for religious difficulties compelled him to remove to Germany, where he might have found encouragement to pursue bibliographical studies.

THE DISCUSSION OF SUBJECT-INDEXES BETWEEN 1549 AND 1598

In the fifty years between Gesner's *Partitiones* (1549) and Spach's *Nomenclator* (1598) the utility of a subject-index was discussed in Italy and the Netherlands and German scholars promised more than once to compile one. While nothing came of the discussion and promises, they indicate a general interest in this kind of reference work that was to bear fruit at the end of the century.

Marcus Antonius Majoragius (Angelo Maria Conti)

Around the middle of the sixteenth century a professor of eloquence at Milan, Marcus Antonius Majoragius (1514–1555), wrote an oration on subject-indexes. I owe the reference to Daniel G. Morhof, but did not discover the pertinent passage in the rare volume of the *Orationes* (Venice, 1582) in the University of Pennsylvania Library during an all-too-brief visit.[29] Majoragius's remarks do not seem to have been the inspiration of the men in Germany, Switzerland, and the Netherlands who contemplated the task a few years later. In bibliographical history Majoragius is an interesting figure for another reason. He was born Antonio Maria Conti, but being a specialist in Cicero, he preferred Marcus to Maria, which was a woman's name and unknown to the Romans. He also rejected the trivial Conti in favor of Majoragius, derived from Maragia (the name of his birthplace) near Canzo in Lombardy. For these acts he was called to account before the Milanese senate. He defended himself in an oration that has some importance in bibliographical history for its historical review of the practice of changing names. He won the day and continued to lecture at the university.[30]

[29] See *Polyhistor*, I, xvii, § 23 (ed. 1747, I, 92). Morhof says, "De Petri Blanchot Idea Bibliothecae Universalis jam supra diximus. Habentur apud Majoragium & Heinsium Orationes hujus argumenti." Heinsius' oration and Blanchot's well-conceived plan are mentioned below. I have not seen an earlier edition (Milan, 1547) of Majoragius, *Orationes et praefationes omnes* edited by J. P. A. Marcellinus or the life (Leipzig, 1731) by J. P. Kohlius.

[30] For discussion of the incident see Archer Taylor and F. J. Mosher, *The bibliographical history of anonyma and pseudonyma* (Chicago, 1951), p. 51.

A Subject-Index by Michael Neander of Sorau

In 1565 Michael Neander (1525–1595) of Sorau in Silesia described rather fully a subject-index that he proposed to make, but his failure to mention it again in the remaining thirty years of his life suggests that he gave up the task. This Michael Neander is not to be confused with two others having the same name and living about the same time.[31] He was a favorite pupil of Melanchton and the author of successful introductions to the study of Greek and Hebrew. All we know about his plan consists in an often-reprinted program found in his *Erotemata linguae graecae* (Basel, 1565).[32] He says that he intends to list all the important libraries that the world has seen and all writings, including even the classical works that are known only by title. He had shown an inclination for studies of this sort in his *De bibliothecis deperditis, ac noviter instructis,* a survey of ancient libraries that had been destroyed and new ones that had been established. In his index he intends to cite and classify books and other works according to subjects and disciplines. He will give the time and place of writing or publication and the number of pages. He will also quote scholarly criticisms. The arrangement will make it possible to find readily information on any subject. In bibliographical details this admir-

[31] For identification of him and biographies of him see Struve-Fischer, pp. 39–40, note *o;* Johannes Fabricius, *Historia bibliothecae Fabricianae* (6 vols.; Wolfenbüttel, 1717–1723), III, 512–513, VI, 303–304 (My copy of vol. I is dated 1717; some copies are dated 1718); Saxe, III, 354–355, 646.

[32] See p. 416. For reprintings of the pertinent passage see Morhof, *Polyhistor,* I, xviii, § 11 (ed. 1747, I, 199); Struve-Fischer, pp. 39–41; Struve-Jugler, I, 25–26. In the last of these the reference to "Collect. Maderianae de Biblioth. p. 37. sq." is to J. J. Maderus, *De bibliothecis* (2d ed. by J. A. Schmidt; 3 vols.; Helmstedt, 1702–1705), I, 37–53. I have not found the original edition of *De bibliothecis deperditis.*

able and ambitious plan shows some advance beyond Gesner's work. The proposal to list libraries foreshadows Louis Jacob, *Traicté des plus belles bibliothèques publiques et particulières qui ont esté et qui sont à présent dans le monde,* 2 pts. (Paris, 1644); and the proposal to cite criticisms foreshadows such a book as Thomas Pope Blount, *Censura celebriorum authorum* (Geneva, 1694).

For a long time Neander's promised work was mentioned in highly laudatory terms and bibliographers who referred to it as lost or unpublished made efforts to find the collectanea. A century after his death Daniel Georg Morhof said that it would have replaced Gesner's bibliography. True enough, if it were executed according to the announced plan. What Neander had published justified such hopes, but it is not clear that Morhof had any firsthand knowledge of the collectanea. All that we can safely say is that Neander saw the need for a subject-index, planned to satisfy it, and apparently gave up an impossible task. This is the first of many unfulfilled plans to make a comprehensive subject-index and also one made by a man who did not have access to adequate library resources.

Josias Simler and Johann Jakob Frisius, A Subject-Index to Gesner's Bibliotheca

The first volume of Gesner's *Bibliotheca,* that is to say, the bibliographical dictionary of 1545, had the good fortune to be supplemented. Incorporating a supplement of 1555 and considerable additions, it was reissued in a condensed form by Josias Simler (1530–1576) in 1574. This epitome included many new names but condensed drastically the long biographical articles. Simler says that Johannes Jacobus Frisius (d. 1611) had done much of the work on it. He and Frisius planned, he says, to publish a

subject-index with the *Bibliotheca* of 1574, but time did
not permit. The index was almost ready (*iam fere absoluta
est*) and should appear the next autumn unless the printer
was forced to postpone publication. Definite as this is,
nothing came of it. It is amazing that Wilhelm Stuckius
says nothing about the subject-index in his biography of
Simler.[33] They were intimate friends and Stuckius cannot
have been unaware of Simler's labors on a task that must
have occupied him for many months or even years. He
praises Simler's remarkable memory for details and his
ability to quote references precisely. In such a context
mention of the subject-index would have been very appropriate. After Simler's death in 1576 Frisius continued
the task and published a final enlarged edition of the epitome in 1583. In this he repeated the final paragraph of the
Praefatio of 1574 with a promise to publish the subject-
index in time for the spring book-fair. He now said that it
had been completed (*iam absoluta est*), but it was never
published.

[33] See Wilhelm Stuckius, *Vita clarissimi viri D. Iosiae Simleri
Tigurini* (Zurich, 1577). He writes (pp. 6b–7a): "Bibliothecam quo-
que illa Gesneri, quam mirum in modum auxit, & locupletauit, totam
memoria videtur tenuisse, quippe cum de cuiusuis auctoria, scriptique
nomine interrogatus, promptissime de illo respondere sit solitus, vt &
ego, & plurimi alij, qui illo familiariter vsi sunt, saepenumero summa
cum admiratione experti sumus. Atque huiusce quidem & memoriae
& iudicij admirabilis bonitate fretus, non ordinata accurateque, sed
vaga plerumque & tumultuaria quorumuis liborum scriptorumque
de lectione vsus est, ita vt praepostero fere ordine a postrema saepe
libri alicuius parte lectionem illius exorsus, modo hanc illam paginam
non tam perlegere, quam quasi per transennam inspicere, nihilque
annotare sit solitus. Et tamen nihilominus totius libri summam,
praecipua capita, extrema cum primis egregie contexendo, acute,
expediteque videre, intelligere, alijsque explicare potuit." There is
more in the same vein. Such comment as this makes us regret the
loss of the subject-index all the more keenly. I am indebted to Max
Lüthi for running down the rare biography of Simler and quoting
this passage.

The unfulfilled promises of Simler and Frisius were bad auguries for the future. The history of subject-indexes is strewn with such promises, but the record for a generation after 1583 is a happy one. Several large and important subject-indexes were compiled and their authors found means to print them.

Petrus Bertius and the Catalogue of the University of Leiden Library

In the preface to the catalogue of the University of Leiden library (1595. Not seen). Petrus Bertius (1565–1629), librarian and compiler of the catalogue, comments on the lack of a subject-index. This lack was painfully felt because he had adopted an alphabetical arrangement of authors. His decision was important and influential because this was the first catalogue of an institutional library to be published. This Leiden catalogue, which was enlarged in later editions in 1640 (with a reprinting of Bertius's preface to the 1595 edition), 1674, and 1716 (with a supplement in 1740), set a model to be imitated. For this reason among others few catalogues of institutional libraries included a subject-index. Petrus Bertius's conversion to Catholicism and his subsequent departure to France, where he became royal geographer to Louis XIV, were more interesting to the age than his remarks on subject-indexes.

ISRAEL SPACH, *NOMENCLATOR SCRIPTORUM PHILOSOPHICORUM ATQUE PHILOLOGICORUM* (1598)

Israel Spach (1560–1610), who had published a classified medical bibliography entitled *Nomenclator scrip-*

torum medicorum (Strasbourg, 1591),[34] must have been pleased with its reception, for he undertook a few years later a similar work devoted to philosophy and philology. These two books with the already existing bibliographies of theology and law [35] surveyed the four university disciplines. Thus, at the end of the sixteenth century, which we do not ordinarily regard as a time blessed with many handy bibliographical aids, a scholar could easily assemble references in all fields. The title *Nomenclator* signifies that he intended to offer only a bald list of names with brief titles and without critical comments. I shall discuss here only the *Nomenclator scriptorum philosophicorum atque philologicorum* (1598). After the contemporary fashion Spach described his *Nomenclator* in a subtitle: "A concise survey of those who have described, discussed, and written on philosophy and all its parts at any time or in any language down to 1597 [classified] according to the categories (locos communes) of philosophy itself,

[34] For references to this handlist of some 1400 writers on medicine see Petzholdt, p. 573; Besterman, *Beginnings*, pp. 27, 71, and WBB, col. 2495. Petzholdt's remark that it is entirely out of date (*durchaus veraltet*) is of course correct, but shows a failure to appreciate the usefulness of the book in 1591 and its present value for historical studies. Besterman and Petzholdt differ in their collations, and in the *Beginnings* Besterman says that there were at least two issues. Lynn Thorndike refers to Spach only as a translator of a medical book.

[35] For early theological bibliographies see Ch. II above. For legal bibliographies see Johannes Baptista Zilettus (Giovanni Battista Ziletti, fl. 1559), *Index liborum omnium nomina complectens, in utroque jure tam Pontificio quam Caesareo* (Venice, 1559). For its various editions and a revision see Petzholdt, p. 623; Besterman, *Beginnings*, pp. 24, 66–67 and WBB, col. 2263. Note that the second edition (Venice, 1566) contains an "Index legum omnium quae in pandectis continentur" and an essay on its use. The interest in legal subject-indexes grows rapidly after this time. See in general Wilhelm Fuchs, "Die Anfänge der juristischen Bibliographie im 16. Jahrhundert," *Archiv für Bibliographie, Buch- und Bibliothekwesen*, II (1929), 44–54. Compare Schardius, *Lexicon*, cited below.

with a double index, one of subjects [and] one of authors."
At this time philosophy included, it will be remembered,
everything but theology, law, and medicine. In his preface
he gives a more ample description in the following words:

I published a few years ago a catalogue (nomenclator) of those
medical writers whose works are extant in print or manuscript.
I am [now] making a similar catalogue of philosophers and
philologians. Various men have written various books on various subjects with various titles. As far as they have come to my
attention, they are cited in my survey, whether they are in print
or in manuscript. Some frivolous works have appeared without
the names of the authors or publishers. There is also an almost
infinite number of writings for the vulgar and of notorious book-
lets that fly about by night and avoid the light of day, but I have
not included them here. For a different reason I have for the
most part passed over those who have translated books from one
language into another, those who have written philosophical
disputations (for these are easily obtainable from the academies
in question), and the authors of minor articles (these are available in sufficient numbers to anyone who wants them). Under
the special headings I have not cited again those who have dealt
with the subject in a general treatise: a treatise on mathematics
that deals with optics is not mentioned under optics. I have cited
authors without adding words of praise or saying where they
lived or what language they used. I have abbreviated titles in
order to reduce the size of the book. Although I cite 5,490
authors, many have escaped me and perhaps many will escape
you, my reader.

Since the *Nomenclator* has no table of contents, it is not
easy to survey its range from philosophy in the modern
sense (Aristotle and the commentators) on page 1 to the
applied arts and technology (painting, the art of war, and
navigation) on page 727. A brief index of catchwords and
an index of authors make it possible to find a particular
subject. A few examples will suggest the quality and
quantity of the information that Spach offers. Before passing a harsh judgment, let the reader put himself in the

position of a scholar in Strasbourg in 1598. Such a man had few reference works comparable to those on a modern desk. He had Latin, Greek, and Hebrew dictionaries and collections of the standard works in various fields, but little in the way of general bibliographies. Only the Leiden University catalogue (1595) might have been available to him in print as a general catalogue of miscellaneous books. No printed catalogue of a private library was yet available. He might have consulted manuscript catalogues of public and private libraries in Strasbourg or on his travels. He no doubt had access to some relatively large collections of books that he could use in the owner's house. The only general account of books in print was the semi-annual Frankfurt fair catalogues of current publications that had begun to appear in 1564 and the cumulation (1592) by Nicolaus Bassé (see below).

It is amazing to see what Spach accomplishes with scanty resources. His account of English historians suggests skill and diligence. The books he cites can scarcely have been known to him in any large number, yet he can name nearly a score. In addition to a dozen general, regional, or other historians, he knows three histories by Catholics in exile and the replies to them. Errors in spelling proper names make it clear that he was citing them at secondhand, but not all of them will be found in Bishop William Nicolson, *The English, Scotch and Irish libraries, giving a short view and character of most of our historians* (new [4th] ed., London, 1776). Spach deserves appreciation for solid work accomplished under great difficulties.

Spach's account of bibliography (pp. 20–22) is surprisingly good. It contains only titles that we would now recognize as pertinent and all are mentioned in Theodore Besterman's *Beginnings of Systematic Bibliography*. He knows "Bostonus de scriptoribus in Ecclesiae in Anglia"; Anton Francesco Doni, *La libraria;* various continuations of St. Jerome's old list of Christian authors; John Bale's account of English writers; and sixteenth-century theological, legal, and medical bibliographies generally. He includes somewhat more theological material than we might expect in a bibliography announced to deal with philosophy, but seems to hold the balance as even as can be hoped for. Astronomy (pp. 357–363) with more than sixty titles (often several editions of a work are cited) makes an equally favorable impression. Both Geometry (pp. 400–407) and Italian history (pp. 527–539) with many subdivisions for provinces and cities are generously surveyed. A reference (p. 359), "In bibl. Diegi Hurtadi," i.e., Hurtado de Mendoza, raises an interesting question. This library was in Venice, but there was no printed catalogue of it. Did Spach get the information from someone who had used the books in Venice or, as is more probable, at secondhand from a treatise?

Spach, a collector and compiler, does not have an original mind. His activities in gathering bibliographical information go along with work in a similar but slightly different direction. His *Gynaeciorum . . . opera* (Strasbourg, 1598), which appeared in the same year as the *Nomenclator scriptorum philosophicorum,* is a compilation of writings on women's diseases. Caspar Wolff of Zurich had published a forerunner in 1566 and Caspar Bauhin (1550–1624) of Basel had enlarged it in 1586. In his book of 1080 pages (neglecting 36 pages of preliminaries and 17 pages of indexes) Spach assembled once more the corpus of gynecological treatises. The making and revising of such treatises was a recognized scholarly procedure at the time and even much later. A few examples will be instruc-

tive. Fifty years before Spach L. Vitruvio Roscio published
*De docendi studendique modo . . . cui adiecemus statim
alios eiusdem argumenti libellos aliquot* (Basel, 1541), a
collection of works on educational matters in 616 pages.
A rare and neglected work is Pierre Pacci (Angelus Are-
tinus, pseud), *Tractatus de maleficiis . . . cum additionibus
. . . Aug. Bonfrancisi, ac H. Cuchalon, Hispani . . . cum
apostillis B. de Landriano, necnon aliorum modernorum*
(Cologne, 1599. Pp. 42, 2 ll., 512), a handbook of writings about witchcraft. The pertinent handbook for library
science is Johannes Lomeier, *De bibliothecis* (Zutphen,
1669) with a revision and enlargement in J. J. Mader,
De bibliothecis atque archivis (2d ed. by J. A. Schmidt,
3 vols.; Helmstadt, 1702–1705). It includes 27 treatises
and excerpts.

Spach's *Gynaeciorum* is an excellent illustration of the
contemporary custom of re-editing and improving a standard work. In two generations this expensive book enjoyed
three editions by different editors. It is not fantastic to
imagine such a course of events in the history of subject-
indexes, but it did not occur. The bibliographical portion
of Gesner's *Bibliotheca* was twice revised and enlarged,
but the *Pandectae* and *Partitiones* were neglected. The
oldest and most famous Christian bibliography, St. Jerome's *De scriptoribus ecclesiasticis,* had a happy career.
In the thousand years after A.D. 392 men supplemented it.
These were assembled into a single volume in Suffridus
Petrus, *De illustribus ecclesiae scriptoribus, authores prae-
cipui veteres* (Cologne, 1580. See WBB, cols. 4022–4023).
The tradition continues in Aubert Le Mire, *Bibliotheca
ecclesiastica* (Antwerp, 1639. See WBB, col. 4024) and
comes to an end in Johann Albert Fabricius, *Bibliotheca
ecclesiastica* (Hamburg, 1718. See WBB, cols. 4024–4025),

which contains all the editions of these early theological bibliographies. It is therefore not impossible to imagine Spach reprinting Gesner's work and supplementing it, but there are good reasons why he did not do so. Perhaps the chief one was that he did not perceive clearly the nature of his own *Nomenclator* and its similarity in purpose to Gesner's *Pandectae*. Probably also he was unwilling to employ Gesner's classification.

PHILIBERT MARESCHAL, *LE GUIDE DES ARTS ET SCIENCES* (1598)

A French counterpart to Spach's *Nomenclator* of somewhat limited scope was published in the same year.[36] This *Guide des arts et sciences et promptuaire de tous livres, tant composez que traduicts en François* (Paris, 1598. Pp. viii, 421) by Philibert Mareschal, Sieur de la Roche is restricted to works in French and excludes those in manuscript. For more than a century longer bibliographers continue to waver about accepting or rejecting manuscript materials but finally end by excluding them or relegating them to a special category. Half a century before Mareschal, Gesner had included them on the same basis as printed books and his contemporary Robert Constantin included them, designating them by a special symbol.

Mareschal's *Guide* is the first subject-index in a vernacular language and restricted to it. The quality of the books cited is more popular than scholarly, but this is to be ex-

[36] For information about this rare book I rely on notes generously made for me by Professor Isidore Silver, who used the copy in the Bibliothèque nationale, and on a microfilm in the Newberry Library. It is not mentioned among the 22106 titles in Alexandre Cioranesco, *Bibliographie de la littérature française du seizième siècle* (Paris, 1959).

pected because scholarly writing was still largely in Latin. Mareschal saw very clearly what he was doing, for he writes (pp. ij^a-ij^b):

D'autant qu'un Espirit est bon plus il est curieux de science, toutefois il est souēt retenu en ignorance par plusieurs accidens ou par faute de docteurs, ou à faute de sçauoir s'il y a liure composé du subject qu'il desire: Ce qu'on ne peut apprendre sinon par la frequentation des hommes doctes, ou lecture entiere des Bibliotheques: qui est de tant de labeur & si long-temps, que presque aussi tost on pourroit auoir appris la mesme science. Car il n'est pas facile de trouer és Biblio-[p. ij^b] theques si aucun Autheur à escrit d'vn subiect, sinon qu'on sçache le nom de l'Autheur mesme. Mais à telle difficulté ce liure sup-plera, & à son ouverture enseignera ce qui a esté traduict & composé en Frãçois sur chacune des Sciences, Facultez, Ars liberaux & Mechaniques, le tout disposé selon l'ordre suyuant.

Mareschal's *Guide* begins with four preliminary leaves containing a table of contents. It is divided into "Ars lib-eraux" (pp. 1–50) and "Facultez" (pp. 64–216). Between these two he places "Philosophie" (pp. 50–63), which is divided into "Physique, Metaphysique" (pp. 50–57) and "Physionomie" (pp. 57–63). Mareschal is following his own devices in the classification of knowledge. According to the table of contents, "Alchimie" should be under "Phi-losophie," but it is actually the first subject (pp. 216–219) for which he has no place in the two main categories. Other subjects treated in this fashion follow: "Poesie sacree" (pp. 219–243), "Poesie Fabuleuse et Fables" (pp. 243–314), "De l'Art Militaire" (pp. 314–321, citing 42 titles); "Architecture, Peinture, Escriture, Sculpture, Ven-erie, Agriculture" (pp. 321–332), history (pp. 338–388), and "Meslanges ou oeuvres traictans de divers subjects" (pp. 388–421). The last section is, it needs scarcely to be said, so large that it is unwieldy without subdivisions. The first division, "Ars liberaux" (pp. 1–50), contains more or less what we might expect: "Grammaire" (pp. 1–4, citing 32 titles dealing with French, Latin, Greek, and German languages), "Rhetorique" (pp. 5–15), "Langues" (pp. 16–20), "Dialectique" (pp. 20–21), "Arithmetique" (pp. 21–24), "Musique" (pp. 24–30), "Geometrie et de tous Poids et Mesures" (pp. 31–34); "Cosmographie, Geographie, Topographie" (pp. 34–41), and "Astrologie" (pp. 41–50, citing some 70 titles). The second division, "Facultez," includes theology (pp. 64–140), jurisprudence (pp. 140–163), "Ethique, police ou moeurs" (pp. 164–190), and medicine (pp. 190–216). The lack of subdivisions in theology makes consultation difficult. The survey of medicine gives, it seems to me, a good idea of actual practice in the sixteenth century.

PAULUS BOLDUANUS,
BIBLIOTHECA PHILOSOPHICA (1616)[37]

A series of bibliographies (*bibliothecae*) by Paulus Bolduanus (fl. 1620), pastor at Vessin in Pomerania, a village not far from Stolp (which was his birthplace), deal with theology, philosophy in the older sense, and history. He is unknown to the authors of the larger biographical dictionaires and is scantily mentioned in those for Pomeranian worthies. His uninformative autobiographical remarks in the preface to the *Bibliotheca philosophica* strike a strange apologetic note suggesting a realization that he would make no great stir in the world. The brief and damning remarks in Struve-Jugler (which I quote in paraphrase) explain his little esteem among bibliographers:

He was a minister of the gospel in a certain Pomeranian village, a man not very well known in his own day, not provided with

[37] By exception this subject-index is included in this chapter because it continues the sixteenth-century tradition.

the aids for so many enterprises, and not sufficiently suited to the task of gathering information about books, all of which should also be said about Draud, who served in the same capacity in Bavaria.[38] The bibliographies are jejune selections made without judgment from hither and yon and especially from the Frankfurt fair catalogues. The *Bibliotheca historica* (1620) is the best of them, being arranged in a better order than the others and showing rudiments of historical knowledge that should not be despised. The *Bibliotheca theologica* (1614) is, however, the most useful.[39]

In these harsh criticisms Morhof, who is Struve's source, and other bibliographers after 1685 concur, and Julius Petzholdt repeats them in 1866. How many of them ever saw and studied the books they damned must remain uncertain. One qualified word spoken in defense of Bolduanus may be quoted. J. C. Daehnert, librarian at the University of Greifswald and a competent judge, says that the bibliographical writings of Bolduanus deserve to be purged of their many errors (this is a cliché in criticisms of bibliographies).[40] He may only be defending him against the criticism implied by their inclusion in the *Index librorum prohibitorum et expurgandorum* (Madrid, 1667), pp. 819–820. Daehnert took the trouble to inform himself about Bolduanus, for he quoted a few lines from a very obscure biographical dictionary: M. Franciscus Wokenius, *Collectio nominum plus quam C. eruditorum alibi vel plane nulla vel manca fit mentio* (Stettin, 1723. Pp. 16. Not seen).[41] According to Wokenius, Bolduanus

[38] Draud compiled subject-indexes mentioned below. He was a pastor in Oberhessen, not Bavaria.

[39] See I, 88–89. The remarks are based on Morhof, *Polyhistor,* I, ch. xviii, § 12 (ed. 1747, I, 199).

[40] *Pommersche Bibliothek* (Greifswald, 1753), II, Pt. 4, No. 4, p. 136.

[41] *Pommersche Bibliothek* (Greifswald, 1756), V, No. 6, pp. 231–232. For other Pomeranian biographical works that I have not consulted see *Serapeum,* XXX (1869), 232–233, 241.

left some unpublished genealogies of Pomeranian noblemen. Wokenius's title indicates that Bolduanus was virtually unknown in 1723. Since his pamphlet deals with more than a hundred scholars in sixteen pages, one is not tempted to run it down to learn more about Bolduanus.

Bolduanus's reputation explains the neglect of his bibliographies. It does not rest on a just appraisal of his work in comparison with that of his contemporaries. Nor does it take into consideration the facilities available to anyone in 1610–1620, whether he lives in a "certain village in Pomerania" or elsewhere, or the usefulness of his work in either his age or ours. Bolduanus's *Bibliotheca*—I refer particularly to the *Bibliotheca philosophica*—was the third large general subject-index to be compiled. It had been preceded by Gesner's *Pandectae* of 1548, from which he could have learned little about organization and could have taken little in the way of materials. In contents and execution Bolduanus's *Bibliotheca philosophica* is altogether superior to Spach's *Nomenclator* of 1598. One cannot say with any justice that Bolduanus's work shows serious faults caused by his residence in a tiny Pomeranian village where few books were within his reach. The implication that he is to be condemned for having gathered information from the Frankfurt fair catalogues is, to say the least, unkind. Everyone knew the faults of the fair catalogues, but where else could he have found the information he needed in 1610–1620? The University of Leiden catalogue of 1595, the Oxford catalogue of 1605, and such manuscript catalogues of public and private libraries as he might have consulted were no doubt more accurate than the fair catalogues, but none of them contained more than a small fraction of the titles in Bolduanus's *Bibliothecae*. What value his work may have to a

modern student will appear in the following remarks. I
would praise him for being a modest, intelligent, and diligent man rather than damn him.

Bolduanus's *Bibliotheca philosophica* (1616) resembles
Spach's *Nomenclator* in being an account of all subjects
other than theology, law, and medicine. History and theology Bolduanus dealt with in separate bibliographies. In
its plan of arrangement the *Bibliotheca philosophica* differs somewhat from the *Nomenclator* and Bolduanus is a
more competent workman than Spach. He offers a classified list of headings and often subdivides the headings.
The authors cited are arranged according to their Christian names, as was then the practice of bibliographers. A
table of contents and an index of authors are lacking.
These deficiencies and a brief and inadequate alphabetical
index of subjects make the *Bibliotheca* difficult to use.
Nevertheless, the blurb on the titlepage is no more of an
overstatement than one expects: "a book of the very greatest usefulness to the students of all the arts and sciences
and very necessary to them in pursuing their studies."

Bolduanus found a plan of arrangement in the seven
liberal arts, to which he made some additions at the end.
The scope of his *Bibliotheca philosophica* and the variety
of subjects with which it deals will appear in the following analysis. He begins with general works (pp. 1–20) on
philosophy in the narrow sense with brief additional sections (pp. 20–23) devoted to the agreements and differences of Aristotelian and Platonic philosophy, the *Insti-
tutes* of Petrus Ramus (Pierre de la Ramée), Stoic, heathen
(Chaldee and Hindu), Epicurean, and Sacred philosophy,
and the Praise of philosophy, a page on Mnemotechnics
(p. 24), and a long account of books dealing with the
"Ratio studiorum" (pp. 25–31). Some general subjects

reserved for the end might, I think, have been included here. He also treats Alphabeta varia (pp. 31–32), the art of Writing (pp. 32–33), and books on Languages (pp. 33–36) in this prefatory section. These details will suggest how finely Bolduanus subdivides his materials. Then, with a section Artes liberales followed by the minor subdivisions Artium dignitas and Artium contemptus (pp. 36–44) the book begins. Grammar extends from p. 44 to p. 93; Dialectics from p. 93 to p. 131; Rhetoric, which is designated as "3" (the previous sections are not numbered), from p. 131 to p. 177; Music, like the following sections, is designated by a Roman numeral and extends from p. 177 to p. 255; Arithmetic from p. 255 to p. 266; Geometry from p. 266 to p. 308; and Astronomy from p. 308 to p. 356. We can reckon with an average of perhaps ten titles to a page. Although Bolduanus includes a great variety of materials under these headings, he does not find a place for everything he wishes to mention. In what follows, his arrangement is not altogether easy to understand but shows an intention to proceed from the general and abstract to the specific. It continues from Metaphysics (pp. 356–362) to Physics (pp. 362–391), which embraces Magic, Divination, Physiognomy, Chiromancy; Man, the Soul, and Immortality; Ethics (pp. 391–402); Political science, which includes sections on the State (Respublica) and Economics (pp. 402–414). There follow sections on the Practical arts (pp. 414–429): the Mechanic arts, Agriculture, Architecture, Military science (with sections on Firearms and Fencing), Cookery, Business and Trade, Shipping, Hunting and Falconry, Painting, and Weaving. The *Bibliotheca* concludes with a long account of Greek and Latin authors (pp. 430–577), writers on Literature (pp. 577–638) including the literary genres, and compilers of handbooks of Poetics. Post-classical authors are not included, and there are no lists of writers of comedies and tragedies. There is a geographico-historical account of universities that cannot be called bibliographical. Bolduanus ends his book with Bibliography (pp. 638–644). The very brief index of subjects is an unsatisfactory guide to the contents of his book.

The *Bibliotheca philosophica* deals, as any book of 1616 with this title would be expected to, with every subject but theology, law, and medicine. In this and the preceding paragraph the quotations of headings have been numerous in order to stress what philosophy included then. Bolduanus has excluded history because he devoted a special bibliography to it. His collections seem valuable to me. There is, for example, a rich account of Aristotelian commentaries (pp. 437–470). They interested students in 1616 perhaps more than they do today. Johann Albert Fabricius, *Bibliotheca graeca*, Lib. III, c. vi (3d ed, 1717–1754, III, 183), which was written a century later and after substantial improvements in the theory and practice of bibliography, cites Bolduanus's account and three other seventeenth-century bibliographies as sources of information. The thirteen titles that Bolduanus cites with adequate bibliographical details under Mnemotechnics (p. 24) represent a considerable advance over Spach's eleven names and three titles (*Nomenclator,* pp. 320–321). Even if we deduct four books published after 1598 and therefore not within Spach's reach, Bolduanus's list is still greatly to be preferred for giving bibliographical details. Since he cites both the 1593 and 1603 editions of a book known to Draud only in the latter edition (see *Bibliotheca classica,* ed. 1611, p. 1032) and adds two titles not known to Draud, he cannot have obtained the information from

Draud. A marginal note in my copy suggests that he took it from Chytraeus. Bolduanus is a competent workman, wherever he found his materials. In *Studiorum formandorum ratio* (pp. 25–31) he is far more critical about the choice of titles than Spach (pp. 10–20) had been and more generous than Draud (*Bibliotheca classica,* ed. 1611, pp. 1105–1106, and, considerably rewritten, ed. 1625, pp. 1494–1495). The long and carefully subdivided review (pp. 116–123) of books by or about Petrus Ramus (Pierre de la Ramée) might well be useful to a modern scholar interested in this Renaissance philosopher and educator. The section devoted to Astronomy (pp. 308–356) makes a substantial impression. The four pages of Bibliography (pp. 644–648) are well-done, being both relatively complete and relatively accurate. A special merit of the *Bibliotheca philosophica* is a long account of Music (pp. 177–255) that lists titles under the following heads: musicae praecepta, opera musica, cantiones sacrae insigniores, cantiones ecclesiaticae, cantiones dominicales, cantiones festivae, natalitia Christi, Passio Christi, harmonica, harmoniae, missae, motetae, vespertinae, psalmi Davidis, hymni, magnificat, threni Jeremiae, psalmi penitentiales, litaniae, moralia, madrigalia (pp. 220–223), nuptialia, bicinia, tricinia, musica instrumentalis, and choreae. It seems unnecessary to turn these categories into English. The titles of collections of German hymns and songs fill pp. 229–235.

Bolduanus's *Bibliotheca philosophica* is not a negligible book and it is not a bad book. On the contrary, it is a good book and superior to much bibliographical work of its day. It no doubt contains chaff, but many will prefer to winnow Bolduanus's harvest rather than to seek the grain in more inconvenient places.

SUBJECT-INDEXES TO
BIOBIBLIOGRAPHICAL DICTIONARIES

The making of subject-indexes to biobibliographical dictionaries reaches back to at least the early years of the seventeenth century. In national and regional dictionaries an index according to subjects is often found along with indexes of authors of noble origin, authors resident in various places and regions, and the like. The tradition of such indexes is especially clear in the Romance countries, and particularly in the provincial and city dictionaries made in Italy in the seventeenth century. In northern Europe, where biobibliographical dictionaries seem to represent an independent bibliographical and historical tradition, subject-indexes are rare. International biobibliographical dictionaries almost never contain subject-indexes. Gesner's *Pandectae* and *Partitiones* require the use of his dictionary but are not based on it. There might have been an exception to the rule in the huge *Pandectae brandenburgicae* planned by Christoph Hendreich (1650–1702), but only two volumes A-B were published (Berlin, 1699) and nothing of the subject-index appeared. Subject-indexes to biobibliographical dictionaries are usually not very helpful because they ordinarily list only names in large categories: theologians, philosophers, or historians. They rarely name the books for which these men are famous and require the reader to turn back to the author's name.

In biobibliographical dictionaries of ecclesiastics and especially members of religious orders the categories in the subject-indexes differ somewhat from those employed in the national or regional dictionaries and have, in general, a greater usefulness. The categories are more specific, often listing commentators on the Bible, writers opposed to heresies, or writers on miracles, especially those of the Virgin Mary.

Both the national or regional and the ecclesiastical bio-bibliographical dictionaries are lists of men, and so are the subject-indexes to them. This Renaissance conception of bibliography explains, at least in part, the lack of titles in these subject-indexes. I discuss them only briefly, beginning with the national and regional dictionaries and using Portugal as a chief example because a continuing tradition there is clear and cataloguers assure me that these indexes are still useful.

SUBJECT-INDEXES IN SECULAR BIOBIBLIOGRAPHICAL DICTIONARIES

A subject-index in a manuscript Portuguese biobibliographical dictionary that I have not seen appears to be the beginning of a long tradition and will serve as my chief example. The Portuguese dictionaries are valuable for information that has not found a way into the general store of European learning. The *Theatrum Lusitaniae litterarium sive Bibliotheca scriptorum omnium lusitanorum* (1665) by João Soares de Brito (1611–1664) contains three indexes, of which the second deals with subjects.[42] The *Theatrum* was superseded by a work that is still a standard authority and enjoyed a reprinting a generation ago: Diogo Barbosa Machado, *Bibliotheca lusitana histó-*

---

[42] See António Anselmo, *Bibliografia das bibliografias portugêsas* (Lisbon, 1923), p. 18, no. 10, citing a manuscript copy of the *Theatrum* in Fundo Geral 6915 (Pp. 1059) in the Biblioteca nacional and another in the library of the Academia das ciências at Lisbon (Pp. 927). Ramiz Galvão cites more copies; see *Boletim da Sociedade de bibliófilos Barbosa Machado*, II (1913), 27–28. Barbosa Machado (1st ed., II, 764; 2d ed, II, 702) cites the title as *Theatrum Lusitaniae litterarium* and the date as 1645.

rica, crítica e cronológica (4 vols.; Lisbon, 1741–1759).
This also contains a subject-index [43] and Ramiz Galvão
points out (pp. 27–28) that Barbosa Machado drew upon
his predecessor. Specialists in Portuguese bibliography
assure me that it is very useful. I have been content to
test its completeness by confirming the references to a
score of titles chosen from the text. The detailed classification in sixty-two categories is both convenient and helpful.
Barbosa Machado and presumably Soares de Brito cite
works in manuscript. The former also used a "succincta
noticia" of the chief Portuguese authors classified according to disciplines by Francisco Manuel de Mello (1608–
1666).[44] Much later Innocêncio Francisco da Silva (1810–
1876) planned to make a similar subject-index for his
standard work, the *Dicionário bibliográphico portuguêz*
(22 vols.; Lisbon, 1858–1923), but did not live to complete
it. He left the task to P. V. Brito Aranha (1833–1914),
who brought it to an end in 1923. Martinho da Fonseca
published *Aditamentos ao Dicionário bibliográfico português* (Coimbra, 1927), but this is not always regarded as
part of the set and bears no volume number. The promised
subject-index did not yet appear. José Soares de Souza,
*Índice alfabético do Dicionário bibliográfico português de
Inocêncio Francisco da Silva* ([São Paulo], 1938) is only
an index of names and has been replaced by a twenty-
third volume entitled *Guia bibliográfica*[45] by Ernesto

[43] See 1st ed., IV, 435–642 (2d ed., IV, 488–721), "Index VII. Das
materias, emque escrevêrao os autores, distribuídas nas seguintes
Classes." The title pages of the *Bibliotheca*, I–III read *cronologica*,
that of vol. IV reads *chronologica*.
[44] For references see Anselmo, p. 110, nos. 808, 809.
[45] This is rare. It was published as a supplement to the *Boletim da
Bibliotheca da Universidade de Coimbra*, XXIII (Coimbra, 1958.
Pp. 30, 763) in five hundred copies, of which a hundred and fifty
were for sale. There is a copy in the Newberry Library.

Soares. Ernesto Soares says (*Guia*, pp. ix-x) that he spent thirty-two years of a laborious life on the task and cannot make the promised subject-index. He recognizes its value and hopes that some stronger hand than his will undertake the task. The popularity of the idea in the seventeenth century and its persistence down to our own time is remarkable.

The following examples will suggest the variety of subject-indexes appended to secular biobibliographical dictionaries and the possibility that a new bibliographical tradition is developing. In the long history of Italian provincial and city dictionaries we see a shift from purely historical compilations to dictionaries containing bibliographical information and subject-indexes. In Spain Nicolás Antonio's (1617–1684) huge national dictionary—*Bibliotheca hispana, . . . haec . . . de his agit, qui post annum secularem M.D. usque ad praesentem diem floruere* (Rome, 1672) and *Bibliotheca hispana vetus . . . Complectens scriptores omnes qui ab Octaviani Augusti imperio ad annum M [–MD.]floruerunt* (Rome, 1696) is still after the passing of three centuries a standard work noteworthy for the extent and variety of its indexes. Homero Séris commends the index to the second volume as a work that has not yet been superseded.[46] Many have overlooked the last words in the title of S. Austin Allibone (1816–1889), *A critical dictionary of English literature and British and American authors living and deceased from the earliest accounts to the latter half of the nineteenth century . . . With forty indexes of subjects* (3 vols., 2 vols. supplement; Philadelphia, 1859–1891. See WBB, col.

[46] *Manual de bibliografía de la literatura española,* I (Syracuse, 1948), 93. For collations of both voumes in both editions see WBB, col. 3873.

1256). The forty indexes (III, 2911–3139) list only names in large categories and thus lead indirectly to 250,000 titles (according to Besterman). The supplement follows the same pattern. The first dozen and the last half-dozen categories are sufficient examples: Agriculture, Antiquities, Architecture, Astronomy, Bibliography, Biography and Correspondence, Botany, Chemistry, Divinity, Domestic economy, Drama, Education . . . Political economy, Politics, Topography, Trade and Commerce, Travels, Voyages. These headings are not subdivided, but there is an index of almost two hundred subheadings comprehended in them. Writers of Proverbs will, for example, be found under the heading Moral and Mental philosophy, and one must refer back from the 1412 names listed there to the individual biographies to discover collections of proverbs. Allibone lists the same author under several headings. According to his recapitulation (III, 3139), the dictionary contains 46,499 authors and the indexes 75,158 names. In other words, half of the authors are mentioned in two places.

The subject-index to the *Bibliotheca danica* (6 vols.; Copenhagen, 1872–1931) by Christian V. Bruun (1831–1906), chief librarian of the Royal Library at Copenhagen, and others, may be mentioned here, although it is an index to a list of books and not to a biobibliographical dictionary. The *Bibliotheca* lists all books published in Denmark from 1482 to 1830. In addition, it includes works by foreign authors on Denmark and Danish subjects, works on Schleswig-Holstein, and the works of men who lived in Norway (until 1814), Iceland, and Greenland. It is based on the collections in the Royal Library and certain other libraries. The original edition with a supplement of 1914 and a volume of indexes published in 1931 has long been out of print. An additional volume (Copenhagen, 1944. See WBB, cols. 987, 3710) by H. Ehrencron-Müller that is not always regarded as belonging to the set lists the literature of Schleswig-Holstein more generously and includes Danish books printed between 1831 and 1840, when the currently appearing *Dansk bogfortegnelse* began. A reprint with the addition of books acquired by the contributing libraries since 1914, a corrected and enlarged subject index, and other aids to reference use is now appearing. As the prospectus says, the *Bibliotheca* will give information about what has been written in Denmark on the making of Brandy, Pestilences, Ailments of the eyes, Money, Insurance, Music, Birds, Maps, Dictionaries, the Postal system, the building of Roads, and in all, 2200 subjects. Since it includes foreign books concerning Denmark and Scandinavia and translations into Danish, it extends somewhat beyond the obvious limits.

While a subject-index attached to a biographical dictionary is obviously useful, makers of such dictionaries have not often recognized its value and have done their job all too hastily or have neglected it entirely. As we have seen, it is by no means so novel an idea as the author of a leading article in the (London) *Times Literary Supplement* would have it. In commenting on *The concise dictionary*, Part II, 1901–1950. *Being an epitome of the twentieth century D. N. B. down to the end of 1950* ([Oxford], 1961), "Select subject index," pp. 465–528, he says that it "incorporates a new feature in a select index of subjects which, in spite of the omissions, will certainly be useful to those who may have occasion to turn to it for light on matter rather than on men." [47] This index is so selective in the choice of headings that its usefulness is limited. It

[47] See the issue for Dec. 29, 1961, p. 929.

offers a strange mixture of references to events as well as books in Politics, Technology, Literary history, and other fields that, while it can be called a subject-index of sorts, it has no great resemblance to those cited in this study. Much the same may be said of the index attached to J. O. Thorne, ed., *Chambers's biographical dictionary* (New ed., Edinburgh, 1961). In the latest edition it has been tripled in size and now fills 35 pages, but as this figure suggests, its scope is very restricted.

SUBJECT-INDEXES IN ECCLESIASTICAL BIOBIBLIOGRAPHICAL DICTIONARIES

Cardinal Robert Bellarmine, De scriptoribus ecclesiasticis (*1613*)

De scriptoribus ecclesiasticis (1613) by Cardinal Robert Bellarmine (1542–1621), perhaps the most widely circulated and often-reprinted seventeenth-century bibliography, is a brief biobibliographical dictionary of ecclesiastical writers in chronological order down to 1500. Although the cardinal was a noted controversialist, both Catholics and Protestants used his book.[48] The subject-indexes in it consist in lists of (1) commentators on the Scriptures, (2) writers against heretics, (3) scholastic theologians, (4) collectors and expositors of sacred canons, (5) writers who

[48] I cannot say whether the subject-indexes in the Lyons, 1613 edition, "recognita & ab autore ipso auctior facta," are found in the first edition (Rome, 1613), but assume that they are. According to Besterman (WBB, col. 4023), both editions contain 38 pages (separately paginated) at the end. These pages in the Lyons edition, which I have seen, correspond to 34 pages in my copy of the Paris, 1631 edition. I cannot say whether these indexes were retained in Philip Labbé's much improved edition (Paris, 1660) or whether André du Saussay's continuation (Cologne, 1684) that brought the work down to 1600 followed the same plan.

dealt with cases of conscience, (6) Christian orators, (7) sacred poets (subdivided into Hebrews and Christians), (8) church historians, (9) chronologers, and (10) pious pamphlets. Except for the last, which gives only titles, the lists contain only proper names and the reader is expected to refer to the text and then to biobibliographical dictionaries for details. Except for the choice of categories, these subject-indexes resemble those in secular biobibliographical dictionaries. Cardinal Bellarmine's indexes amount to a rough subject-index of ecclesiastical writings according to large categories. They would scarcely call for mention but for the fact that his book was influential and widely known. We need not insist on seeing a direct connection between his indexes and the admirable subject-indexes in De Backer and Sommervogel's Jesuit bibliography next to be discussed, but we can regard both as representative of the same tradition.

Pierre Bliard, Tables (1909)

The tenth volume of Carlos Sommervogel and Augustin de Backer, *Bibliothèque de la Compagnie de Jésus* (11 vols.; Brussels, later Paris, 1890–1909. See WBB, cols. 2157–2158) is an account of the writings of members of the Society of Jesus and contains a large and carefully made subject-index by Pierre Bliard (pp. xi, cols. 1916). It is an admirable modern representative of a long-standing tradition in biobibliographical dictionaries of the religious orders. Since the authors named in it are chosen according to their affiliation, I shall not cite parallels to it. In dictionaries of this sort the books listed are largely ecclesiastical in nature, have been published in small editions and in towns usually not regarded as publishing centers; for all these reasons the bibliographies offer very useful information. Astronomy, English history, and Medicine that have been ordinarily used as subjects to be examined in characterizing subject-indexes cannot be used here. The short section on Bibliography (cols. 1902–1904) contains some interesting bits of information. Mario Praz consulted this dictionary for authors who wrote Emblembooks, but I am not sure that he used Bliard's *Tables* (cols. 1331–1332) which names some titles that seem to have escaped him. It is not surprising that we find here much useful information for the study of Neo-Latin literature, Languages and Linguistics, and Riddles (col. 1331). It may be remarked in passing that some sections of the articles dealing with Conduct of Life promise to reward study.

A LOOK BACK

With three classified subject-indexes—Conrad Gesner, *Pandectae* (1548) and *Partitiones* (1549); Israel Spach, *Nomenclator* (1598); and Philibert Mareschal, *Le Guide* (1598)—and two of the early seventeenth century—Cardinal Robert Bellarmine, *De scriptoribus ecclesiasticis* (1613) and Paulus Bolduanus, *Bibliotheca philosophica* (1616)—bibliographies of this kind came to an end before 1620. Classified subject-indexes will appear later in this study, but the modern examples have no connections with their Renaissance predecessors unless, as I have suggested, there is a line of descent from *De scriptoribus ecclesiasticis* to the subject-indexes attached to biobibliographical dictionaries.

The five early classified subject-indexes lack any connections with one another. Each has its own plan of arrangement and represents its author's independent labors.

The *Pandectae* and *Partitiones* contain many references to classical Greek and Latin authorities, relatively generous citations of scholarly writings in Latin, virtually no mention of vernacular writings, abundant references to miscellanies of encyclopedic quality, and some materials we cannot regard as bibliographical in nature. The later bibliographers—Spach, Mareschal, and Bolduanus—reverse Gesner's procedure on every point. They include little or nothing that is not bibliographical. They make no references to encyclopedias and miscellanies. They recognize some vernacular writings, but there was very little available to them. Mareschal recognizes almost nothing but vernacular works. They go far beyond Gesner in listing contemporary scholarly work and reject classical Greek and Latin authorities. They have made a first step toward the modern subject-indexes limited to contemporary authorities. For obvious reasons Cardinal Robert Bellarmine goes his own way. The categories in his subject-index are determined by the nature of the bibliographical dictionary to which it was attached and have no similarity to those in the other bibliographies. His ecclesiastical interests and training set his work apart. These men took little or nothing from one another. We must therefore consult them all to obtain as complete a record as possible.

Between Gesner's *Pandectae* (1548) and *Partitiones* (1549) and the subject bibliographies published at the end of the century including Bolduanus, *Bibliotheca philosophica* (1616) a great change occurred. A medieval spirit clings to Gesner's work; the later writings have a modern air and technique. Gesner includes lists of themes; the later bibliographers have nothing of the sort. Gesner gives references to encyclopedic works; the later bibliographers cite only books on specific subjects and expect readers to consult general reference works without being sent to them. Gesner is medieval in the details of bibliographical technique and his citations often lack preciseness; the later bibliographers usually give titles with dates and places of publication and formats. Gesner must yield in the matter of typographical arrangement to the later bibliographers who employ varieties of type, headings, and other devices much as we do.

In reviewing the bibliographical history of the sixteenth century we see clearly the consequences of the failure to publish a subject-index to the University of Leiden catalogue and to revise Gesner's work. Had Gesner's book been less expensive and had Simler and Frisius printed their index, we can reasonably conjecture that subject bibliography would have developed rapidly. Had a subject-index to the University of Leiden library been made, we can suppose that other institutional catalogues might have been provided with one. The idea of a subject-index to a biographical dictionary was readily grasped and developed and has persisted to our own time. It had from the beginning certain obvious defects, but a wider acceptance of it would have led men to remedy them.

4

Alphabetical Subject-Indexes in the Seventeenth Century

THROUGHOUT THE SEVENTEENTH CENTURY MEN MADE SUB-
ject-indexes in an alphabetical arrangement. Exception
may perhaps be made for a few indexes announced as
being in preparation that are not sufficiently well described
for us to know how they were arranged. This shift from
the classified arrangement exclusively employed during
the sixteenth century is not the subject of particular comment in the prefaces. It is already foreshadowed in Johannes Molanus, *Bibliotheca materiarum* (1618), which
was actually compiled before 1585, when Molanus died.
It is here considered according to the year when it was
published.

One reason for the abrupt change from a classified to
an alphabetical arrangement is perhaps to be seen in the
fact that the sources used were almost without exception

classified bibliographies: the semi-annual fair catalogues
and the catalogues of both public and private libraries
employed a classified arrangement. It may well be that
the makers of subject-indexes found it easier to arrange
their materials according to alphabetical headings than
to adjust and elaborate the subject headings in their
sources and to reconcile differences in terminology. They
were not following models employing an alphabetical arrangement. Only in Italy, Holland, and England did makers of library catalogues employ it at this time and subject-
indexes, with one exception, were not made in these countries. This exception is the *Index universalis alphabeticus*
(1612) by Fabianus Justinianus, whose work stands somewhere between a library catalogue of the Vallicelliana at
Rome and a subject-index. It was altogether natural for
him to employ an alphabetical arrangement. Georg
Draud's summaries of the fair catalogues (1611–1625)
were subdivided according to large categories and within
them headings were arranged alphabetically. After the
middle of the century both methods of arrangement were
employed, either a single alphabet embracing all headings
or a subdivision into a few large categories within which
the arrangement of headings was alphabetical. The classified arrangement continued to be characteristic of lists
in the book trade and public or private library catalogues.

The seventeenth-century alphabetical subject-indexes
were much more convenient reference works than their
predecessors. A classified subject-index implies a generally
accepted and readily understood system of classification,
a good table of contents, and exhaustive indexes of authors
and subjects. The sixteenth-century classified indexes left
much to be desired in all of these regards. Gesner had
supplemented his inadequate table of contents by analyses

of individual chapters but even these were incomplete. The indexes he offered were unsatisfactory. Spach, Mareschal, and Bolduanus gave users even less help. Perhaps the most serious deficiency was the lack of a generally recognized classification. Even today we do not have one, as the variation in the organization of reference works shows. An alphabetical arrangement of general subject-indexes was gradually adopted during the seventeenth century. This change seems to have been an independent development hit upon by various bibliographers in various countries. In an interesting account of medical reference works Loren C. Mackinney traces its earlier spread in the Middle Ages and the Renaissance:

From the eleventh century on, medical compendia showed a decided improvement. . . . In arrangement much progress was made. Alphabetizing was often carried out to the second and third letters. Many of the later treatises demonstrate real organizing ability and a high appreciation of the value of citations and detailed references. Precision of organization seems to have become common in almost every class of medical literature—not only in the herbals and books of simples but also in glossaries, concordances, dictionaries, and indexes.[1]

Little or nothing of this was transferred to the practice of general bibliography. Men were unaware of the bibliographical techniques employed in unfamiliar fields of study or, what is less probable, were unable to generalize them and apply them in another field. MacKinney goes on to say in a footnote:

[C. H. Haskins, *The renaissance of the twelfth century*, Cambridge, Mass., 1928, p. 78] has an interesting comment on this point to the effect that "the Middle Ages did not care much for

[1] "Medieval medical dictionaries and glossaries" in J. L. Cate and E. N. Anderson, eds., *Medical and historiographical essays in honor of James Westfall Thompson*, Chicago, [1938], pp. 240–268. See pp. 267–268.

alphabetical order, at least beyond the initial letter, and they would have faced a telephone directory with the consternation of an American office boy." This vivid characterization is perhaps true of the earlier centuries, but medical compilers of the later Middle Ages seem to have been quite fond of the alphabetical order, and on a large scale, at that. Dondus' stout volumes of indexes are as thick as a metropolitan directory, and they contain not one but a series of indexes. The same is true of many nonmedical compendia; e.g., Vincent of Beauvais and Bartholomeus Anglicus. . . . Even some of the early *glossaria* (e.g., the *Liber glossarium* and the *Glossarium Salmonis*) were as large as a Webster's unabridged dictionary. And, as to complexity, it is well to remember the cross-referenced indexes of Macer Floridus, and the alphabets within alphabets of the *Holme de simplicibus medicinis.*

An alphabetical arrangement was employed in medical reference works even before the time of Galen (see Mac-Kinney, pp. 244; 248, n. 16; 251, n. 27; 253; 255, citing Pamphilus of Alexandria, Galen's model). A similar discussion of developments in theology and law would be instructive. There seems to have been no borrowing of bibliographical techniques in philology and literary history or at least the seventeenth-century bibliographers are unaware of it. The subject needs more study than it can be given here.

While some old standard works of reference like those by Caelius Rhodiginus, Raffaele Volaterranus, and a few others survived in their original forms into the early seventeenth century, their days were numbered. Some were reworked, enlarged, and reconstituted: a thirteenth-century collection of excerpts useful for the discussion of moral ideas passed through the *Flores pene omnium doctorum* into an alphabetical *Polyanthea.* The awkwardly arranged texts in the *Speculum exemplorum* were made available with substantial additions in alphabetical order in Johannes Major, *Magnum speculum exemplorum.* A very conspicuous instance of the development is seen in Erasmus's *Adagia*. Although it had been provided with large indexes during the sixteenth century, J. J. Grynaeus rearranged it entirely in 1629. The change brought with it serious inconveniences, for Erasmus had often made references back and forth and Grynaeus made it hard to find them. Such a popular sixteenth-century encyclopedia as the *Theatrum vitae humanae* (Basel, 1565) by Theodore Zwinger the Elder (1533–1588) was replaced by alphabetical reference works, especially those by Johann Heinrich Alsted (1588–1638), who has been called the founder of the modern encyclopedia.

Further comment on this change from a systematic organized view of human knowledge to a survey of unrelated items of information in an alphabetical order needs more discussion than would be in place here. It is worth saying that at a much later time there are interesting efforts to counteract it. In its last editions the *Encyclopedia britannica* provides a systematic reader's guide. In the arrangement of titles the *Bibliotheca Osleriana* (Oxford, 1929),[2] a catalogue of Sir William Osler's medical library, offers an instructive example of an endeavor to give an organized historical view of the development of medicine.

There are several kinds of alphabetical subject-indexes. The two earliest examples discussed in this chapter— Molanus, *Bibliotheca* (1618) and Justinianus, *Index* (1612) —alphabetical without divisions according to faculties. Later a subdivision according to the four faculties—the-

---

[2] See my *Book catalogues*, pp. 132, 156–157. The books are now in McGill University Library, Montreal. Hermann Escher comments all too briefly on the seventeenth-century alphabetical subject catalogues suggested by J. H. Hottinger and Gabriel Naudé; see *Zentralblatt für Bibliothekswesen*, LI (1934), 517–519.

ology, law, medicine, and philosophy—is usually preferred and within them subjects may be arranged logically or alphabetically.

JOHANNES MOLANUS, *BIBLIOTHECA MATERIARUM* (1618)

With these preliminary remarks in mind, we turn now to the first alphabetical subject-index. Since it was published in 1618, I shall refer to it according to that date, when it became available for general use. It was actually written more than thirty years earlier by Johannes Molanus (Jan van der Meulen, c1533–1585), papal censor in the Low Countries and professor of theology at Louvain. Although the anonymous editor says he made an effort to bring it up to date, very few additions are identifiable. This *Bibliotheca materiarum quae, a quibus auctoribus, cum antiquis, tum recentioribus sint pertractae, docentibus, concionantibus, ac scriptoribus pernecessaria* (A subject-bibliography most useful to teachers, preachers, and authors that contains subjects dealt with by both ancient and modern writers) does not belie its claim to usefulness.[3] Its author, a churchman and professor of theology, naturally paid special attention to ecclesiastical matters, but clearly intended to include anything of scholarly value. According to Besterman, WBB, col. 4024, Molanus cites 12,500 titles. There is an index recapitulating the headings but no index of authors.

Molanus announces an intention to serve writers (scriptores) generally, but quite naturally conceives them to be

[3] See G. W. Freytag, *Analecta litteraria de libris rarioribus* (Leipzig, 1750), pp. 1069–1071; Saxe, III, 438, 652, citing especially B. G. Struve, *Bibliotheca antiqua* (Jena, 1705. Not seen), pp. 214 ff.

theologians or men who based their studies on theology. What he offers to those interested in the classics, philosophy, history, law, or medicine is limited in extent and quality and is characteristically seen from a theologian's point of view. It probably represents what was available to him. The article Bibliotheca (p. 20), lists collections rather than bibliographies: an edition of the works of the church fathers, a *Bibliotheca concionum,* i.e., a handbook for sermon-writers; "Photii Patriarchae Bibliotheca de scriptoribus ecclesiast. versa ab Andrea Schott," and Diodorus, *Bibliotheca historica.* The reference to Photius concerns Schott's edition of the *Myriobiblon* published in 1611.[4] Since this is one of the rare references to a book published after 1585 and since it was edited by Andreas Schott, whose *Catalogus catholicorum S. Scripturae interpretum* is a supplement to the *Bibliotheca* and is mentioned on the titlepage, I venture to conjecture that Schott may have been responsible for getting the *Bibliotheca* into print. This list of "bibliothecae" shows that Molanus, like many other makers of subject-indexes, was guided by titles. Photius's *Myriobiblon* and Diodorus's *Bibliotheca* differ considerably from the other works named in this list. The article Scriptores (p. 144), where we find references to bibliographies, includes such standard bibliographers and bibliographies as St. Jerome, Johannes Tritheim, and Cardinal Robert Bellarmine; Jacob Pammius's list of commentators on the Bible;[5] Wilhelm Eysengrein's rare *Catalogus testium veritatis* (Dillingen, 1565), a reply to Matthias Flaccius Illyricus's book with the same title

[4] For references to this see WBB, col. 626; Brunet, *Manuel,* IV, 624; J. G. T. Graesse, *Trésor de livres rares et précieux* (7 vols.; Dresden, 1859–1869), V, 276.

[5] The author is Jacobus Pamelius (1536–1587), bishop of St. Omer; see Saxe, III, 438.

(this fanatically Protestant book is not included); and Cornelis van Loos, *Illustrium Germaniae scriptorum catalogus* (Mainz, 1582). A strongly theological tinge is obvious here and elsewhere. Conrad Gesner's *Bibliotheca* and its continuations and revisions are lacking. The editor's failure to bring Molanus's book up to date shows itself in many ways, especially in the neglect of bibliographies by Antonio Possevino.

It is hardly necessary to stress the Catholic quality of the references. Martin Luther's name does not appear in the article Gratia (grace). Articles like Calvinistae Haeretici (p. 23) and Mart. Kemnitius Haereticus (p. 36) cite only refutations of unorthodox ideas. As bibliographers, we may object to Molanus's doctrinal limitations but we can find compensating advantages. His book is one of the few subject-indexes by a Catholic hand to get into print. Molanus leans no farther in one direction than Protestant compilers lean in the other. The editor of the *Bibliotheca* did not draw upon the *Index universalis alphabeticus* by Fabianus Justinianus published in 1612 (see below) as a casual comparison of Apophthegmata, Bestia, Cabbala, or Daemones (Justinianus: Demon) shows.

Molanus's competently made reference book contains a great variety of information, as a dozen headings will show: Gabella (salt tax), Gallia (France), Gaudium (joy), Geldri (Gelre, a province in the Low Countries), Gemmae (gems), Genesis, Genethliaci (poems celebrating a birth), Gentiles, Gentium mores (customs), Geographia, Germani, Gigas (giant), Gladius (sword), Gloria (glory), Gothi (Goths). With such a choice of abstract and concrete, literary, historical, scientific, geographical, and other headings Molanus offers a view of contemporary scholarly interests. The number of references under a heading is usually three or four except when he is more generous than usual with a theological term. In Cambium (exchange) he cites four representative theologians. Articles like Education and Puer (boy) with five each and Studium (studies) with twenty-two are typical. A few subjects of current interest around 1600 are dealt with at some length: Calendarium lists thirty titles. Except for the Virgin Mary and a few heretics, individuals are rarely named as headings. Many place names are present but others that seem equally obvious are lacking, and a principle determining their inclusion is not readily perceived. Brixia (Brescia) and Brugae (Bruges) are mentioned, but Augsburg, Leiden, London, Lyons, Orleans, and Paris are not.

Molanus offers little on astronomy, which he does not recognize as a heading. Astrologia brings titles chiefly by theologians and is of interest primarily to them. Cometa names only two theological titles, and Coelum (sky) with two and Sol (sun) with one offer as little. Luna (moon) and Stella (star) do not appear as headings. Medicine receives the same short shrift. The article Medicus contains six chiefly theological titles, and nothing of particular value to a medical student appears in the rest of "M." The article Pestis with seven chiefly theological titles has a cross-reference to "Plura vide in Cathalogis medicorum," implying that Molanus thought it unnecessary to excerpt medical bibliographies. The two articles on English history—Anglia with seventeen references and Britannia with six—show a perhaps adequate command of the subject, but articles on English cities—London, Canterbury, Oxford, or York—are lacking.

An estimate of the value, either in its own day or now, of the *Bibliotheca materiarum* is not altogether easy to make. Molanus does not seem to have chosen titles from a wide general knowledge of books or a large library. He does not make clear what sources he consulted. For example, he does not seem to have used the Frankfurt fair catalogues that began to appear about twenty years before his death. He preferred Catholic to Protestant sources. This has certain advantages. Contemporary subject bibliographers from Gesner (1548, 1549) to Draud (1610, 1611, 1625) with whom we might compare him have Protestant backgrounds. Only Mareschal (1598), who made a list of French books, might be compared as a Catholic bibliographer and he differs in all regards from Molanus. Molanus did not use Gesner's *Pandectae* and *Partitiones,* which was the only general subject-index available during his lifetime. The *Bibliotheca materiarum* has some value as an independent compilation but can be said to be almost completely superseded by Justinianus's *Index* of 1612. It is easy to use. The alphabetical list of headings duplicates the arrangement of the book. There is no index of authors cited. The references usually lack dates and places of publication and often titles, but the bibliographical technique of Molanus's day did not insist upon these details.

THE *BIBLIOTHECA EXOTICA* (1610, 1625); GEORG DRAUD, *BIBLIOTHECA CLASSICA* (1611, 1625) AND *BIBLIOTHECA LIBRORUM GERMANICORUM CLASSICA* (1611, 1625)

The books offered for sale at the Frankfurt book-fair were listed in semi-annual fair-catalogues (Messkataloge) that began to appear in 1564. Within a generation these catalogues became so numerous and difficult to consult that compilations of them were needed. Although these were intended for booksellers, they also had considerable usefulness to scholars. The three earliest compilations did not get far beyond the bookshops [6] and were so quickly replaced that we may pass over them in favor of the three Bibliothecae that scholars used for more than a century as a subject-index. Rudolf Blum has discussed all these compilations in great detail with special attention to their origins, interrelations, and bibliographical techniques. These are the first examples of indispensable aids for booksellers.[7] They have continued to be made down to the present time. Histories and bibliographies give the necessary information about their titles and contents, but do not always make clear which ones are convenient sources of subject information.[8]

The anonymous *Bibliotheca exotica*, a classified list of books in languages other than Latin and German, was,

[6] These are Nicolaus Bassé, *Collectio in unum corpus omnium librorum . . . qui in nundinis francofurtensibus ab anno 1563 usque ad . . . 1592 venales extiterunt* (3 pts.; Frankfurt a.M., 1592); Henning Grosse, *Elenchus, seu Index generalis, in quo continentur libri omnes qui . . . post annum 1593 usque ad annum 1600 . . . novi auctive prodierunt* (Leipzig, n.d. [1600]); Johannes Clessius, *Unius seculi eiusque virorum literatorum monumentis tum florentissimi, tum fertilissimi ab anno domino 1500 ad 1602 inclusive, elenchus* (2 vols., Frankfurt a.M., 1602). For collations and estimates of the numbers of books cited in these works see Besterman, WBB. For the biography of Bassé see Josef Benzing, *Die Buchdrucker des 16. und 17. Jahrhunderts im deutschen Sprachgebiet*, Beiträge zum Buch- und Bibliothekswesen, 12 (Wiesbaden, 1963), p. 117.

[7] For Blum's admirable discussion see his *Nationalbibliographien*, pp. 249–255.

[8] LeRoy H. Linder, *The rise of current complete national bibliographies* (New York, 1959) deals hastily and incompletely with the early period. For bibliographies see R. L. Collison, *Bibliographies, subject and national; a guide to their contents, arrangement and use* (New York, 1951); Olga Pinto, *Le bibliografie nazionali*, Biblioteca di bibliografia italiana, 20 (2d ed.; Florence, 1951); R. A. Peddie, *National bibliographies, a descriptive catalogue of the works which register books published in each country* (London, 1912); Schneider, pp. 158–368; Malclès, *Les sources* I, 112–212.

like the *Bibliotheca classica* (1611) and the *Bibliotheca lirororum germanicorum classica* (1611) by Georg Draud (1573–1635), based on Johannes Clessius's *Elenchus* of 1602 but included the fair-catalogues down to 1610 and much additional material.[9] All three bibliographies were printed in the same style and have been usually treated as a unit, as they were intended to be. The *Bibliotheca exotica* does not bear Draud's name and it is uncertain what share, if any, he had in it. Throughout the seventeenth century booksellers and scholars used these books as subject-indexes. Scholars damned them and the fair-catalogues on which they rested with one voice. They are now extremely rare books.

The *Bibliotheca exotica* of 1610 lists more than four thousand French titles, smaller numbers in Italian and Spanish, a few in Dutch, and two in Hungarian. English titles are lacking. According to Paul Lacroix,[10] the com-

---

[9] One collation will suffice: *Bibliotheca exotica, sive Catalogus officinalis librorum peregrinis linguis usualibus scriptorum, videlicet Gallica, Italica, Hispanica, Belgica, Anglica, Danica, Bohemica, Ungarica, &c. omnium, quotquot in officinis bibliopolarum indagari potuerunt, & in nundinis Francofurtensibus prostant, ac venales habentur.*
La bibliotheque universail, contenant le catalogue de tous les livres, qui ont esté imprimes ce siecle passé, aux langues Françoise, Italieñe, Espaignole., & autres, qui sont aujourdhuy plus communes, despuis l'an. 1500. jusques à l'an present 1610. distribuée en certain ordre selon les matieres y contenues, & les surnoms de Autheurs (Frankfurt a.M., 1610, Pp. 219).
I have included the French title because some bibliographers have identified the book by it. Blum gives facsimiles of all three titles of the first editions of these bibliographies and that of the 1625 edition of the *Bibliotheca classica*. He and WBB give collations and estimates of the numbers of books cited in them.

[10] P.-L. Jacob (pseud.), *Recherches bibliographiques sur des livres rares et curieux* (Paris, 1880), p. 144. The compiler of the *Bibliotheca exotica* cannot have used the articles on Guillaume de Salluste (pp. 154–155), Michael de Nostradamus (p. 330), or Pontus de Tyard (p. 421) in La Croix du Maine, *Bibliothèque* (Paris, 1584). A more de-

piler consulted French bibliographies by François Grudé de la Croix du Maine (Paris, 1584) and Antoine du Verdier (Lyons, 1585) in making the edition of 1625. Neither of them is mentioned in the book and a comparison of the first of them with the *Bibliotheca* shows that the compiler did not use it.

In the *Bibliotheca exotica* the compiler divided the titles according to languages, then according to subjects, and within the subjects, arranged them alphabetically according to authors with groups of anonymous works at the end of each subject. The categories are rather small and are convenient for reference. He separates Protestant and Catholic Theology and sets up categories for Law; Medicine; "Libri politici" (Economics and Political Science); Ethics or casuistry; "Libri economici" (Agriculture, Trade, History, and Geography); "Libri ad studia politica spectantes," which include also Military Science and Hunting; Mathematics with Architecture and Geometry, Astronomy, Arithmetic; Physics and Metaphysics; Physiognomy and Oneiromancy; Philology; Dialectics, Rhetoric, and Oratory; Grammar; Poetics and Metrics; Women and Love; Jestbooks; and Music. A modern user will not understand the classification, but will find the running head a sufficient guide and will complain about the lack of an index of authors. In the companion works Draud or the publisher perceived its value and provided it.

In the following year (1611) Draud published a compilation of Latin books in a fashion similar to that employed in the *Bibliotheca exotica* but with some modifications in bibliographical style that Rudolf Blum has de-

---

tailed comparison seems unnecessary. Du Verdier's book is not available to me in the edition that the compiler might have used and seems scarcely worth running down for comparison.

scribed.[11] This *Bibliotheca classica* bears his name on the
titlepage. It is classified, that is to say, subdivided according to major disciplines and arranged alphabetically according to headings and within the headings alphabetically
according to authors. He begins with Theology, which he
divides into Lutheran, Zwinglian, and Catholic sections
and concludes with "Patrum Sanctorum Ecclesiae scripta
theologica." Typical subdivisions are Hebrew books (pp.
431–450), Law (pp. 451–631), Medicine and Chemistry
(pp. 633–712), History, Geography, and Economics, which
last includes Political Science (pp. 713–935), Philosophy,
the Arts, and the Humanities (pp. 937–1114), Poetry and
Metrics (pp. 1015–1021), Music (pp. 1203–1236). The
book ends with additions and corrections (pp. 1237–1253)
and an author index according to family names. Besterman lists it (WBB, col. 2258) as a bibliography of the
classics, but it is general in scope.

Draud inserts many cross-references indicated by as-
terisks and brought out to the left-hand margin. The section of Lutheran theology begins, for example, as follows:

*Abbreviatura linguae sanctae.   Vide Grammatica.
*Abelis historia.   Vide Martyres.
*Abstractive locutiones.   Vide Persona Christi.
*Absurda absurdorum absurdissima.[12]   Vide Calviniani.
*Academia Jesu Christi.   Vide Fidei purioris fundamenta.
*Accidentarij.   Vide Peccatum originis.
          Acta Apostolorum & in ea commentarij
                [Nine titles follow]

If Draud had continued to be generous with cross-
references, he would have vastly increased the reference

[11] See pp. 23–25. The sections for Music in both the 1611 and
1625 editions have been recently reprinted by K. Ameln (Bonn,
1957. Not seen).
[12] The title of a book (Jena, 1512) by Albert Grauer (b. 1575).

value of the *Bibliotheca classica*, but after the first few letters in the first section of theology he reduces the use of them considerably. He continues to make them occasionally through the theological sections. Those he made for law and medicine are collected in an appendix (1247–1250); it does not appear that he made any for the remainder of the book containing the sections most likely to interest a reader today. Perhaps the printer objected because cross-references on the scale employed at the beginning would have meant a substantial enlargement of the book.

In his bibliographical technique Draud follows the contemporary fashion: titles are abbreviated and editions of a standard work or books by a recognized authority are cited casually, often without a title. His analyses of large collective works must have been very helpful to all users of the *Bibliotheca classica*. For example, he summarizes in great detail (pp. 603–627) a standard legal encyclopedia called *Tractatatus tractatuum* (29 vols., Venice, 1584–1586).[13] Rudolf Blum finds his manner of excerpting and arranging titles very interesting and discusses it in the light of modern practice. It is unnecessary to repeat or digest his informative and instructive discussion.

Draud relies on the fair catalogues and the publishers' catalogues that he could obtain. He goes beyond them in elaborating the classification and in setting up, for example, a category of collections of medical writings (p. 686). At times, but less often than we would wish, he ceases to depend on titles. Thus, his account of guides to university studies and the curriculum (Ratio studiorum, pp. 1105–1106) shows some familiarity with the contents of the books. It is not altogether clear whether he aims

[13] A copy in the Newberry Library.

at something more encyclopedic than a mere collection of the titles available. For example, he gives (pp. 802–809) a list of chronicles or universal histories that begin with Creation, a chronological list of historians from Moses to Guicciardini, and a tabulation of historical works according to the dates with which they begin or end.

It is difficult to speak in moderate terms of the *Bibliotheca classica* as a summary of Renaissance learning. It contains many errors and ghosts, but even they may be clues to a forgotten book or a plan that failed of execution. Ghosts may owe their origin to the practice of announcing books in the fair catalogues before their actual publication. Errors and confusions may arise because the publisher gave the book a new title or announced it inexactly. The errors that beset bibliographers and ordinary men in copying titles were present in 1610 just as they are today. One must accept the situation as one finds it and take the chaff with the wheat. The chaff is by no means worthless until it has been thoroughly thrashed. There are often more recent sources of information than Draud's bibliographies and one will ordinarily prefer to consult them. But, for historical purposes and especially those in which one wants to follow every clue to its end, one dare not pass by the *Bibliothecae*. For example, there are twenty-seven closely printed lines listing editions under the caption "Euclidis Elementa Geometr." (pp. 998–999). A century later Johann Albert Fabricius gave a more judicious and reliable selection of the editions, but he was not interested in old schoolbooks.[14] Three tightly printed quarto pages (pp. 973–976) with sections entitled "Dia-

[14] See *Bibliotheca graeca* (3d ed., 14 vols.; Hamburg, 1717–1754), III, 367–377. Charles Thomas-Stanford has collected the schoolbooks in *Early editions of Euclid's Elements*, Bibliographical Society, Illustrated Monographs, 20 (London, 1926). I am not sure that he consulted Draud.

lectica Rami, Dialecticae Rameae impugnatio," and "Dialectica Philippo-Ramea" suggest the impact of the ideas and methods of Pierre de la Ramée (Petrus Ramus). The identification of the titles promises to be vexatious and is not to be undertaken without previous familiarity with pertinent books, especially the studies by Walter J. Ong. These examples will suggest what sort of information Draud gives.

Even a casual turning of the pages of the *Bibliotheca classica* yields tempting clues to follow further. For example, a Finnish scholar has recently called attention to Simon Roth, the author of what has been called the first dictionary of foreign words in the German language. Neither he nor any other student of the subject has, so far as I know, commented on a title reported by Draud (p. 1001): "Wolff. Hungeri linguae Germanicae vindicatio, contra exoticas quasdam, quae complurium vocum & dictionum, mere Germanicarum, Etymologias, ex sua petere conati sunt. Argentorati 1586. in 8." In addition to long lists of editions of Plautus, Seneca, and Terence, the sections entitled Comoediae (pp. 1132–1136) and Tragoediae (pp. 1195–1196) cite titles of more recent plays. Draud does not regularly indicate whether they are in Latin or a vernacular language, but in any case he lays a foundation for the bibliography of Renaissance drama. H. B. Wheatley, who wrote an entertaining book on Renaissance anagrams,[15] could have profitably consulted Draud. William Hammer, who wrote a doctoral dissertation on poems in praise of cities,[16] would have found much to his purpose in Urbium incolarumque descriptio.

[15] *On anagrams* (London, 1862). See *Bibliotheca classica* (ed. 1611), pp. 1116–1117.
[16] *Latin and German encomia of cities* (Diss.; University of Chicago, 1937). See *Bibliotheca classica* (ed. 1611), pp. 1200–1201.

Inasmuch as Draud strove for completeness it seems scarcely necessary to comment on his success or failure in particular directions. He gave booksellers and scholars as complete an account of books published before 1610 as circumstances permitted. We can correct his ignorance of incunabula, enlarge his inadequate survey of books published outside Germany, and repair his many defects. In considering his achievement it is carping criticism to point out deficiencies and errors.

After the lapse of fifteen years new editions of the three bibliographies appeared. The general plan remained unchanged except that cross-references were completely omitted. Draud canceled many headings and reclassified the titles. Unfortunately he still did not see the utility of a table of contents and an index of headings. Comparison of the 1611 and 1625 editions of the *Bibliotheca classica* will illustrate his methods. He discarded titles for reasons that I do not understand. Perhaps examination of these books might make his procedure clear. Thus, in Globi (ed. 1611, p. 1002; ed. 1625, p. 1377) he repeated no title from the earlier edition. In Graecae linguae commendatio (ed. 1611, p. 1002; ed. 1625, p. 1377) he carried over two and omitted four titles. He made minor improvements of details and added titles (these are not necessarily titles of books printed between 1611 and 1625). This, in Graecae epistolae (ed. 1611, p. 1003; ed. 1625, pp. 1377–1378) he kept all the titles and corrected an error in a date. In Memoria artificialis (ed. 1611, p. 1032; ed. 1625, p. 1416) he kept all the earlier citations and added as many new ones. Draud subjected the first edition to a careful and methodical revision. Users must consult both editions. A seventeenth-century owner of my copy of the 1625 edition says in a manuscript note that he bought the 1611 edition because he found it necessary.

A somewhat larger sample will give an idea of Draud's book and the nature of his revision. The first dozen entries [17] in the section entitled "Philosophici, artiumque humaniorum, adde tamen et (pro ingeniorum petulantia, atque abusu) inhumaniorum, libri . . ." are as follows:

Bibl. classica, 1611	Bibl. classica, 1625
Academica 6	Academica 6 —4, *4
Adverbia 1	Acromatica Aristotelis 2
Adversaria,	Adagia 6
Animadversiones 2	Adversaria,
Aenigmata 7	Animadversiones 4 *2
Aequator 1	Aenigmata 5 —3, *1
Affectuum motio 1	Aequationes 1
Alexandra [by Lycophron] 1	Aequinoctia 1
Alphabeta varia 15	Aeris transmutatio 2
Amatoria 8	Alloquia 2
Amicitia [18] 4	Alphabeta varia 10 —5
Anagrammatismi [19] 2	Analytica Aristotelis priora
Analytica Aristotelis priora	[13 lines]
[16 lines]	

Draud's thoroughgoing revision concerned both the headings and the titles cited under them. Many headings were transferred to more appropriate places. Alexandra (a Greek romance), Amatoria (love-stories), and Anagrammatismi were moved to the section entitled "Libri poetici." Aenigmata remained, but also appeared in the section for literature (ed. 1611, p. 938 [47 titles]; ed. 1625, pp. 1387 [5 titles] and 1505 [1 title]). I cannot explain the startling reduction in the number of titles. Aequator, which concerns the sidereal equator, was transferred to

[17] See ed. 1611, pp. 937–940; ed. 1625, pp. 1306–1308. The first Arabic number is the number of titles cited. A dash precedes the number omitted in 1625, and a * precedes the number added in 1625.

[18] Editions of Cicero, Laelius, seu de amicitia are not counted.

[19] These two titles were transferred to "Libri poetici," ed. 1625, p. 1507 (17 titles), which included the 11 titles in "Libri poetici," ed. 1611, pp. 1116–1117.

Planetae (ed. 1625, p. 1468). The only title under Adverbia, an anonymous *Connubium adverbiorum Ciceronianorum* (Lyons, 1583), disappeared in the reshuffling. At least I cannot find it under Ciceroniana, Grammatica latina, or Phrases. Draud made substantial additions to the number of headings, especially those for literature and the sciences. Many titles added in 1625 refer to books published before 1611. It can only be a matter for conjecture why he failed to cite them in the earlier edition. These comparisons must suffice, for a more critical study of Draud's procedure calls for use of the fair-catalogues.

The 1625 edition of the *Bibliotheca classica* was substantially larger and, on the whole, more carefully made than the 1611 edition. If we disregard the preliminary pages and the indexes of authors, we can compare the 1253 pages of the 1611 edition with the 1654 pages of the 1625 edition. The format and typography of the two editions is the same, but the omission of cross-references in the later edition meant an increase in the number of pages available for bibliography. All in all, the 1625 edition is perhaps one-third larger than the 1611 edition. If we accept Theodore Besterman's estimated 30,000 titles in the 1611 edition—the figure is not at all excessive—those in the 1625 edition must amount to at least 40,000 (Besterman's figure is 35,000). In any case the *Bibliotheca classica* is a very substantial record on the books printed before 1625. Some bibliographers cite an edition of 1643 (Petzholdst, p. 71, says 1644), but it seems to be a ghost.

With all their faults, many and grievous as they are, the *Bibliotheca exotica* and Draud's bibliographies of Latin and German books are valuable guides to sixteenth- and early seventeenth-century books. No doubt titles are cited inaccurately; no doubt ghosts haunt their pages; and no doubt books are classified incorrectly because Draud has relied on titles. These defects do not justify the complete neglect that has befallen him. Morhof has no kind word for him except a commendation of his method; eighteenth-century bibliographers follow Morhof blindly. In damning him Petzholdt rises (pp. 70–71) to unusual eloquence (I paraphrase):

Whoever is not balked by the not inconsiderable trouble of consulting now and again these bundles (first published in 1611) of many thousands of notes excerpted from the unreliable fair catalogues, may perhaps in occasional instances find something useful. The benefit to be obtained does not in the remotest degree correspond to the efforts that the use of the book requires.

More recent scholars scarcely know his name. Johannes Franck, the author of a brief biographical sketch in the *Allgemeine deutsche Biographie*, the standard German biographical dictionary, mentions various books by Draud as valuable for the cultural history of his day, but omits the *Bibliothecae* entirely. Theodore Besterman does not name him in *The Beginnings of Systematic Bibliography*. Like prophets, bibliographers enjoy only a very limited fame, but fate has dealt more harshly with Draud than most other bibliographers. There are other reasons for the neglect of him than the defects in his work. Scholarship of all kinds began anew in the eighteenth century and refused to recognize or use the scholarly writings of the seventeenth and earlier centuries. Draud's bibliographies disappeared from the scholarly scene because eighteenth-century theologians had little inclination to thresh the straw of seventeenth-century controversy and could consult bibliographies much more to their liking when they did. In theology, for example, such an old-fashioned work of enormous scope as Casimir Oudin (1638–1717), *Commentarius de scriptoribus ecclesiae antiquis illorumque scriptis* (3 vols.; Leipzig, 1722. See WBB, col. 4026), meant little to the new age, and a little more than a century later Petzholdt does not even mention it. Students of the classics made better tools than Draud's books to meet their needs. Here Johann Albert Fabricius led the way. Like theologians, they demanded works containing critical comments that Draud did not provide. Students of law and medicine had their own bibliographies that were larger, more accurate, and more convenient than Draud's *Bibliothecae*. There was no important category of scholars likely to consult them. Bookdealers did not want them and there were then few historians of scholarship such as flourish today. Draud's *Bibliothecae* were awkward to use, the bindings were dilapidated, the references were out of date and unreliable, and the editions and commentaries cited were chiefly of little value. Successful dealers and scholars threw the *Bibliothecae* on the ashheap, and they have now become rarities of the first order.

I cannot leave Georg Draud without saying a word about his other writings and trying to get closer to the man himself.[20] My remarks will be brief because his works are scantily represented in the shelves of the great libraries I have visited. Georg Draud was born in 1573 in the village of Dauernheim in Hesse as a son of the third wife of the pastor Peter Draud. Being one of twenty-five children, he was soon forced to make his own way in the

[20] See Johannes Fabricius, *Historia,* V, 529–530; Saxe, IV, 217–218; F. W. Striedler, *Grundlagen zu einer hessischen Gelehrten- und Schrift-stellerlexikon* (15 vols.; Kassel, 1781–1806, and continued by other hands), III, 213; Johannes Franck, *Allgemeine deutsche Biographie,* V, 383.

world. He studied theology at Marburg and received an
M.A. As I have already said, he often made a living as a
proofreader and hack. From 1599 to 1614 he was pastor in
Gross-Karben, a pleasant Hessian village. Its intellectual
resources are limited and its pastor can have received no
generous stipend. One can only conjecture how Draud
managed to compile the thick volumes of the *Bibliothecae*
at the distance of a day's journey from Frankfurt. He removed to Ortenberg and finally to Dauernheim, from
where he fled to Butzbach on account of the plague. He
died in 1635.

Draud's writings are more numerous and varied than
we might expect from his circumstances. The first was an
edition (1603) of Solinus with notes that are said to be
valuable. Salmasius's edition (1629) replaced it and it
has disappeared from sight. Solinus with his miscellaneous
interests is just the sort of author we would expect to at-
tract Draud's attention. He brought to theology a practical
turn of mind, for he wrote a *Duodenarius historico-bibli-
cus,* which is also referred to as *Pandectae Veteris et Novi
Testamenti* and seems to have been a guide to the writing
of sermons. Such titles as *Hortulus senilis animae* (A garden of an old man's soul) or *Remedium stultitiae* (A cure
for folly) suggests that village life gave him subjects, and
Colloquia principum mensalia (The tabletalk of princes)
and *Praxis & prudentia aulica* (Court life and prudence)
may be subjects of his own choice or subjects suggested by
a publisher who thought such books would sell well. Some
of these were written in German, and others in Latin. His
Theatrum urbium (A conspectus of cities) is, like the *Bibliothecae,* a compilation. What reference works can he
have had in a small Hessian village in making it? Presumably the publisher commissioned him to do the edition of

Dies caniculares, an encyclopedic work by Simon Majolus, to which he made considerable additions. A *Discursus typographicus cum praecipuorum typographorum insignibus* (A treatise on printing with the printer's marks of the chief printers. Frankfurt, 1625) shows that his interest in publishing continued to the end. This record leaves the impression of extraordinary diligence and a great variety of interests.

FABIANUS JUSTINIANUS, *INDEX UNIVERSALIS ALPHABETICUS* (1612)

While Georg Draud was compiling the first edition of his *Bibliothecae,* Fabianus Justinianus (Fabiano Giustiniani, 1578–1627), bishop of Ajaccio in Corsica (1616) but resident in Rome and librarian of the Oratorians, was at work on a large alphabetical subject-index.[21] The brave title of his *Index universalis alphabeticus materias in omni facultate consulte pertractans, eorumque scriptores et locos designans* (1612) raises high hopes, and by their number its 648 folio pages might seem to confirm them. Unfortunately the *Index* does not satisfy the expectations that its title and size might awaken.[22]

For a long time libraries had been flourishing at Rome. Sixtus IV continued the tradition of his predecessor Nicholas V and lavished money on books and buildings. Not

[21] He was born Fabriano Taranchetti, but was adopted into the Giustiniani family. He was admitted into the Oratory in 1597.

[22] For comment on the *Index* see Rudolf Blum, p. 27; I. Fraschetti Santinelli, *Il catalogo alfabetico per soggetti* (Milan, [1941]), pp. 32–34, quoting the article "Biblioteca"; Giuseppe Fumagalli, *Cataloghi di biblioteche e indici bibliografici* (Florence, 1887), pp. 180–181. Augustino Oldoini, *Athenaeum liguisticum* (Perugia, 1680), p. 172 says that a second edition was in the "Collegium Milanese d. C. d. G." It has been discovered and is discussed below.

long before the compilation of the *Index universalis* Sixtus
V had erected (1587–1589) the present Vatican library.
Angelo Rocca (1545–1620) had founded (1605) the Biblioteca Angelica, which was the only real public library
at Rome, and had written some of the first books on library
science. The Biblioteca Vallicelliana, of which Justinianus
was librarian, acquired the books of St. Philip Neri, Achille
Stazio, Cesare Baronio, and Odorico Rinaldi. A few years
later, in the papacy of Urban VIII, the number and importance of humanists and book-collectors resident in
Rome or visiting the city during the years 1630–1632 inspired Leone Allacci (1586–1669), librarian of the Vatican,
whose own books came later to the Vallicelliana, to write
a *Who's Who* (*Apes Urbanae* [Rome, 1633]) listing them.
This enthusiasm continued for another century or even
somewhat longer. The *Index universalis alphabeticus* is
part of the joy in books and libraries that marks the last
years of the sixteenth and the whole of the seventeenth
century at Rome. By his dedication to Cardinal Scipio
Borghese, then librarian of the Vatican, Justinianus suggests this happy background.

Justinianus, a bibliographer and exegete, was experienced
in the task of making a subject-index that he undertook.
Two years after the publication of his *Index* he printed
a bibliography of commentators on the Bible with a catalogue of those who had written or preached on particular
texts: *De sacra Scriptura eiusque usu, ac interpretibus
commentarius. In quo non solum ad sacrorum Bibliorum
studium, et sacras conciones formandas institutio traditur:
sed etiam selectorum librorum in universam theologiam
speculativam, practicam, et positivam, singularis; et in
totam sacram Scripturam universalis notitia perhibetur*
(Rome, 1614. Pp. [xiv], 280, 151, [16]). This or more pre-

cisely Liber Tertius (pp. 1–151, separately numbered after
p. 280) entitled "Catalogus universalis eorum, qui tum
universe, tum singulatim in sacrorum Bibliorum libros
scripsisse noscitur" differs but little in title and presumably
in contents from an *Elenchus* announced on the titlepage
of the *Index* of 1612.[23] This *catalogus*, which seems to be
competently made, might have been mentioned in the
preceding chapter on bibliographies based on the Bible.
A portion of *De sacra Scriptura* (Liber II, pp. 145–280)
was published separately (Cologne, 1619. Not seen) as
De sacro concinnatore and is especially interesting because
the publisher says that it should be regarded as a supplement to the *Bibliotheca materiarum* by Johannes Molanus
that he had just brought out. In 1621 Justinianus published
a commentary on Tobit and was presumably continuing
work on a second edition of the *Index*. He was a diligent
man but does not give enough of himself in his prefaces
to come alive to a modern reader.

The *Index universalis alphabeticus* is, as Fraschetti Santinelli points out, based on an inventory of the Biblioteca
Vallicelliana and cites many books according to their titles
without attempting a closer analysis. The Oratory had acquired by gift or purchase some large collections and libraries that Justinianus put in order. Nevertheless, he went
much farther than an inventory or shelflist by adding references to specific passages in books. His citations are so
numerous that one must suppose that he kept some encyclopedic works within easy reach. Typical works of this
sort are Johannes Schenkius (1530–1598), *Observationes
medicae* (7 vols.; Basel, 1584–1597 and later eds.), which
he consults for medical subjects; Tommasso Garzoni

[23] This Elenchus is not present in my photographic copy of the
Index.

(c1549–1589), *La piazza universale di tutte le professioni* (Venice, 1585 and later eds.) and Hieronymus Cardan, *De rerum varietate* (1551?),[24] which he cites for secular subjects; Joseph Langius, *Nova polyanthea* (Lyons, 1604 and later eds.), which he cites for philosophical and abstract subjects; and various theological compendia. He turned occasionally to the *Theatrum vitae humanae* (Basel, 1565 and later eds.), a standard sixteenth-century encyclopedia. This list of reference works, to which perhaps as many more might be added, is instructive. Justinianus did not use Caelius Rhodiginus and Raffaele Volaterranus, whom Conrad Gesner cited often, although they were Italians and their encyclopedic works were available in many editions. Probably their emphasis on classical rather than contemporary sources made them unsuitable.

Perhaps the most curious source used by Justinianus is Garzoni's *Piazza*, a remarkable encyclopedic account of trades and professions. Books of this sort have a long history and in some instances contain bibliographical information that justifies us in regarding them as akin to subject-indexes. In my copy of the *Piazza* (Venice, 1599), and no doubt in others, there are many references to authorities in the margins. The adaptations of the *Piazza* in various languages are praised as important and useful. The first of them may have been Cristóval Suárez de Figuera, *Piazza universal de todas ciencias, y artes, parte traducida de Toscano, y parte compuesta* (Madrid, 1615).[25] A substantially enlarged edition was published more than a century later: *Nuevamente, corregido, y addicionado para esta impressión. En que se comprehende*

---

[24] David Clement doubts the existence of an edition of 1551; see *Bibliothèque curieuse* . . . (9 vols.; Göttingen, later Leipzig, 1750–1760), VI, 279–281.

[25] 8 ll., 368 pp. 2d ed.; Perpignan, 1630 (8 ll., 379 pp.).

*una universal noticia de cada una de las ciencias, sus
inventores, origen, introducción en varias provincias y
reynos, sus professores mas distinguidos, progressos, etc.
De todas las religiones, etc., de las órdenes militares . . .
de varias artes liberales y mechánicas, su origen, inventores.*[26] The German *Piazza universale. Das ist, allgemeiner
Schawplatz Marckt und Zusammenkunfft aller Profes-
sionen Künsten Geschäfften Händeln und Handtwercken
. . .* (Frankfurt a.M., 1641, repr. 1659) is also augmented.[27]
It is noteworthy for 146 woodcuts, chiefly or perhaps exclusively by Jost Ammann, that greatly increase its value.
They were originally made for Hans Sachs, *Eygentliche
Beschreibung aller Stände auff Erden* (Frankfurt a.M.,
1568) and were purchased for use in the *Piazza* at a price
that made the publisher wince. Like other books of this
sort, it contains accounts of arts and crafts of all kinds,
makers of musical instruments, painters, printers, book-
binders, rulers, clerics, physicians, and alchemists. The
Beschreibung is not important for bibliographical uses,
but some examples of this genre occasionally are. By way
of conclusion to these remarks I mention a similar older
work: Barthélemy de Chasseneux (1480–1541), *Catalogus
gloriae mundi laudes honores excellentias ac praeminen-
tias omnium fere plurimarumque rerum illus[trium] continens* (Lyons, 1529 and later eds.).[28]

In its plan the *Index universalis alphabeticus* is truly

[26] Madrid, 1733 (8 ll., 676 pp., 27 ll.).
[27] 14 ll., 1084 pp., 7 ll., with a folding map of the world. See Curt
Faber du Faur, *German baroque literature. A catalogue of the collection in the Yale University Library* (New Haven, 1958), p. 299,
no. 1191. There is a copy in the University of California Library at
Berkeley.
[28] See Brunet, *Manuel*, I, col. 1819; Robert Brun, *Le livre illustré
en France au XVIᵉ Siècle* (Paris, 1930), pp. 170–171; J.-H. Pignot,
*Un jurisconsulte au xviᵉ siècle. Barthélemy de Chasseneuz, . . . sa vie
et ses oeuvres* (Paris, 1880), Ch. III, pp. 143–209.

universal, but Justinianus does look very far beyond matters suggested by his training and experience or those
suggested by general reference works. The headings
through *ab-* are typical of what he chooses to include. The
following list shows how numerous they are and how
neatly he subdivided them. The numbers in parenthesis
in the following list refer to the subdivisions:

Aaron (2), abba (explanation of a word in Matt. 14), abbas (4),
abbatissa, abbatia, S. Abbo, abdomen, Abel (4), Abgar, abjura-
tio, ablactio, ablutio (2), abortum, abortivus, Abraham (4),
Abrahami eremitae vita, Abrahae abbatis vita, abbreviatura (2),
abrogatio, Absalon, absens, absolutio (7), abstentia (10),
abstractio interna, abstractum et concretum, S. Abundantius,
S. Abundius, abusio et abusus (4), abyssus (2).

Here we find an abundance of ecclesiastical headings
(Old Testament names, the names of saints and others of
like interest, ideas useful to a preacher and a theologian),
a generous selection of medical terms, and a few legal and
philosophical terms. Geographical and historical names,
except those associated with the church, are comparatively
rare. Except for medicine, references to the sciences are
rather scanty. Those associated with the seven liberal arts
are rather numerous. On the whole, one can say that the
headings are well-chosen. The typographical arrangement
is also excellent. See, as a sample (references are omitted):

Abel

de Abel primo Iustorum, & quod in hominibus Iusti a principio
Mundi maxima Dei bonitas semper claruit
de Abel secundo filio Adam, figura Sacramentorum
de Abel & Cain
de eorundem Sacrificiis

In spite of all I have said, the *Index* will disappoint
anyone who takes the trouble to run down this rare book.
We cannot quarrel with the citations by authors' names

without titles, for this was acceptable bibliographical procedure in 1612. Nor can we quarrel with abbreviated titles
and the lack of dates and places of publication. What we
can quarrel with is the choice and use of authorities. Justinianus gives information that had little value in 1612
and even less today. Few at any time can profit by such a
reference as "Aaron. Liber Ariamontani, in Regijs Bibliis."
He could have given more and better references, although
we may thank him for naming a location of the book cited.
Nor does he always deal adequately with subjects about
which he was well-informed. The article Abbatissa contains nothing that his readers could not have found immediately in contemporary reference works. We can praise
a cross-reference beginning "Vide etiam . . . (See also
. . .)," for such an aid was rare at this time, but Justinianus's contemporaries could not have found three references to systematic treatises that they ought to know very
helpful. We, who are perhaps less familiar with them, may
find them welcome, but there are now better sources of
information about abbesses.

Under the headings for non-ecclesiastical subjects we
do not ordinarily find much useful information. The article Abdomen consists, for example, in a citation of "Io.
Schenkius, lib. 3. observationum Medicarum." A modern
student of medical history might very likely turn this up
without consulting the *Index universalis*. In Academiae
Justinianus cites Garzoni's *Piazza* and a well-known treatise by Jacob Middendorpius. Justinianus probably did
not have a desire or the resources to go beyond the ordinary reference works of his day. According to Besterman
(WBB, col. 451), he cites an impressive 60,000 titles. In
brief, the book is a handy compendium that readers in the
Vallicelliana no doubt found useful.

The articles for the subjects that I have used as a stand-dard in comparing subject-indexes confirm what has been said. The article Astronomia (pp. 43–44) cites more than a score of names and is followed by as many sub-articles with bibliographical references. One or another of them may perhaps be helpful to a modern historian, but the whole does not get beyond a hasty survey. The articles Anglia (p. 23) with sub-articles of a religious nature particularly interesting to Catholic readers and Britannia (p. 61) represent what could be easily put together in the Vallicelliana and contain little of value to others than students there. In Bibliotheca (p. 57) Justinianus cites nothing of consequence and mingles Apollodorus, *Bibliotheca* (i.e., a citation according to title) with treatises on libraries, while Scriptor et Scriptura (p. 482), where we might hope for something on bibliography, deals with the art of writing and not with authors and books. Medicine does not interest Justinianus.

This discouraging report is to be corrected by recognizing that many articles seem worth turning to. For example, I quote (p. 123):

Critici Dies

de Criticis diebus. Abrahae Ravennatis libri. Andreas Laurentius. Antonius Petitaeus in suo Crisimenologion. Augerius Ferrerius in libro de diebus decretorijs. Augustinus Nyphus. Boderus, Fredericus Bonaventura, in 6. lib. sui tract. de Octomestri. Frid. Chrysogoni in lib. de Prognost. Io. Guidons (sic) de temporibus altiorum. Lucas Gauricius. in lib. de diebus decretorijs. Michael Angelus Blond. in lib. de diebus decretorijs.
de Eorum causis per se. quae in nobis sunt. liber incerti.[29]

[29] Since this article is quoted as an example of Justinianus's bibliographical style, I do not identify the references and offer no translation. By exception, however, Lucas Gauricius (1475–1558), *Super diebus decretoriis* (Rome, 1546) may be identified because it is very rare. Justinianus's article might have been useful for such modern discussions of the subject as Hans Hilferding, *Bacons Schriften über*

Some of these references may be helpful even today, but
the reference to a "liber incerti" perhaps could not have
been easily found in the Vallicelliana in 1612 and will now
probably elude a diligent effort. The citations of Andreas
Laurentius and Augustinus Nyphus without the titles of
their books were not troublesome then and can very likely
be clarified today with little trouble. The reference to
Boderus without a Christian name was more vexatious in
1612 than it is now. Another and better example of an
article likely to be useful today is the long article Studium
(p. 507), but I am unwilling to quote it without identifying the references.

References to Justinianus's *Index universalis alphabeticus* are few, brief, and unfavorable. For this reason it is
all the more curious that John Wilkins, Bishop of Chester,
should cite it in his *Ecclesiastes; or, A discourse concerning the gift of prayer* (1646) [30] and should recognize it as
an alphabetical subject-index. This very popular preacher's guide might have directed someone to the *Index* or
might have induced a librarian to buy it. Bodley's librarian
did so, but no one else in England as far as I can see.
Wilkins cites the *Index* along with a dozen other bibliographies:

Amongst whom there are some that go by an Alphabetical
order of the Authors names, as Photius, Sextus Senensis, Posse-
vinus, &c. others observe an Alphabetical order in setting down

---

die kritischen Tage (Diss.; Erfurt, 1913); Friedrich Palitzsch, *Bacons
zweite astrologische Schrift über die kritischen Tage* (Diss.; Leipzig,
1918); Max Förster, "Die altenglischen Verzeichnisse von Glücks-
und Unglückstagen," *Studies in English philology. A miscellany in
honor of Friedrich Klaeber* (Minneapolis, 1929), pp. 258–277;
Gustav Jungbauer, "Unglückstage," *Handwörterbuch des deutschen
Aberglaubens,* VIII (Berlin, 1936–1937), cols. 1427–1440.

[30] I have used the seventh edition (London, 1693). He is wrong in
citing Gesner as alphabetical.

the several matters and subjects they insist upon; as, Bolduanus, Draudius, Gesner, Justinianus, &c. So that it a man would know either what Subject any particular Authors have treated upon, or what Authors have treated particularly upon any Subject, he may in them see references to this purpose.

Petzholdt damns the *Index* in a sentence (p. 70). Besterman notes (WBB, col. 459) the canceling of p. 223 in some copies [31] and the replacement of the preface and indicates (col. 440) that the *Elenchus* containing the theological index was printed together with the *Index* in 1612.

The second edition of Justinianus's Index, which is dated 1627, remains in manuscript and is now in the Braidense in Milan with the shelfmark AE XII. 17.[32] The manuscript had been left in Ajaccio when Justinianus died and passed into the possession of the Jesuits in Milan and finally into the Braidense. It has been thoroughly revised and substantially enlarged: much of the preliminary matter is omitted, many articles are brought up to date by minor additions, and others are reorganized and rewritten. Adam and Administratio have been reorganized; Academiae, Aedificatio, Confirmatio, and Confessio contain important additions. Duellum fills a column. Apparently Justinianus made the changes and had the whole copied, leaving some gaps to be filled in by a second hand. These changes do not alter the character of the book; it remains a subject-index with a strong emphasis on ecclesiastical matters and interests. For reference purposes one should

[31] This page contains references to Hispania and Historia. There may be an objectionable political allusion in one or the other of these articles, but I have not tried to identify it.

[32] I am indebted to Professors Vittorio Santoli of the University of Florence and Cesare Segré of the University of Milan for discovering it. I have used an enlargement from a microfilm in the Newberry Library. The microfilm is in the University of Pennsylvania Library.

consult the second edition, but it represents no development of historical significance.

INDEX ALPHABETICUS
[BIBLIOTHECAE ANGELICAE]...
RERUM ORDINE CONCINNATUS (c1620)

A manuscript subject-catalogue of the Angelica entitled *Index alphabeticus librorum impressorum rerum ordine concinnatus* made about the same time as Justinianus's *Index universalis* may be mentioned briefly for the sake of comparison. It is Mss. 616, 617 in the Angelica and is briefly described by I. Fraschetti Santinelli.[33] I have seen it. The similarity of titles is curious and may suggest some connection. The Angelica subject-catalogue was kept up to date (assiduamente aggiornato). The *Index universalis* was rather more a bibliography than a catalogue and the Vallicelliana does not have a copy containing either additions or the shelfmarks of the books cited. The maker of the Angelica catalogue was more careful in classifying titles than Justinianus was. For example, he correctly entered F. Moncaejus (Francesco Money), *De vitulo aureo* (The golden calf) under Aaron, where a reader would be glad to find it. He excerpted more standard authors and miscellanies than Justinianus did and gave more precise references. His emphasis was less severely ecclesiastical and involved at times the use of Italian terms (*Canto fermo*) along with Latin (*Casus conscientiae*). The Angelica catalogue will serve as an example of the manuscript catalogues used by readers and officials in libraries.

[33] *I Cataloghi*, pp. 34–36. See pp. 31, n. 1 and 38, n. 1 for references to catalogues of manuscripts at Monte Cassino that suggest an opportunity for further study of developments in subject cataloguing.

Fraschetti Santinelli cites other Italian examples but I shall not discuss them, since they were intended to serve only the scholars who visited the library. It would appear that Italian librarians indexed their books very carefully.

PLANS FOR SUBJECT-INDEXES (1630–1670)

With the second editions (1625) of the *Bibliotheca exotica* and Draud's *Bibliothecae* and Justinianus's revision (1627) of his *Index universalis alphabeticus* the making of subject-indexes ceased for a generation. Political and social conditions were unfavorable to large projects that called for leisure and the use of many resources. The unrest in England that culminated in the execution of Charles I and the Commonwealth, the Parisian riots in which Cardinal Mazarin's first library was dispersed and the Fronde; and the Thirty Years War that dragged on in Germany were unpropitious. Bibliography itself was in flux. Catalogues of public and private libraries beginning with the University of Leiden catalogue of 1595, the Bodleian catalogues of 1605, 1620, and 1635, and catalogues of private libraries like that made by Gabriel Naudé for Jean des Cordes (1643) or the Dutch auction catalogues that increased rapidly in number in this century were bibliographical aids that at first satisfied scholarly demands for guides to subject matter. As time passed the need for information suggested its accumulation in reference works. Men began to write specialized bibliographies of various fields, and Philip Labbé published a bibliography of bibliographies in 1653.

Although no subject-index was compiled in the second and third quarters of the seventeenth century, the notion of one appears in widely separated places. Men in France,

England, and (after the Thirty Years War) Germany made plans and in some instances collections. At times they show some familiarity with earlier work of this sort, but in general they work and think independently.[34]

Petrus Blanchot, Idea bibliothecae universalis (*1631*)

In 1631 Petrus (Pierre) Blanchot (1589–1637), "ex ordine Minimorum S. Francisci de Paula," described a plan for an enormous subject-index and said that he had already made good progress with it. He intended to list virtually everything that had been written, citing editions according to dates and places of publication. It was truly a work to be desired by all scholars, an "Opus sacro-pro-phanum, Theologis positivis & scholasticis, concionatori-bus, canonistis, jurisconsultis, politicis, medicis, historicis, philosophicis, mathematicis, philologiis, bibliopolis, om-niumque artium professoribus collectoribus voto nuncupa-tum." According to a prospectus entitled *Idea bibliothecae universalis* (Paris, 1631. Pp. 8), by which he hoped to enlist collaborators, he planned a subject with small head-ings that he would assemble alphabetically in indexes of the various disciplines. Within the headings he intended to arrange titles chronologically to show historical devel-opments. It was a cumulation of already existing cata-logues. He had already worked through the shelves of libraries at Paris (probably the library of the Minorites), Passy, and Vincennes. He expected help from Italy, Ger-

[34] D. G. Morhof alludes to Daniel Heinsius (1582–1655) in this context; see *Polyhistor,* I, ch. xviii, § 23 (ed. 1747, I, 92). I find no clear allusion to a subject-index in his oration (1607) thanking the faculty for the honor of the librarianship. Adrien Baillet also refers to this oration, but rightly thinks it is of little consequence; see *Jugemens des savans* (17 vols., Amsterdam, 1725), II, i, 236–237. It is the third in his *Orationes* (new ed., Leiden, 1615).

many, Belgium, Spain, and even England, which "the
ocean shuts off from the rest of the world, [but] not from
common needs and from mankind."

An excellent brief bibliography of bibliographies that
he has used or intends to use shows how clearly Blanchot
conceives his task. It gives a most favorable impression of
his competence. In four pages he lists under the heading
"Bibliotheca" more than a hundred titles. They include 22
general bibliographies, 13 collections of the church fathers (such collections were called "Bibliotheca"), 7 bibliographies of positive theology (i.e., theology based on
the revealed word of God), 6 bibliographies of scholastic
theology, and 8 bibliographies of theological scholarship.
After naming these he sets up headings for bibliographies
of the Carmelites, Augustinians, Benedictines, Carthusi-
ans, Dominicans, and Jesuits, citing one for each order and
two for his own, the Minorites. He then names 3 legal, 2
historical (actually 3, since he does not give a separate
number to G. J. Vossius, *De historicis latinis*), 17 national,
3 philosophical, and 6 medical bibliographies and 6 catalogues of manuscripts. He has recognized the modern
categories and has neatly arranged them.

His remarks about the twenty-two general bibliographies show his knowledge of the field and his skill in organization. He regards Photius, *Myriobiblon* as the first
general work and assigns three numbers to three seventh-
century editions. The one number given to Conrad Gesner
includes the *Bibliotheca universalis*, the *Pandectae*, the
Partitiones, the *Appendix* of 1555, the epitome edited by
Josias Simler in 1583, and *De libris a se* [Conrad Gesner]
editis epistola [Zurich, 1562. Not seen]. This summary
treatment of Gesner may awaken a suspicion that he has
not seen the books. Both Robert Constantin's *Nomencla-*

tor, a selective bibliography that has already been mentioned, and Antoine de Verdier's biobibliographical supplement (1585) to Gesner's *Bibliotheca* receive separate numbers. Blanchot knows the compilations of the Frankfurt fair-catalogues by Bassé, Clessius, and Draud (see above, p. 99, n. 6), but not the one by Henning Grosse, which may have escaped him or may have been omitted because Clessius's book superseded it. Since he does not mention either the *Bibliotheca exotica* or Draud's bibliography of German books, we can infer that he did not intend to include books in vernacular languages. He seems unaware of the 1625 edition of Draud's *Bibliotheca classica.* He cites Christopher Ferg's catalogue of the University of Ingolstadt library with the date 1599,[35] and Thomas James's 1605 and 1620 catalogues of the Bodleian and, in the preface but not in the bibliography, the University of Leiden catalogue (1595). At this time few institutional catalogues had been printed and all of them were hard to find at any distance from the institution that issued them. David Hoeschel's catalogue of Greek manuscripts at Augsburg (1595) that is mentioned here among general bibliographies would be better placed in the final section for catalogues of manuscripts. The mention of catalogues of manuscripts shows that he probably intended, like contemporary bibliographers generally, to list manuscripts as well as printed books. He knows Fabianus Justinianus, *Index universalis alphabeticus* (1612) and Johannes Mo-

[35] This catalogue was never printed. Blanchot cites the imprint as "Ingolstad. apud Andream Vviller. 1599. fol.," and therefore did not take the reference from Bolduanus, who has "Ingolst. 1600 in fol. apud Eliam Willerum." These references are curious because Josef Benzing knows no Willer as a printer at Augsburg; see *Die Buchdrucker des 16. und 17. Jahrhunderts im deutschen Sprachgebiet* (Wiesbaden, 1963).

lanus, *Bibliotheca materiarum* (1618), which were, I suspect, of infrequent occurrence. If he had commented on
them, we should have a better idea of the place and
purpose of his own book.

Blanchot names a few books that bibliographical practice of the time justified him in citing and two that I have
not seen. We should not cite today the publisher's catalogues issued by Johannes Oporinus [36] and the Goltzius
firm.[37] In the sixteenth and early seventeenth centuries
bibliographers mention them more than once and pass
over the Aldine, Stephanus (Estienne), and Elzevir catalogues. The situation is now reversed. The catalogues of
the latter publishers are objects of study, and the Oporinus and Goltzius catalogues are scarcely noticed. There
is little listing of books in Henri Estienne, *Francofurdiense
emporium* (1574), but bibliographers of Blanchot's day
cite it.[38] Two rare books of bibliographical quality have
not been within my reach: Wolfgang Lazius, (1514–
1565), *Catalogus partim suorum, partim aliorum scriptorum nuper inventorum* (Vienna), which does not appear
in ordinary reference works, and L. Andreas Resendius
(André de Resende, O. P., 1498–1573), *Scriptorum nunc
simul editorum tomus alter* (Cologne, 1600).[39] The lack

[36] See John W. Spargo, "Some reference books of the sixteenth
and seventeenth centuries: a finding list," *Papers of the Bibliographical Society of America*, XXXI (1937), 145, citing a catalogue of 1569
and a larger one of 1571. Blanchot specifies the latter. Paul Deschamps and Gustave Brunet, *Supplément* [to Brunet's *Manuel*], II,
col. 1224 cite a catalogue of 1552.

[37] Both Blanchot and Bolduanus, *Bibliotheca philosophica*, p. 645
cite this as "Joannis Castelli Catalogus officinae Goltzianae. Antwerp.
ap. Plantinum."

[38] See James Westfall Thompson, *The Frankfort book fair. The
Francofurdiense emporium of Henri Estienne edited with historical
introduction* (Chicago, 1911).

[39] The date of Resende's birth is uncertain; see *Livros antigos
portuguêzes 1489–1600 da bibliotheca de sua majestade fidelíssima*

of a date for the first of these suggests that Blanchot has not seen it. Lazius, the son of a Strasbourg physician who was a friend of Beatus Rhenanus, was educated at Ingolstadt, and spent his life as a medical professor and historian in Vienna. His books are now in the Austrian national library. He traveled widely in central Europe in search of historical antiquities, once with an Austrian nobleman to visit France, Belgium, and northern Germany and another time in southern Germany and Switzerland. The Dominican Resende, a humanist and a friend of Erasmus and Damião de Góes, brought the Inquisition to Portugal and invented the word *Lusíadas* that Camoens used as the title for his epic.

Blanchot is a good bibliographer. His chronological arrangement of the general bibliographies and the completeness of his list are evidences of his skill. The remainder of the *Idea bibliothecae universalis* is as well organized as the portion we have seen. He is diligent in naming "Bostoni volumen de Scriptoribus Ecclesiast. in Anglia," [40] a medieval biobibliographical dictionary of English churchmen, that was known to few in his day, and perhaps even more diligent in naming the *Bibliotheca Chi-*

[King Manuel II] (3 vols.; London, 1929–1935), I, 500, suggesting "probably in 1500." For the curious explanation of the "L." prefixed to his name see I, 507–508 and II, 175–177. For his invention of *Lusíadas* see I, 510–511.

Anselmo Braamcamp Freire, "Bibliographia Resendiana," *Arquivo histórico portuguêz*, X (1914), 286–322, especially pp. 302–304, gives the contents of the *Tomus alter*. It contains a small subject-index of some minor historical works by Resende, but nothing of greater importance.

[40] See Ernest A. Savage, "Notes on the early monastic libraries of Scotland with an account of the Registrum liborum Angliae and of the Catalogus scriptorum ecclesiae of John Boston of the abbey of Bury St. Edmunds," *Publications of the Edinburgh Bibliographical Society*, XIV (1928).

nensium (1605).[41] His citations are in some instances at secondhand, but this is excusable, for he is listing books he intended to consult and not necessarily those he has seen or used. We must regret that only six years of life remained to him at the time when he published the *Idea* and said that much of the task was already done (Et non minima parte affectam). With his death in 1637 his bibliographical collections disappear from sight.

Georg Hieronymus Welschius and His Plan for a Bibliography

Nothing seems to have survived of a bibliography planned by Georg Hieronymus Welschius (1624–1677), an Augsburg scholar famous in his day for his knowledge of medicine and the Oriental languages.[42] No one in the seventeenth century reported the extent and nature of his collectanea, and we have only his somewhat vague intimations of a work that seems to have been more or less a classified list of the best books. His ability and training as well as the interest shown by later bibliographers in what he promised to do suggest that his book would have been both curious and instructive.

Welschius studied at Tübingen and Strasbourg and interrupted his university work to spend three years in Padua. He carried to Padua a letter of introduction to the Danish professor and bibliographer Johan Rode (Rhodius), who had settled in Italy.[43] Welschius's keen interest

---

[41] See my *Renaissance guides to books* (Berkeley, 1945), p. 145, citing Henri Cordier, *Bibliotheca sinica* (2d ed., 4 vols. and suppl.; Paris, 1904–1924), III, col. 1813.

[42] *Allgemeine deutsche Biographie*, XLI, 681.

[43] Rode wrote the first list of pseudonyms (published by Vincent Placcius in 1674); see Archer Taylor and F. J. Mosher, *The Bibliographical History of Anonyma and Pseudonyma* (Chicago, 1951), p. 262.

in Arabic studies led him to ask his parents for permission to visit Egypt, but they refused it, and perhaps wisely, as the event showed. After his return to Strasbourg his teachers thought him ready for the examination for the doctor's degree, but, overcome by melancholia, he went home to Augsburg, where he remained for the rest of his life, except for a brief stay in Basel, where he received the doctor's degree in 1645. In addition to a knowledge of Arabic, Syriac, and Greek Welschius knew enough Turkish to plan a history of Turkish literature. He is said to have had also some acquaintance with Armenian and Chinese. He devoted the last thirty years of his life to private studies, chiefly medical. Just before his death he was admitted to a company of learned physicians, and although he seems not to have practised medicine, doctors often asked for his advice. Evidence of his attainments in medicine remains in the *Somnium Vindiciani sive Deside-rata medicinae* (Augsburg, 1676), a curious list of medical problems that has been described as the first collection of medical subjects that call for investigation.[44] His posthumous annotated edition of medical lectures by Johannes Walaeus at the University of Leiden was published in 1679.

These biographical and bibliographical details suggest Welschius's remarkable knowledge of languages, his wide-ranging interests, and his gift for synthesis and organization. According to a list of seventy tasks that he had in hand he planned a *Notitia scriptorum panglotta*, which was to be a selective list of works accepted as authorita-

[44] For a good account of this book see Gottlieb Stolle, *Anleitung zur Historie der medicinischen Gelahrheit* (Jena, 1731), pp. 285–288. See also Georg Paschius, *Tractatus de novis inventis, quorum accuratiori cultui pacem praetulit antiquitas* (2d ed. Leipzig, 1700), pp. 502 ff., cited from Stolle, p. 288, note *e*.

tive. It may be the same as a *Varia scriptorum genera,* which Nicolaus Hieronymus Gundling says, was to be a small octavo for scholars to read on their travels.[45]

Within a dozen years after Welschius's death Daniel George Morhof celebrated his learning enthusiastically, but showed no firsthand acquaintance with his literary remains. He appears to be giving only what he gathered from a biography by Schröckius and from general report. A little more information may be gleaned from Theodor Jansson Van Almeloveen, *Bibliotheca promissa et latens,* a bibliography of unfinished and published writings.[47] Around 1710 Mauritius Huselitt promised to look for Welschius's notes, but regarded the search as a forlorn hope (see below). As a matter of fact, he might have been successful if he had actually gone to Augsburg. A few years later both Gottlieb Stolle in his previously mentioned history of medicine and B. G. Struve[48] show themselves to be little better informed than Morhof was. A clue in N. H. Gundling's history of learning was perhaps not easy to follow even around 1730, when he was lecturing.[49] It concerns a reference to some fifty manuscripts in a "Catalogus Spizelianorum." The *Catalogus bibliothecae a Theophilo Spizelio collecto et Gabriele Spizelio* ([Augsburg], 1705) lists, however, only printed books. The manuscripts may have been listed in a supplement that I have been unable to see. Although Welschius's bibliography is

[45] *Vollständige Historie der Gelahrheit* (5 vols. and suppl., Frankfurt a.M., 1734–1746), I, 404 and 290–291.

[46] *Polyhistor,* I, ch. vi, § 38 (ed. 1747, I, 51).

[47] Gouda, 1688. See pp. 121–122.

[48] See *Introductio in notitiam rei litterariae* (5th ed., Frankfurt a.M., 1729), pp. 39–42; Struve-Fischer, pp. 60–63 (with abundant references); Struve-Jugler, I, 33–34.

[49] *Vollständige Historie,* I, 404. See my *Book catalogues,* p. 263. There is a copy of the *Catalogus* in the Newberry Library.

not specifically mentioned, it may well have been in the manuscripts acquired by Raymond von Krafft from the Spitzel collection and owned by him around the middle of the eighteenth century.[50] They dealt with "Latinity, poetry (i.e., belles lettres), chronology, the study of theology, and other subjects" and are said to have been listed as Nos. 232–240 in a Spitzel catalogue "in 4°." This cannot be the folio catalogue of 1705 or the duodecimo supplement. From Struve-Jugler, I, 35, we learn that some of Welschius's manuscripts were in the possession of M. F. Beckmann in the seventeenth century,[51] but I cannot trace them further. It is not altogether certain that Welschius's bibliography is lost, but Huselitt could have found it more easily than we can. I have cited these references to show the value that contemporaries attached to Welschius's literary remains.

Welschius left a brief description of his proposed bibliography in an *Epistola de scriptis suis ad bibliopolas et typographos S. R. Imperii,* which Almeloveen printed. He proposed to publish no fewer than seventy books, and of these the sixty-ninth is the *Notitia auctorum panglotta.* He says it will not be exhaustive, as Gesner's *Pandectae* had been intended to be. The notion that it was a subject-index rests upon this comparison. On the contrary, he goes on, it will name the best authors in various languages, will identify the best editions of their works, and will in-

[50] See *Catalogus historico-criticus bibliothecae Krafftianae* (Ulm, 1753) in a separately paged appendix listing manuscripts (p. 108, No. 96 b). J. G. Schelhorn comments at length on the library, but mentions only six volumes of autograph letters as coming from the Spitzel library; see *Amoenitates litterariae* (14 vols., Frankfurt, 1725), III, 115–118.

[51] This information comes from R. M. Meelführerus, *Accessiones ad Almeloveeni Bibiliothecam* . . . (Nürnberg, 1699). See a photographic copy in the Newberry Library.

clude quotations of criticisms. G. J. Vossius, who had made a beginning with the task, had suggested it to Welschius as well as others and had given them collectanea. The form in which Welschius received the collectanea, whether in print, in manuscript, or by dictation, is not clear. By adding "Orientales et linguarum omnes" Welschius was enlarging the scope of the undertaking. Although contemporary bibliographers cite the *Notitia* as a subject-index, it is not altogether clear that it was. It may have been a list of best books with critical comments or something like Tobias Magirus, *Eponymologicum criticum* (2d ed., Frankfurt, 1687) and Thomas Pope-Blount, *Censura celebrium authorum* (Geneva, 1694). Whatever it was, men of the time attached much importance to it.

Sir William Petty, Office of common address (1648)

A third seventeenth-century proposal to make a subject-index is part of a curious and interesting plan suggested by Sir William Petty (1623–1687) in connection with various proposals made by Samuel Hartlib. Richard Foster Jones summarizes well these proposals in a chapter entitled "Projects, inventions, and the progress of science" (pp. 154–187) in *Ancients and Moderns. A study of the background of the "Battle of the books."* [52] I shall deal only briefly with Petty's plan because it was not realized and because the subject-index is a relatively minor aspect of what Petty, Hartlib, and others intended. As Jones says (p. 154), "Those who were seeking man's salvation not in books borrowed largely from antiquity but in more efficient marshalling of the factors making for his practical good are not far removed from the scientists themselves."

[52] Washington University studies, n.s., Language and literature, 6 (St. Louis, Mo., 1936).

Their emphasis is on agriculture, anatomy, chemistry, and experimental science in general. Although religion, learning, and ingenuities, "which are Objects of Contemplation and delight unto the Mind, for their strangenesse and usefulnesse unto the life of Man" are mentioned (p. 158), no clear picture of a subject-index is drawn.

In a rare pamphlet entitled *The advice of W. P. to Mr. Samuel Hartlib, for the advancement of some particular parts of learning* (1648),[53] Petty suggested the establishment of an "office of common address, . . . where men may know what is already done in the business of learning, what is at present doing, and what is intended to be done." The means he proposes are "first, to get labourers together; then, to see what is well and sufficiently done already, by perusing all books, and taking notice of all mechanical inventions, for which there must be appointed able readers of all such books; and every book must be read by two several persons aprt, to prevent mistakes. Out of all these books, one book or great work was to be made, though consisting of many volumes, with proper indices, or tables, for the easy finding, remembering, and well understanding all things contained in these books."

Petty's suggestion with its strong emphasis on technology and science had no immediate response, but it has been realized in more recent years. The "one book or great work" that he foresaw has not been compiled and cannot be because the extent and variety of inventions and discoveries defy listing. Yet patent lawyers have no difficulty

[53] See Wing, P 1914 and the reprint in *The Harleian miscellany* (10 vols.; London, 1808–1813), VI, 1–14. The passages quoted are on pp. 13–14. See also James Crosley, ed., *The diary and correspondence of Dr. John Worthington,* Chetham Society, Remains &c., XIII ([Manchester], 1847), p. 294, n. l.

in collecting information about new inventions.[54] Chemists, biologists, and scientists generally easily survey new discoveries. Special journals inform nuclear scientists and makers of aircraft about advances in their fields.

Petty believes that

This work will be a help to eloquence, where men, by their great acquaintance with things, might find out similitudes, metaphors, allusions, and other graces of discourses in abundance.
To arithmeticians and geometricians, supplying them with matter, whereon to exercise those most excellent sciences . . .
Divines, having so large a book of God's work, added to that of his word, may he (read "then") more clearly from them deduce the wisdom, power, and goodness of the Almighty. Physicians, observing the use of all drugs, and operations in the production of artificials, may with success transfer them to their uses in their art. And lawyers, when they plead concerning trades and manufactures, would better know what to say on such occasions.

In his reply; *A further discoverie of the Office of Publick Address for Accomodations* ([London], 1648. See Wing, H987),[55] Samuel Hartlib makes practical applications of the idea that are scarcely bibliographical in nature. This plan has Baconian roots and may have been stimulated by ideas derived from John Amos Comenius. A third pamphlet, which is anonymous but has been ascribed to Hartlib, is entitled *Cornu-Copia: a miscellaneum of liciferous and most fructiferous experiments, observations, and discoveries, immethodically distributed; to be really demonstrated and communicated in all sincerity* also enlarges upon practical applications.

[54] See WBB, "List," cols. 5112–5119, and "Patents," cols. 5328–5356. See also the remarks on R. A. Peddie below.
[55] *The Harleian Miscellany*, VI, 14–27. For the *Cornu-Copia*, see *The Harleian Miscellany*, VI, 27–36. Wing H 982 assigns the conjectural date 1652 to it and cites the title with minor differences.

Sir William Petty's life and experiences enabled him to estimate readily both the nature and the difficulties of the task and its value. He was born as the son of a clothier but showed a marked taste for mechanical things. At an early age he went to sea and was left with a broken leg on the French coast. He supported himself by teaching English and navigation and gained an education at the Jesuit college at Caen. He served in the royal navy but retired from it to study at Utrecht, Amsterdam, and Leiden. Then he went to Paris, where he met Hobbes in a group at Mersenne's house. He returned to England in 1646, became a doctor of physics at Oxford in 1649, and was associated with a society that was a forerunner of the Royal Society. For a time he was active in medicine and later in government affairs, especially finance. He wrote a great variety of books, particularly in political economy. Such a man readily appreciated the usefulness and the difficulty of the task that he proposed.

A few years later William Simpson, a Wakefield physician, proposed a similar idea on a smaller scale. He proposed to deal only with medical treatises. Since his plan was limited it calls for mention here only as evidence of an active interest in subject bibliography. I have not seen the rare *Hydrologia chymica* (London, 1669) [56] and quote the following remarks from Colin Richardson's *Catalogue 139*, No. 104:

Extremely interesting, too is the suggestion that a body of experts should examine technical treatises as they appear, analyse their contents and publish from time to time the best features. Atlhough Simpson's scheme echoes Bacon, Hartlib and Comenius, his own development has some original features.

[56] See Wing, S 3833; D. I. Duveen, *Bibliotheca alchemica et chemica; an annotated catalogue of printed books* (London, 1949), pp. 511–512.

Baron von Boineburg's Plan

While Welschius in Augsburg was making notes for a subject-index, Johann Christian Freiherr (Baron) von Boineburg (1622–1673) also proposed to make one. This nobleman, who resided on his estate and in Frankfurt am Main after his conversion to Catholicism in 1656 and his arrest in 1665 for suspicious acts (he was released as innocent after five weeks), can perhaps have had knowledge of Welschius's plans. He does not appear as an author in the history of bibliography, but he was famous at the time for the possession of a great library and for correspondence with scholars, especially bibliographers. Hermann Conring addressed to him an often-quoted letter, *De bibliotheca Augusta quae est in arce Wolfenbuttelensi . . . epistola qua simul de omni re bibliothecaria disseritur* (Wolfenbüttel, 1661; ed. nova, Helmstadt, 1684).[57] It concerned the possibility of making a catalogue of the treasures at Wolfenbüttel and came to the conclusion that the enterprise was not feasible. Since it gave a brief critical summary of general bibliographies and library catalogues, it was for a short time valuable as the only general work of the kind. Later writings soon superseded it and it is now only historically interesting.

According to Struve-Jugler, I, 35, Baron von Boineburg described his plan for a subject-index in letters to Zacharias Prüschenkius and J. C. Dietericus.[58] His remarks have

[57] For these and other editions of the *Epistolae* see my *Book catalogues,* pp. 207–208 and F. L. Schönemann, *Serapeum,* IV (1843), 193–204, especially pp. 203–204.

[58] Meelführerus (see above) reprints the pertinent passages; see p. 12. See also Struve-Fischer, pp. 63–64. A review of *Jo. Christiani L. Baronis de Boineburg ad . . . Jo. Conradum Dietericum Epistolae* (Nuremberg, 1703) in the *Acta eruditorum* that Struve-Fischer cites makes clear how greatly men desired the baron's work but gives no

been excerpted or commented upon in various places. It does not appear that he had gone very far. We are told that almost every book in his library contained annotations citing not only parallels in pertinent books but also additional materials of polymathic interest. His library was, after his death, kept in Mainz for a time but is now in the library of the University of Erfurt. As late as 1885 Paulus Cassel busied himself with the baron's books and papers at Erfurt, but gave no notion of what he found.[59] It would be curious and important to the historian of bibliography to know whether anything remains of an index to von Boineburg's library that G. W. Leibniz compiled. This very detailed analytical subject catalogue in which a single work was cited in as many as ten places [60] does not appear to be the subject-index of general useful-

clear idea of it. B. G. Struve, *Acta litteraria ex manuscriptis eruta,* I (Jena, 1705), fasc. 3 (with separate pagination), pp. 1–70 also contains excerpts of letters written between 1649 and 1665. The writers give much bibliographical information, but I see no references to a subject-index. See also S. J. Arenhold, *Conspectus bibliothecae universalis . . . epistolarum* (Hannover, 1736), pp. 14, 29.

[59] He writes (*Aus dem Lande des Sonnenaufgangs* [Berlin, 1885], p. 9): Ich habe in Erfurt mich viel mit dem Schriften und der Bibliothek des Freiherrn v. Boineburg beschäftigt, der im 17. Jahrhundert Staatsminister des Kurfürsten von Mainz und ein Convertit gewesen ist."

[60] See Zischka, *Index lexicorum* (Vienna, [1959]), p. xxxvi and G. E. Guhrauer, "Bibliothekarisches aus Leibnizens Leben und Schriften," *Serapeum,* XII (1851), 1–16, 17–30, 35–42. The catalogue was made about 1670 and was given up on von Boineburg's death (Guhrauer, p. 3). Leibniz says that he spent almost a whole winter on it. I have not seen the two volumes of correspondence between Leibniz and von Boineburg edited by J. D. Gruber (Hanau, 1745). Oskar Thyregod's chapter entitled "Une encyclopédie ou science universelle" arouses one's interest in Leibniz's later efforts to devise and apply a classification of books; see *Die Kulturfunktion der Bibliothek* (The Hague, 1936), pp. 34–38. These references are extremely difficult to decipher and do not concern an actual subject-index or plans for one.

ness that men at the time expected. The fact that an
"Eques auratus, S. Caes. Maiest. Camerarius, Archiepis-
copi et Electoris Mogunti intimus Consiliarius et supremus
Mareschallus" could occupy himself with such a task be-
tokens a general sympathy with bibliography and a particular understanding of the need for a subject-index.
Probably the baron's unfortunate experiences, which involved a promise on his release to take no revenge, made
him hesitate to publish anything. My inquiries about his
papers have yielded no positive result. The librarian of
the Wissenschaftliche Bibliothek der Stadt Erfurt kindly
informs me that only von Boineburg's books came to that
library and no manuscripts are there or in the Erfurt
Stadtarchiv. What manuscripts may have survived are in
the Landesarchiv of Magdeburg or in Mainz or in Würz-
burg.

To what a low estate subject-indexes had fallen by the
middle of the seventeenth century we learn from Mathias
Prideaux, Master of Arts and sometime Fellow of Exeter
College, Oxford. In *An easy and compendious introduction
for reading all sorts of histories* (Oxford, 1648) he writes:
"To this pile of Histories are reducible, 1. All Catalogues,
as that of *Gesner, Molanus, Draudius;* those of Libraries
and Marts constantly increased. 2. All *Journals, Naviga-
tions, and Discoveries.* 3. All *Jesuitical,* and other relations
of strange things done in *China,* or the like, which (to examine the method all along observed) may be shut up
with these." [61] The full force of his remarks appears in the
fact that the "Histories" to which he is referring are collections of observations in natural history (which he does
not reject as useless), memorabilia of various kinds such as
Valerius Maximus, Hakluyt, and others (which he does

[61] I have used the fourth edition (Oxford, 1664). See p. 350.

not wholly reject), and romances, to which he devotes two pages. He classifies them briefly as "Such Brats of Invention and Spawn of idle hours, are well [sic] most found to be either, 1. Rude, or 2. Endless, 3. or Depraved, 4. or Superstitious, or else 5. Moral, 6. Political, or 7. Satyrical" (p. 348) and illustrates each category by examples. Gesner, Molanus, and Draud would have been surprised to find themselves in such company, but Prideaux's distaste for bibliography is obvious.

THE GOLDEN AGE
OF SUBJECT-INDEXES, 1670–1700

Although the years from 1631 (Blanchot) to the 1670s (Welschius, Boineburg, and others) saw only promises, the last generation of the seventeenth century saw the completion of at least five large subject-indexes: the six folio volumes of Martin Lipenius, *Bibliotheca realis* were printed; Raffaelo Savonarola's *Orbis litterarius universalis* was compiled and announced as ready for publication and in the next century a portion was printed; a second German index—the *Bibliotheca enucleata* by Johann Georg Schiele(n)—was published; Francesco Marucelli's *Mare magnum* was completed and announced and still survives in a revision; and André Baillet finished a subject-index to the large private library of Chrétien-François de Lamoignon. Others were called for and still others were planned, although characteristically on a somewhat limited scale, down to 1710.[62]

[62] François Pomey, S. J. (1618–1673), *Indiculus universalis rerum fere omnium quae in mundo sunt scientiarum item artiumque nomina* (Lyons, 1667) is classificatory rather than bibliographical in quality and needs mention only for its title. See A. and A. de Backer and Carlos Sommervogel, *Bibliothèque de la Compagnie de Jésus* (new ed., 12 vols., Brussels, 1890–1909), VI, cols. 986–989.

Apart from these indexes one of the most important events in bibliographical history between 1670 and 1710 was the publication of Thomas Hyde, *Catalogus impressorum librorum bibliothecae Bodlejanae in Academia Oxoniensi* (Oxford, 1674). As Hyde says more than once in his preface, it was a catalogue of the largest collection of books then in existence. At the end of the preface he recommends the user to read the catalogue and make his own subject-index of matters interesting to him. In the *Polyhistor* (1685) D. G. Morhof praised the catalogue and remarked briefly: "And besides, the catalogue is arranged according to authors, not according to subjects. Consequently the second part, the index of subjects, which will equal the first part of the catalogue in bulk, is lacking; but nonetheless it is very useful." [63] This comment shows Morhof's unfamiliarity with alphabetical catalogues, which were rare north of the Alps. He goes on to quote Baillet's preface to the subject-index of the Lamoignon library, in which Baillet condemns Hyde's failure to arrange books according to subjects. This quotation is incidentally the only bit of Baillet's index that survives. The value of a subject-index was clearly recognized in the last years of the seventeenth century, and men undertook tasks of an amazing extent to meet the demand.

Johann Jäcklin, Catalogus universalis omnium librorum (*1674*)

I cannot trace this book beyond Josef Benzing's reference to it.[64] He did not see it and conjectures that it may

[63] I, ch. xvii, §§ 29–32 (ed. 1747, I, 93).
[64] *Die Buchdrucker des 16. und 17. Jahrhunderts im deutschen Sprachgebiet*, Beiträge zum Buch- und Bibliothekswesen, 12 (Wiesbaden, 1963), p. 317.

have been a "Sortiments-katalog," i.e., a wholesaler's list.
Such lists often bore titles of this sort and were classified
for the convenience of purchasers. If the *Catalogus* belongs in this category, it would have more than a little in
common with a subject-index. But guesses about it are
vain. Jäcklin (fl. 1656–1710) was a printer at Munich who
published many Italian books.

Martinus Lipenius, Bibliotheca realis (*1679–1685*)

The only late seventeenth-century general subject-
index to be published in full is the *Bibliotheca realis* (6 v.,
1679–1685) by Martinus Lipenius (1630–1692). Like
many bibliographers who essayed to conquer the world of
learning and books, Lipenius was of modest origin, being
born of peasant stock in a Brandenburg village.[65] He was a
pupil of Johann Andreas Quenstadt (1617–1688), the author of an international biobibliographical dictionary on a
novel geographical plan, the *Dialogus de patriis illustrium
doctrina et scriptis virorum, omnium ordinum ac facultatum* (Wittenberg, 1654). He taught at Wittenberg, Halle,
and Stettin, and finally served as conrector of the gym-
nasium at Lübeck. Although one might perhaps infer some
unhappy personal qualities from these frequent changes
of residence, biographers call him an upright man, loving
peace and concord and most disinclined to participate in

---

[65] The collation is too lengthy to give in the text above: *Juridica*
(1679). Pp. 560, [ii], citing 20,000 titles; see WBB, col. 2266.
Medica (1679). Pp. [xix], 492, [xlii], citing 12,500 titles; see WBB,
col. 2495. *Philosophica* (2 vols., 1692). Pp. [viii], 864, [ii]; 865–
1594, [cvi], citing 40,000 titles; see WBB, col. 3192. *Theologica* (2
vols., 1685). Pp. [clviii], 748;[ii], 748, [ii]; 944, [iv], citing 60,000
titles; see WBB, col. 4026.

For the biography of Lipenius see Johannes Fabricius, *Historia
bibliothecae* (6 vols.; Wolfenbüttel, 1717–1724), III, 175–177; Saxe,
V, 588; F. L. Hoffmann, *Serapeum*, XXX (1689), 17–19; Johannes
Franck, *Allgemeine deutsche Biographie*, XVIII, 725–726.

quarrels. He had several helpers in making the *Bibliotheca*, for he thanks Christian Zeissius and his son Christian Valerius as well as Daniel Springinsgut for aid. In enlisting helpers Lipenius differs from many compilers of subject indexes who have carried out their arduous task single-handed.

The *Bibliotheca realis*, an expensive work luxuriously printed in six folio volumes, did not circulate widely and did not, except for one part, tempt successors to revise and improve it. At the time of its appearance the custom of revising bibliographies was beginning to decline. The volume for law (Jurisprudentia) was reworked several times, by F. G. Struve in 1720, by G. A. Jenichen in 1736 with a supplement in 1743 and an enlarged edition in 1757, and finally by several hands in an edition in four volumes that was begun in 1775 and completed in 1823.[66] If the other volumes had had as fortunate a fate, the name of Lipenius would be remembered by others than students of legal history and the development of subject bibliography would have been more rapid and happier than it proved to be.

A revision did not quite come to pass in the case of the two volumes for philosophy. For his own convenience the great bibliographer Johann Albert Fabricius made some notes in his copy, which is now in the Royal Library at Copenhagen (Fabricius 52. 2°). An accompanying envelope contains pp. 337–348 of the volume for theology. Here the annotation to Mystica Theologia adds perhaps 25 titles. Elsewhere it is only a title or two to a column. In the volume for philosophy there are perhaps 14 additions to Algebra, somewhat more to Amicitia, and a considerable number to Anglia. Anglicana Religio is black

[66] See Petzholdt, p. 624; WBB, col. 2266.

with notes. So also are Fortificatio, Invidia, Memoria, Musica, Polonia, and Schola. Except for a possible preference for abstract subjects I see no principle in Fabricius's choice of subjects for annotation.

These notes are worth mentioning because H. S. Reimarus listed them in his biography of Fabricius among the "Libri mss. vel praelo prope parati, vel coepti, affectique." [67] He cites them only as "Accessiones et castigationes" without further comment. J. F. Jugler, who refers to them and says they can be had from Fabricius's "very learned son-in-law (i.e., Reimarus)," continues, "if only some Hercules, following the path of Jenichen [who re-edited the volume for law], would wish to cleanse this Augean stable (i.e., the four volumes fcr philosophy and theology)!" [68] The suggestion that Reimarus would take the trouble to communicate Fabricius's notes to an inquirer throws a bright light on the cooperative spirit of eighteenth-century scholarship.

Bibliographers of Lipenius's own time found the *Bibliotheca realis* altogether unsatisfactory. Daniel Georg Morhof, Gottlieb Stolle, and Burkhard Gotthelf Struve damned it briefly and emphatically. Johannes Fabricius, who owned the two theological and the two philosophical volumes, was equally severe, supporting his judgment with insignificant corrections. Surprisingly enough, he regarded Lipenius's use of the term "philosophia" as far too broad and failed to see that it had the general sense that was disappearing in the latter half of the seventeenth century.

In order to describe the *Bibliotheca realis* and to sug-

[67] See *De vita et scriptis Joannis Alberti Fabricii* (Hamburg, 1737), p. 210, no. 12.
[68] See Struve-Jugler, I, 92.

gest what usefulness it may have for a modern reader I
begin with the bibliographical articles in the volumes for
philosophy. The article Catalogus, which lists publisher's
catalogues, sale catalogues, and catalogues of public and
private libraries, falls far short of modern standards. The
titles are, it must be granted, hard to list conveniently.
The list contains serious confusions and errors, but there
is no earlier guide to this difficult bibliographical category.
An enthusiastic and informed bibliographer can glean information from it. There is more good than bad in the two
folio pages of Bibliotheca, a list composed almost exclusively of books having that word in their titles. It is not the
earliest bibliography of bibliographies and is a rather casual piece of work to set beside Philip Labbé's earlier
Bibliotheca bibliothecarum (1664), which he could profitably have studied. Lipenius is careful to exclude collections of various kinds that were also called "bibliotheca"
and therefore shows somewhat more bibliographical sense
than he is usually credited with displaying. Half a dozen
titles should have been included in Catalogus, but the
remainder are bibliographies, indexes, and lists of various
kinds. He has not verified his references, for such bibliographical ghosts as a 1643 edition of Georg Draud's *Bibliotheca classica* and Jodocus à Dudinck's bibliographies
are present.[69]

[69] For Draud see above. In the seventeenth and eighteenth centuries scholars sought vainly for Dudinck's bibliographies; see my
History of bibliographies of bibliographies (New Brunswick, N.J.,
1955), pp. 21–23 and Johannes Fabricius, *Historiae bibliothecae* (6
vols.; Wolfenbüttel, 1717–1724), V, 496, citing H. A. Groschuffius,
Conlectio rariorum librorum, Fasc. I, p. 25 (not seen). I add a
strange bit of information that does not help us much further.
J. F. K. Johnstone and A. W. Robertson, *Bibliotheca Aberdonensis*
(2 vols.; Aberdeen, 1929, 1930), I, 273, cites a copy of Hugo Sempill,
De mathematicis (Antwerp, 1635) with the remark, "The [Univer-

The rich articles Anglia, Anglicana and Britannia have about the same quality as those for bibliography. A detailed characterization seems unnecessary and might be suggested by a reply to the question whether one would advise a beginner to consult the *Bibliotheca* first or last among reference works. Its convenient plan appeals to a modern student and its large size suggests recommending it as the first, but enough inaccurate, incomplete, or confusing citations are present to baulk anyone who has not already acquired some familiarity with pertinent names and titles and the habits of seventeenth-century bibliographers. At a relatively late stage in one's work one can concentrate attention on novel titles and can solve the puzzles in Lipenius's references.

The nine columns that Lipenius gives to Astronomy show his merits and faults perhaps as well as any other section. They contain perhaps a hundred and fifty titles identified by the occurrence of *Astronomia* in the title. How many ghosts and errors are present would be difficult for anyone but a specialist to say, but a casual reading does not greatly arouse fears. These nine columns are supplemented by six more listing books with more specialized titles like "Institutiones," "Introductio," and "Tabulae." Lipenius has obviously depended on titles in assembling and classifying titles. Two more faults are apparent at once to the eye of even the hastiest reader: far too many titles lack the dates and places of publication and the proportion of books published before 1625 is much too large

---

sity of] Edinburgh copy is inscribed on the title page: Bibliothecae Jodoir à Dudinek." The emendations *Jodoci* and *Dudinck* are obvious. Although his bibliographies are lost, a book from his library has survived. See *Catalogue of the printed books in the library of the University of Edinburgh* (3 vols.; [Edinburgh], 1918–1923), III, 577 (the inscription is not mentioned here).

to give an adequate notion of the development of astronomy during the seventeenth century. These columns are to be supplemented by consulting Cometa, Coelum, Luna, Sol, and Stellae, several of which give a generous number of references. Some headings that one might expect do not appear, e.g., Constellatio, Zodiacus. The lack of cross-references and an index of headings is painfully felt. For all its defects the Bibliotheca may prove serviceable to a historian of astronomy.

On occasion Lipenius's *Bibliotheca* can yield useful information. The brief article Anonymi is perhaps the first bibliography of dictionaries of anonyma. It was useful in its day but more information on the subject can now be found easily elsewhere. This is of course always the case with subject-indexes. In this article there is a reference to Johannes Rhodius (Johan Rode) as the compiler of a dictionary with the remark "Extat cum Placcio," i.e., published in a volume by Placcius. Since Rhodius's manuscript notes, which were published by Vincentius Placcius in his *Syntagma* of 1674 (a collection of writings on anonyma and pseudonyma), have often been cited as an independent work and even within the last generation, this is a useful bit of information. Its value is not immediately obvious to an inexperienced reader, and only one who has stumbled over references to Rhodius will fully appreciate it.

Lipenius fails to serve fully the needs of a student seeking references to a subject because he depends chiefly on significant words in titles and has not always examined the books. Probably he could not. This fault has its compensations. We have no catalogue of books published in the seventeenth century and earlier arranged according to titles. Consequently Lipenius may enable us to identify a book cited only by title. I can, for example, suggest no easier way of identifying the titles named by Krause and Köcher in the passages quoted below. They have definite books in mind, and their readers recognized them.

If a good catchword does not occur in a title or if Lipenius misapprehends a title, he is likely to fail to list the book or fail to list it in the right place. Plays are usually identified in subtitles as "Comoedia" or "Tragoedia" and can be readily classified. Lipenius's long lists of them may be valuable to a student. On the other hand, "Satyra" rarely occurs in titles. Consequently Lipenius's list is altogether inadequate, although it does include some unusual books.

Difficulties may arise in the use of catchwords. For example, Giovanni Bonifazio Bagatta, *Admiranda orbis christiani* (Venice, 1680), an almost unknown dictionary of saints' Miracles, appears under Admiranda in the theological index (I, 15).[70] Perhaps students of miracles will readily turn to this catchword, but I am not certain that they will. Informatio, Ratio studiorum, and Studia & studiendi ratio cite the same kind of titles, but there are no cross-references. Fortunately an index of authors for each of the four fields, theology, law, medicine, and philosophy, enables us to go from the name of a suitably chosen author to the proper heading.

Much useful information can be obtained from the Bibliotheca realis. The articles on literary genres seem to me to be likely to be useful. Lipenius lists Biblica poemata in four columns citing perhaps sixty items. Whatever defects there may be in the list, it should be serviceable to one interested in this minor genre. In this case Lipenius does not show himself to be as tightly bound as usual to the words in the title.

[70] See a copy in the Newberry Library.

Rare and infrequently cited books often turn up. I find a reference to a book dealing with the belief that blood drips from the body of a murdered man in the presence of the murderer or at his touch (see Cadaver). The book may be better known than I suspect it to be; it does not appear in two discussions of the superstition I have consulted. A column of titles under Civilitas morum contains chiefly works dealing with the legal status of a citizen, but some may interest a student of Courtesy books. Ten titles dealing with Cochinchina that were published between 1631 and 1670 are cited. I find unfamiliar titles under Disciplina, Methodus, Pueri, and Studia & Studiendi Ratio, although I have ordinarily read these articles in subject-indexes. The article Encyclopedia might be a start in writing the history of the subject. These are random examples of what one comes upon in the *Bibliotheca realis*.

There are obvious deficiencies in Lipenius's work. Technology comes off rather short, and science on the whole receives no generous treatment. Many articles that Lipenius's contemporaries consulted are no longer important. There are, for example, better guides to old historical writings.[71] Both theology and medicine are more easily accessible in better guides than the *Bibliotheca realis,* and the volume for law was revised as late as 1775–1823. If one should have the courage to cleanse what contemporaries called an Augean stable, one might limit one's efforts to the volumes for philosophy and even in them might be selective. The task would not be terrifying in extent or difficulty. A careful workman might keep his notes on the broad margins or he might interleave the volumes, as

[71] See Nicolas Lenglet du Fresnoy, *Méthode pour étudier l'histoire* (15 vols.; Paris, 1772) and J. G. Meusel, ed., B. G. Struve, *Bibliotheca historica* (22 vols.; Jena, 1782–1804). For collations of these see WBB, cols. 1885–1886.

Fabricius did. In a few years he would find his corrections and additions were a valuable aid to his studies. He might, if he wished, produce a substantial work of general usefulness by excerpting systematically a few good contemporary catalogues of public and private libraries.

It is by no means clear how Lipenius and his helpers gathered titles. One expects them to have leaned heavily on Draud. The article Bucolica with more than a score of titles of which only three were published after 1625, the date of the last edition of Draud, *Bibliotheca classica*, might seem to bear out the conjecture. On looking more closely it appears that Draud (p. 1518) cites only an anthology and six authors of bucolic poetry. Lipenius mentions neither the anthology nor any of the six authors. The failure to mention Baptista Mantuanus characterizes the quality of Lipenius's work. Readers may have been grateful to Lipenius for citing many editions of Virgil (not cited by Draud), but the majority of the titles are critical writings. Many titles published after 1625 appear in Lipenius's article Epigrammata, but the preponderance of early titles is striking. The epigram was a very popular genre in the seventeenth century, but Lipenius's account is scarcely adequate. In places it looks like a somewhat careless copy of Draud (*Bibliotheca classica*, pp. 1531–1534) with errors, a few corrections, and a generous addition of new names (a few earlier but the majority later than 1625). Critical works on the epigram published between 1568 and 1658 (all but one later than 1649) are listed separately and this makes one think a little better of Lipenius as a bibliographer, but the comparison leaves me baffled for an explanation of how he worked. Draud cites (p. 1535) two general works of doubtful pertinence (not in Lipenius) and six writers on Epitheta. The writers are in Lipenius, but there is nothing like Draud's generous account of Johannes Ravisius Textor (Jean Tixier), an authority on the subject. Elsewhere Lipenius often cites many editions of a work, but not on this occasion. The article Homo perhaps depends on Draud (pp. 1593–1594), with characteristic errors and corrections, but includes many new titles. I have assumed that the errors arose in copying Draud, but this is not necessarily the case. However it may be, Lipenius is not likely to be right when he differs from Draud and if he used the *Bibliothecae*, he used them with great freedom.

The prefaces to the several volumes of the *Bibliotheca realis* give rather less information about Lipenius's manner of working than one would wish. Where information is most to be desired, the *Philosophica* (1682) fails us completely. According to the preface to the first of the four volumes, the *Juridica* (1679), he already foresaw at the beginning of the task nine years earlier a division into four faculties. The *Theologica* and *Philosophica* seemed relatively easy, the *Medica* more difficult, and the *Juridica* the most difficult. The volumes appeared, however, in precisely the reverse order. For the *Juridica* he acknowledges (p. [iii]) indebtedness to the inspiration of G. W. Leibniz, who had written an introduction to legal studies, and complains that he had found no bibliographical guide for his task comparable to van der Linden's medical compendium. He has used (p. vii) public and private libraries at Halle, Leipzig, Stettin, and Lübeck, and thanks Caspar Thurmann especially for advice and access to his private library. For all his efforts the *Juridica* was an unsatisfactory piece of work and Lipenius realized it. Strangely enough, it was the only one of the four volumes to be revised and its successful career continued into the nineteenth century! The *Bibliotheca Medica* (1679), which Lipenius regarded as an easier task, was published in the same year as the *Juridica*. He calls it an entirely novel work (p. [iii]), but does not clearly indicate how his procedure differs from that of Israel Spach (see above). His list of predecessors consulted (p. [xiii]) is too long to repeat here; they are standard authorities, among whom van der Linden is his chief aid. His justifiable confidence in his sources of information is so great that he discards the apologetic attitude characteristic of the preface to the *Juridica*. Nevertheless, the book fell completely flat. D. G. Morhof damned it in a sentence (*Polyhistor*, III, vii, 1, § 3; ed. 1747, II, 603) and expressed the hope that someone competent in both medicine and philology would undertake the task. A more devastating criticism is not easily imagined. Gottlieb Stolle does not even mention the book in his extensive *Anleitung zur Historie der Medicinischen Gelahrheit* (Jena, 1731). The brief preface to the *Bibliotheca philosophica* (1682) gives no hint of the sources used. In the *Bibliotheca theologica* (1685) he is, on the contrary, generous with indications of both general works and bibliographers of religious orders. Unfortunately he does not make clear why he regards the earlier indexes by Molanus and Bolduanus as works of a character different from his own books and calls them "Commentatores aut Exegetas." They contain perhaps more historical headings and more headings referring to individuals than the *Theologica* does, but I cannot see any important difference. Lipenius rejected classifications according to loci communes and Biblical texts, but brings much the same information as his predecessors bring. More than one instance of use of Molanus can be easily seen in the *Theologica*. Since sermons were cited in indexes arranged according to Biblical texts and loci communes, Lipenius might, it seems to me, have cited the appropriate texts in his headings. The information was in his hands and would have been useful to readers at the time. Gottlieb Stolle (*Anleitung zur Historie der theologischen Gelahrheit* [Jena, 1739], pp. 24–25) dismisses the *Theologica* with the remark that it calls for an editor who will revise it with the care shown by G. A. Jenichen in the new edition of the *Juridica*.[72] Although Lipenius showed great diligence and consulted the best authorities for the *Medica* and *Theologica*, he failed completely to satisfy scholars of his own time.

With the aids within his reach Lipenius and his helpers could have made a better book than the *Bibliotheca realis*. During the seventeenth century catalogues of public and private libraries had become available in increasing numbers. Scholars complained about the flood of Dutch auction catalogues. Specialized subject-bibliographies were being written. In various countries classified dealer's catalogues and trade-lists were being compiled. Since the early Frankfurt fair catalogues have not been in my hands for detailed comparison, I cannot say how completely he excerpted them. A considerable number of titles that he did not obtain from the sources of information used in the booktrade implies an effort to work in a systematic fashion, but it was neither accurate nor complete.

It is time to close the *Bibliotheca realis* and strike a trial balance. What it will be is already clear. The deceptive ease of getting at references and its size (Besterman estimates that it cites 125,000 titles and the figure is, if anything, too small) recommend it. The quality of the cita-

[72] The remark is a commonplace in bibliographies. I have previously quoted Struve's use of it.

tions, their incompleteness, and the difficulty of correcting errors in them make it desirable to come to the book with a store of information in one's head. The dates of publication (1679–1685) are misleading, for the *Bibliotheca* does not adequately review the production of books in the seventeenth century and least of all in its middle quarters. Lipenius shows an acquaintance with books published outside his own country, but references to them, and particularly to French titles, are unsatisfactory. In spite of its many and grievous faults, the *Bibliotheca* is not without value. It offers a better review of many literary genres that can be obtained from contemporary sources. On occasion it may enable one to identify a book cited by title. It is convenient to use.

Friedrich Adolf Ebert, a great librarian and bibliographer, cried out in 1821:

When will German scholars finally agree to discard completely this careless and wholly faulty compilation that has been the source of thousands of errors? Even its most cautious use is dangerous.[73]

We must qualify this warning. Ebert did not see that the "thousands of errors" means that scholars often consulted the *Bibliotheca realis* because after a century and a half it was still serving, however badly, a real need. For a generation his contemporaries—Bouginé, Lawätz, Eichhorn, Wachler, and the rest—had been making huge classified compilations that met this need less satisfactorily. Had these men devoted themselves to the improvement of the *Bibliotheca realis*, they would have saved themselves untold labor in organizing materials and would have left an invaluable reference work. This did not happen and the

[73] *Allgemeines bibliographisches Lexikon* (2 vols., Leipzig, 1821, 1830), I, cols. 992–993.

Bibliotheca realis was damned and has remained damned. The last to push it deeper into oblivion were J. G. T. Graesse and Julius Petzholdt, Ebert's successors at the royal library at Dresden. The former, who himself wrote a work of similiar nature, buried Lipenius in a list of encyclopedic writers, where no one found him; the latter, who deals with the four parts separately (pp. 459, 477, 574, 625), calls it unreliable and wholly lacking in plan. Causa finita erat.

Raffaello Savonarola, Orbis litterarius (1698)

A second great subject-index of the late seventeenth century seems now most unfortunately to be lost. This is the *Orbis litterarius universalis* by Raffaello Savonarola (1646–1730). Strangely enough, this indefatigable worker has no place in Frati's biobibliographical account of Italian librarians and bibliographers.[74] He is one more of the many bibliographers of modest origin who attempted vast tasks. The eleventh son of his father's third wife (whom the father had married at the age of 68), Raffaello was educated by a priest and entered the Theatine order in 1662. He was sent to the University of Bologna, where, when he fell sick, he was told that he could not expect to have a long life because his father had been over eighty when he was born. The event fortunately disproved the prophecy. Raffaello continued his theological studies in Florence and then preached at Bologna, Venice, Padua, Ferrara, and Florence. When he was sent in 1679 to Munich, he made friends with a Bavarian and an English member of his order. At this time he began his bibliog-

---

[74] See G. Biagi, *Indice del 'Mare magnum'* (Rome, 1888), pp. xi–xvi and especially pp. xxxviii, n. 20–xliv, n. 30; Ottino and Fumagalli, pp. 129–130, no. 1410.

raphical studies. Somewhat later he announced a plan for a work to include all materials and authors in every science and art in any language from the beginning of scholarly studies down to his own time. Books were to be cited with mention of the date and place of publication as well as the format and with critical annotation. His announcement is perhaps flamboyant, even in a baroque age: "Opus ex Mundi totius Bibliothecis praecipuis concinnatum ordine Indicis Generalis materiarum Alphabetice dispositum et characteribus Hebraicae, Caldaicae, Syriacae, Graecae, Arabicae, Persicae, Armenae, Germanicae, Etiopicae, Egyptiacae nonnunquam elaboratum, Italis, Gallis, Hispanis, Boemis, Pannoniis [Hungarians], Anglis, Belgis et caeteris exterarum Nationum Scriptoribus, plerumque Latino, interdum vernaculos sermone appositis." Only the title, from which I quote, was published in 1698 as a prospectus. We may find Savonarola's promises boastful, as his contemporaries did, but even the hastiest examination of what he actually published will make us listen sympathetically to them.

Biagi quotes Johann Burckhard Mencken as a contemporary who poked fun at the *Orbis litterarius* in his *De charlataneria eruditorum,* first published in 1715 and an immediate success.[75] The reference is somewhat inaccurate, for Biagi has in mind a note signed "Kend.," a pseudonym used by J. G. Krause (1684–1736), the editor of a later edition. In this note and not in *De charlataneria* Savonarola's book is mentioned and put in a line descending from Ramon Lull. This derivation is by no means correct, for Lull's writings are more epistemological than bibliographical in nature.

Mencken's generalities and Krause's note may, however,

[75] See *Indice,* p. xlii, n. 23.

be cited here for their lists of titles (they contain no more than titles) of books allied to subject-indexes as surveys of scholarship. Mencken, who is discussing silly and boastful titles, cites "the vast numbers of Golden Keys, Royal Methods, Graduses ad Parnassum, Oceanic Micro-Macro-Cosmoses, Shields of Truth, Bulwarks of Science, Inventories of the Mind," [76] and Krause adds "catalogos titulis magnificis Artis artium, Artis universalis, Artis magnae sciendi, scribendi, disserendi, Operis operum, Phari Scientiarum, Viae regiae ad omnes scientias & artes, sexcentisque aliis" and makes a special mention of Savonarola with a full quotation of the title.[77] Identifications of these titles are difficult and would lead us far afield, but, as examples: the "Ars magna sciendi" is probably Athanasius Kircher (1602–1680), *Ars magna sciendi in XII libros digesta, qua nova & universali methodo per artificiosam combinationem contextum de omni re plurimis prope infinita rationibus disputari, omniumque summaria quaedam cognito comparari potest* (Amsterdam, 1669); "Viae regiae" alludes to various works: one for geometry by Petrus Ramus (Pierre de la Ramée), a more general one promised by Quirinus Kuhlmann (1651–1689), or most probably the very popular *Via regia ad omnes scientias et artes* (Prague, 1682) by Caspar Knittel. The last, if it was intended, has no particular bibliographical value, but was, in spite of Krause's scorn, reprinted as late as 1759. The *Pharus scientiarum* (2 vols., Lyons, 1659. Pp. 401, 272, with an unpaginated "Index rerum" and table of contents) is by Sebastian Izquierdo, S. J., (1601–1681). It appears to be rare, but I saw a copy briefly in Mafra, Portugal. Sommer-

[76] H. L. Mencken, ed., *The charlatanry of the learned* (New York, 1937), pp. 68–69.
[77] *De charlataneria* (5th ed., Amsterdam, 1747), p. 36.

vogel and De Backer call this classification of knowledge
a "cours de philosophie." It contains little or no bibliography. Gratianus Aschpanus, who is J. G. Krause once
more, quoted the note in *De charlataneria* with approval
a few years later in his *De superstitione erudita et litteraria
libellus* and adds more titles: Thesauros, Lexica univer-
salia, Infundibula, Artes artium, Atlantes, Theatra historica, Claues aureas, Methodos regias, Hemaria, Promp-
tuaria, Mellificia, Parnassos, Florilegia & id genus alia." [78]
The *Mellificia* is probably the book by Binchius cited
above. It is by no means clear that either Mencken or
Krause ever saw Savonarola's bibliography of geography
or knew more about him than could be hastily inferred
from the titlepage of the *Orbis litterarius* of 1698. They
cite a jumble of encyclopedic works, biobibliographical
dictionaries, handbooks of historical facts, collections of
maps, and anthologies.

I need only point out a non-bibliographical tradition
exemplified by Izquierdo's *Pharus scientiarum*. Such logical, even mechanical subdividing of knowledge, either
taken as a whole (often with emphasis on nature and its
phenomena) or with reference to a single large field like
jurisprudence, was much favored in the seventeenth century. "Leibniz, for example, by this method comes to the
result that there are no more and no less than 2047 'genera
speciesque possibiles' of governmental arrangements. . . .
[Quirinus] Kuhlmann planned, using this system, to write
a series of encyclopedic studies, covering human knowledge, the sum total of human knowledge at the time. Nothing came of this plan, but his failure to carry it out is

[78] See the first ed. (Cologne, 1728), pp. 91–92, note ***. This, a
later edition, and one with manuscript notes are in the University
of Göttingen library.

lamented by later writers, although they distrusted his reliance upon divine impulse [as the fundamental principle of classification]." [79] As Walter J. Ong shows, there is much of a Ramist tradition in such analytical and classificatory studies.[80] Whether Lullian or Ramist in origin, the classifications were accompanied by very little bibliographical information and did not offer schemes for bibliographies.

Savonarola was a bibliographer on a grand scale. According to Giovambattista Conzatti's edition of Innocenzio Savonarola's biography of his uncle,[81] Savonarola returned to Padua on July 15, 1681, having finished two large works: an unpublished bibliography of authors (*Indice de' scrittori inedito*) and the bibliography of geography. This reference and Savonarola's manner of working suggest that the two works were separate enterprises. During the next twenty years he compiled an alphabetical repertory of texts from the Bible and the Church Fathers, another of texts suggested by the saints and their legends, still another of Biblical and patristic references to the Virgin Mary, an anthology of materials selected from sermons and handbooks for preachers, an anthology of eighty Spanish sermons, and "varie altre cose." Because he announced the *Orbis litterarius* in 1698 we can infer that he continued to work on it, although it was said to have been brought

---

[79] Robert L. Beare, "Quirinus Kuhlmann and his religious apprenticeship," *PMLA*, LXVIII (1959), 828–862, especially pp. 839–840. The reference here to Kuhlmann in Morhof's *Polyhistor* is to I, ch. 20, § 5 (ed. 1747, I, 231). Walter Dietze, *Quirinus Kuhlmann. Ketzer und poetischer Versuch einer monographischen Darstellung vom Leben und Werk*, Neue Beiträge zur Literaturwissenschaft, 17 (Berlin, 1963. Pp. 640, 8 pl.), p. 393 and elsewhere offers rather little to the point.

[80] See "Ramist method and the commercial mind," *Studies in the Renaissance*, VIII (1961), 155–172, for references to modern lists of similar books.

[81] Cited by Biagi, p. xlii. A microfilm in the Newberry Library.

back to Padua in 1681 as a completed work. All of these compilations except the bibliography of geography appear to be lost.

All that we can say about the *Orbis litterarius* must be inferences drawn from the titlepage printed as a prospectus in 1698, an announcement made in 1700, and his bibliography of geography. The announcement in a Venetian journal, *La Galleria di Minerva*,[82] says that the *Orbis* was estimated to be eight large folios when printed and that it was in a single alphabet (geography being included). It concludes with the somewhat despairing remark:

Circa di che nell'Atti della Stampa si risolverà con il Consiglio de più Dotti e Discreti, à fine di maggiormente giovare con un Nuovo MONDO LETTERARIO UNIVERSALE all'Republica de Letterati.

Savonarola proceeded with unusual bibliographical care for his time. Few of his contemporaries cited titles in the original languages and accompanied them with translations. It is altogether likely that the typographical difficulties of printing his book had a share in delaying and preventing its publication. However this may be, his efforts to find a printer were in vain. In 1713 he published under the anagrammatic pseudonym Alphonsus Lasor a Varea the *Universus terrarum orbis scriptorum calamo delineatus, hoc est auctorum fere omnium, qui de Europae, Asiae, Africae, & Americae regnis . . . scripserunt*. It justifies his claim of being almost complete, for Theodore Besterman estimates that it contains 75,000 references (WBB, col. 1570), a figure which may well be an underestimate. To this work we shall return. There is no clear indication that Savonarola continued to work on the *Orbis*, although he

[82] III (1700), 76–77.

lived until 1730. The reference to it as a work of forty volumes folio probably implies that he had enlarged the work that would fill eight printed volumes in 1698. The manuscript was in the library of the Theatines at Padua in 1739, when Innocenzio Savonarola was writing his uncle's biography. It was presumably still there in 1780, when Antonio Francesco Vezzosi compiled a bibliography of the order.[83] It probably disappeared when the books of the suppressed "conventi" were delivered to the University of Padua about 1810. It can have remained in the hands of the order, have been delivered to the university or to the Marciana in Venice or perhaps to the Vatican Library, or have been destroyed. Efforts to find it in 1880 and 1887 proved fruitless, and my inquiry has had a negative answer.[84] While we must resign ourselves to this, I find it hard to believe that the forty volumes of the *Orbis,* which had been the subject of much discussion only two generations before 1810, were thrown on an ash heap in Napoleonic times.

We can guess what the *Orbis* may have been like by looking at Savonarola's remarkable *Universus terrarum,* a bibliography of geography. Ottino and Fumagalli say that it is actually the first two volumes of the *Orbis,*[85] but this cannot be correct, for at least twice in the *Universus* (see I, 6 b, 168 b) Savonarola refers to the *Orbis* as a work awaiting publication. One confusing remark about the

[83] For this work see Ottino and Fumagalli, p. 77, no. 784. Giuseppe Vedova, *Bibliografia degli scrittori padovani* (2 vols.; Padua, 1832–1836), II, 229–230 gives only a digest of his predecessors.

[84] For references to a search made in 1880 see *Il bibliofilo,* I (1880), 12, 26, 80.

[85] See *Bibliotheca bibliographica italiana,* pp. 129–130, no. 1410 and J. G. Keyssler, *Neueste Reisen durch Teutschland . . . Italien* (2 vols., Hannover, 1751), I, 1156.

Universus calls for explanation. Friedrich Ebert [86] cites it under the name of Vincenzo Maria Coronelli (c1650–1716), cosmographer of Venice and general of the Franciscan order, and points out that Coronelli's *Regnorum, provinciarum, civitatumque ac quorumcumque locorum orbis terrarum nomina latina, tam juxta antiquos quam recentes geographos, duobus tomis exposita, quibus congruunt italica, ut facilius inveniantur illa* [sc. *nomina*], *quae impressa, imprimendave sunt in omnibus voluminibus Bibliothecae universalis P. Coronelli* (1716) differs from Savonarola's book only by title. Ebert's description is correct. This *Nomina latina*, as I shall call it, is still in the Dresden library. Ermanno Armao rejects the ascription to Coronelli.[87] Strictly speaking, the *Nomina latina* does not contain such an ascription. It contains the new title-page, on which there is below the title an oval shield with a sailing vessel on a globe and the inscription Argonautae below and a band or ribbon above inscribed *Plus ultra*. The inscription encircling the oval reads P. M. Vincentis Coronelli totius ordinis S. Francisci M. C. minister generalis LXXVIII. On the next leaf is a portrait of Clement XI and some inscriptions. There follow three maps tipped in, two of which the printer has labeled as Coronelli's. The binder's title reads *Orbis terrarum nomina latina Tom. I* (and *Tom. II*). This, I think, makes entirely clear what Coronelli was doing. He had published seven volumes of a huge *Bibliotheca universalis*, planned to fill forty-five volumes of encyclopedic rather than bibliographical quality. Although the seventh and last published volume of this work bears the date 1701 (Ebert, No. 5289), he may

[86] Lexikon, no. 5294. In the Dresden library the volume has the shelfmark Lex. geogr. 18.
[87] *Biblioteca di bibliografia italiana*, 17 (Florence, 1944), p. 268.

still, even in 1716 (the year of his death), have hoped to continue it or, as seems more likely to me, that date may refer to the year when his collections were bound for safekeeping. Coronelli was using the *Universus* as an index of names and this alone (not Savonarola's text) would be published when the *Bibliotheca* was complete. This we might infer from the words "illa [sc. nomina] impressa, imprimendave sunt in omnibus voluminibus Bibliotheca universalis P. Coronelli." Such is the most favorable interpretation I can offer of the facts. In 1739 Savonarola's nephew said in his bibliography of his uncle that Coronelli had offered to incorporate Savonarola's work (apparently the whole *Orbis* is meant) in the encyclopedia at the price of sacrificing Savonarola's authorship and that a member of still another order wanted it at the same price (see Biagi, p. xli). All this does not make pleasant reading and the removal in the Dresden copy of the titlepage with the pseudonym that identified Savonarola after a fashion makes one suspect Coronelli's intentions.

Savonarola's *Universus* is a geographical lexicon based, as the preface entitled "Lectori" says, on two earlier works, Michael Antoine Baudran (1653–1700), *Geographia, ordine literarum descripta* (Paris, 1670; 2 vols., 1682; 1705) and Philippus Alexandrinus Ferrarius (1554–1626), *Lexicon geographicum* (Milan, 1627; London, 1657, 1665). It superseded them and was in turn superseded by Antoine-Augustin Bruen de la Martinière, *Dictionnaire géographique, historique et critique* (10 vols.; The Hague, 1726–1730, with improved editions down to 1768).[88] Such works call for no mention here. Savonarola's *Universus* ranges

[88] I have not pursued these geographical works beyond identifying them in Robert Watt, *Bibliotheca britannica* (for this work see below); finding Ferrarius, *Lexicon* in Wing, F 814, 815; and looking at La Martinière.

more widely than the identification of geographical names with occasional bibliographical notes on them. In including much general bibliographical information it resembles Ulysse Chevalier's *Répertoire . . . Topo-bibliographie* discussed below.

Savonarola begins the *Universus* with a remarkable list of authors cited that fills sixty pages (I, 1–60), an "Index notabilium, & aliquot materiarum, de quibus etiam traduntur scriptores locorum in opere positorum" (I, 61–66), and a list (I, 67–68) of articles citing more than a hundred titles. The "Index" is well worth reading for articles on subjects that are not strictly geographical in nature. There are more than a hundred titles under America, more than three hundred under Anglia, more than six hundred botanical books under Hortus, and more than eight hundred chemical books under Mineralia, including such subjects as the transformation of Metals and potable Gold.

The Universus begins with Abaessinia (I, 2–3) with two-score references,—a very respectable number for 1713.[89] A scholar does not find Savonarola neglectful here or elsewhere of bibliographical details, for almost all the references include the date and place of publication and the format. The titles cited are travels, geographical descriptions, histories, maps, books on language and printing, lists of professors (if the heading is the name of a university town), famous men, and ecclesiastical figures, and books about religious matters associated with the places cited. Classical, Biblical, and Oriental names are

[89] As an example of the best modern bibliographical technique compare with Savonarola's account: Donald M. Lockhart's appendix (PMLA, LXXVIII [1963], 527–528) to his article on "The Ethiopian background of Johnson's 'Rasselas.'" It is entitled "A classified list of original European works containing information on Ethiopia published before 1759."

treated generously. A remarkable account of Anglia fills ten pages (I, 55–65). That of Ingolstadt (II, 35) mentions the elusive catalogue of the university library as well as a book about plants native to the region.[90] The article Latium (II, 82–88) brings many references to Latin dictionaries of various kinds. The bibliographies of the Saracens and Turkey seem rich enough to be still useful.

Savonarola was generous in his definition of what to include. The five columns of references under Infernus (II, 34–35), like the fifteen titles in the article Limbo (II, 107) or the account of the Earthly Paradise (II, 305), might be regarded as pertinent to a geographical subject-index. In the last of these he has caught *Paradisus deperditus* and *reseratus* by John Milton. The fifty titles in Oracles (II, 283) refer to books connected with places and are appropriately included. The two columns on the Sibylline Oracles (II, 502–503) go perhaps a bit farther than one might expect. Six titles on Druids (I, 340), a bibliography of Labyrinths (II, 74) with a dozen titles, the five pages dealing with Medicine, doctors, and medicaments (II, 166–171), a brief review of the Medici (II, 172), eighteen pages given to Minerals (II, 190–208), which approach being a bibliography of early chemistry, three pages on Monarchs (II, 217–219) like the remarks on Dukes (I, 341) with political implications, and a short account of Satyrs (II, 477) can perhaps be said to exceed the limits of a bibliography of geography. The long articles De Imperio and De Rebuspublicis look rich enough to be useful even now to a student of Renaissance political history and theory. A modern reader can still consult Savona-

[90] For comment on this catalogue see my *Book-catalogues*, pp. 45–46, 94–95 and above. Savonarola got information from a source that I have not identified because he cites the compiler's name as "Fers seu Fres" and the date of publication as 1605.

rola's *Universus* and he may not be disappointed. No one
who has looked into it can fail to regret bitterly the loss
of Savonarola's *Orbis litterarius.*

Francesco Marucelli, Mare magnum *(1701)*

The existence of Savonarola's *Orbis* proved in the end
to be an effective hindrance to the publication of another
large subject also composed by an Italian. This *Mare
magnum* made by Francesco Marucelli (1625–1703),[91]
founder of the Biblioteca Marucelliana in Florence, has
survived various accidents and copyings and can now be
consulted in an eighteenth-century copy in the Marucelliana. After the lapse of two centuries Giuseppe Biagi, then
librarian of the Marucelliana, found it in a corner and
described it. Marucelli had announced the *Mare magnum*
and had suggested its contents, as Savonarola had done
three years earlier, by printing a titlepage (1701):

Mare magnum omnium materiarum, sive index universalis
alphabeticus quorumcumque scriptorum cujuscumque idioma-
tis, qui de quacumque arte, scientia, historia, vel re, aut
integrum volumen, aut saltem capitulum conscripserunt cum
tali rerum distinctione, ac divisione, ut nihil exactius, vel copio-
sius desiderari possit. Opus triginta annorum continuato labore,
studioque concinnatum, in quo centum quinquaginta mille
auctores indicantur usque in praesentem diem ubique terrarum
editi materis per alphabetum dispositis, et in earum qualibet,
quantumvis arida, etque jejuna plurimis cumulatis scriptoribus
cum anno, loco, & editionis forma ex pluribus tomis in praelum
jam expeditis. Tomus primus Historalis.[92]

We may hear in the subtitle an echo of the *Index universalis alphabeticus* by Fabianus Justinianus, but I shall
not insist upon it.

[91] See Albano Sorbelli, ed., Carlo Frati, *Dizionario bio-biblio-
grafico dei bibliotecari e bibliofili italiani dal sec. XIV al XIX,*
Biblioteca di bibliografia italiana, 13 (Florence, 1933), pp. 339–340.
[92] Reproduced by Biagi as a frontispiece to his Francesco Marucelli, *Indice del Mare Magnum,* Indici e cataloghi, 9 (Rome, 1888).

The manuscript now in the Marucelliana is not Marucelli's original work but a copy and, in fact, the copy of a copy. After Francesco Marucelli's death in 1703 (Frati prefers this year to 1713), his nephew Alessandro obtained papal permission to read books on the Index and continued to add to the *Mare magnum*. When he discussed its publication in 1735, he had added seven to the original fifteen volumes and had copied and rearranged the whole work. Subsequently he added two more volumes. All these manuscripts appear to be lost. The work survives in 111 volumes copied after 1751 on the order of Angelo Maria Bandini (1726–1803), "primo prefetto della Marucelliana" and, after 1756, also chief of the Laurenziana. According to Biagi (p. xi), some additions were made as late as 1754. Interest in maintaining the *Mare magnum*, which served as a subject catalogue of the Marucelliana, slackened after 1735, when its publication had seemed likely. After the middle of the eighteenth century, when the last additions were made, it disappeared from sight only to be rediscovered by Biagi in 1887.

Although publication of the *Mare magnum* was contemplated in 1735, Alessandro Marucelli expressly forebade it in his will of July 5, 1751 (see Biagi, pp. xxxvii-xxxviii), refusing to permit the use of funds from either his own or his uncle's estate. No doubt the existence of Savonarola's *Orbis* played some part in his decision, but Biagi regards the prohibition as somewhat mysterious. He thinks that search in the archives of the Marucelliana might clarify it (p. xi).

In the course of copying, revision, and enlargement the *Mare magnum* underwent changes. We can only conjecture what Marucelli's original plan may have been from the words "Tomus Primus Historialis" on the titlepage of 1701. Apparently he conceived his work in large sections

that were subdivided in smaller headings arranged alphabetically. In the copy that we now have the work is divided into 42 large headings comprising from one to a
dozen or more volumes containing an estimated 200,000
references. The headings are then subdivided alphabetically in smaller articles. Fumagalli says that they number
5507. The largest headings are Liturgy (6 vols.), Theo-
loglia universalis (12 vols.), Civil and criminal law (14
vols.), Canon law (6 vols.), and Natural history (8 vols.).

If we combine the various subdivisions of history and
biography, we might obtain perhaps six volumes each for
Italian and non-Italian subjects. Such figures give some
notion of what Marucelli chose to excerpt. We see that he
did not zealously excerpt literature or even the Bible
(4 vols.).

The arrangement is at times annoying or at least surprising. We should not expect to find the Hun Attila, the
Dutch Erasmus, and the Albanian Scanderbeg in Vitae
Italorum. Many smaller categories that we might look for
are lacking without an obvious explanation. It is idle to
conjecture whether Marucelli ever compiled them or
whether they were lost in copying and recopying the manuscript. There is, for example, no heading for Anonyma
and pseudonyma, although the subject was much discussed around the end of the seventeenth century. On the
whole, he does not show himself to be much interested in
bibliography. His knowledge of foreign countries except
what is now modern Germany (3 vols., including Russia,
Sweden, and the Turkish Empire) and France (3 vols.) is
not remarkable and is at best contained in a volume for
each.

On the title page Marucelli suggests the usefulness of
the *Mare magnum* to scholars. Guido Biagi enlarges en-

thusiastically on this subject (pp. xviii-xix). He says that the *Mare magnum* lists many books published in the seventeenth century, the most obscure century in Italian bibliographical and literary history. The titles of books published in this century often fail to indicate the contents clearly, and information can be gathered from the *Mare magnum*. In certain regards, he continues, it is more useful than a modern encyclopedia and it supplies materials for solving questions that have occupied scholars of former days and have since been neglected. As examples of such questions he mentions (pp. xviii-xix): "Why have the sons of great fathers failed to equal their fathers?" and the interpretation of a line in Dante's Purgatorio, "Rare volte risurge per li rami" (7. 121). I have not hit upon the headings in Biagi's list that will lead to comment on these questions. He thinks that the *Mare magnum* is valuable for references to forgotten authors and titles. This opinion must be qualified by noting that the genealogical information about Italian families cited in the headings listed by Biagi (pp. 153–177) may be useful, but it will be difficult to find a reference to a particular family and even more to a particular book about which one seeks to know more. He goes on to point out that Marucelli has collected many curious references to the human nose.

Biagi's praise is generous. The *Mare magnum* is an unexplored storehouse, but it does not contain all one might look for. Marucelli does not have much interest in literary subjects. There is little that I can identify as a guide to a famous theme like Sophonisba, Iphigenia, or Medea. Rhetorica et grammatica and Historia litteraria comprise only four volumes with perhaps 200 headings. Virtually all of the latter section is concerned with biobibliographical articles on authors. More general material will be found

in the first section as appears from the following list of
headings (p. 153):

De accentibus, adverbiis, agnominatione, vulgo Bisticcio, alius
vel alii dictione, allegoria, alma et eius significatione, Amazoni-
bus, anachronismo, anagrammate, autonomasia, apologiae di-
versae et responsiones, seu vindiciae, aspiratione in vocabulis,
seu verbis, atramento, bibliothecis et bibliopolis, brevitate.[93]

I leave this and the following list chosen from Miscellanea
(pp. 125–132), of which there are four volumes, in the
original to show the difficulties with which one must contend in using the *Mare magnum*. There is no doubt that
Marucelli has gathered many curious references under the
following headings, but it is a question of finding the right
one at the right time in such a list as this:

De abreviaturis et cifris sive notis literarum contractis; absortis
a terra; accademiis; Accensi, qui essent apud Romam: acu
fortuito deglutita [one would look for this in Medicine]; aenigmatibus et symbolis; amphitheatro; anno, mensibus et diebus,
mane et vespero; ascia; aspersoribus equorum; asylo seu refugio
[one might look for this under Law]; aula et aulicis. Vide etiam
Gratia principum; aulicis et tapetis; aulis et cubiculis loquenti-
bus; aurigis; barba; Barbaris et Barbarie; barbitonsoribus;
bibendo et potu; bibacibus. Vide etiam vino; bravio; bysso.

Theological and historical subjects are carefully analyzed; subjects in natural history, physics, i.e., the physical
world, and medicine perhaps less fully; legal subjects, especially canon law, generously; and other subjects, including literary history, often with notice of unexpected
matters.

Few scholars have looked into the *Mare magnum* or
at least few have acknowledged indebtedness to it. According to Frati the references to Petrarch have been ex-

[93] Here and in the following list the "De" introducing the heading
is omitted after the first occurrence.

cerpted. According to Biagi (p. xxviii) Girolamo Meloni consulted it in 1707 when writing a legal treatise. In 1887 Biagi printed the article De auditu et auribus (Hearing and ears) in a pamphlet published in honor of the birth of a daughter to his friend Vittorio Grazzi. This was intended more to draw attention to the *Mare magnum* than to contribute to medical history. Biagi reprinted this in his *Indice* (pp. xlix-lvi). This reprinting is perhaps the easiest means of getting an idea of the quality of Marucelli's work, but I cannot be sure that the idea one might get is correct. The citations are very full and conform to modern bibliographical style. The citations De aenigmatibus and De bibliothecis, which are before me in photostat, suggest that Biagi corrected or at least modernized Marucelli's references. In these two articles the references are by no means easy to read.

The *Mare magnum* is very much what we might expect an Italian churchman of the end of the seventeenth century to have written. It offers a great deal on theological and legal subjects, on Italian families, and on those individuals who were associated with Italy in some way. The eight volumes for the natural sciences contain much information, but are not the work of one actively studying them. Probably the four volumes for Medicine and the four for Anatomy and Surgery will be useful to a student of medical history. In every way the *Mare magnum* is a great advance beyond the *Index universalis alphabeticus* of Justinianus.

Such comparison of Marucelli's *Mare magnum* and Savonarola's *Orbis* as I can make must rest on the three articles that I have seen and Savonarola's *Universus terrarum*. It can suggest the strength and weakness of both works and their value to a modern student. Probably

Savonarola had a better knowledge of languages and saw
more books than Marucelli. On the other hand, Marucelli
is to be commended for including references to parts of
books. This Savonarola does less frequently. It is important to remember that Marucelli cited many books that
are still in the Marucelliana. For one who is so fortunate
as to be studying in Florence this is a great advantage.
In bibliographical technique Savonarola is superior to
Marucelli. It will already have occurred to the reader that
the two bibliographies might have been conflated, but
there were, we can conjecture, very natural reasons why
this did not happen. The distance between Padua and
Florence is an obvious handicap. The differences in the
arrangement of the two indexes is another. The natural
unwillingness of either author to see his labors swallowed
up in another man's work is still another. Had a combination come to pass, the result would have been a subject-
index of such importance that the history of subject bibliography would have been altogether different from what
it proved to be.

Simon Pauli (or Paulli), Historia litteraria *(1671)*

Simon Pauli's dealer's catalogue may be mentioned here
for its title and as an early example of a dealer's classified
catalogue of current literature. The *Historia litteraria sive
Dispositio librorum omnium facultatum ac artium, secundum materias, in usum philobiblorum congesta* (Strasbourg, 1671) is an early instance of the term "historia litteraria" that was used a generation later to signify a
chronological critical survey. Pauli's rather detailed classification might call for remark, but I shall note only that
he lists (pp. 164–168) novels, comedies and tragedies, and
jestbooks. These categories are rarely mentioned in sub-

ject-indexes. I shall not mention later examples of dealer's catalogues [94] and shall touch only briefly on similar compilations made by publishers.

Antoine Tribler de la Ruë, pseud., Bibliothèque générale *(c1689)*

This offers puzzles that I cannot solve, but is nevertheless a valuable indication that men were thinking about a general subject-index in Paris just before 1700. In Adrien Baillet's *Des satyres personelles* (Paris, 1689), an answer to the *Anti-Baillet* by Gilles Ménage, the reading of a list of twenty-seven fictitious bibliographies fills an intermission at the beginning of the third "entretien." [95] Their titles are given at length and are, in some instances, commented upon. The authors' names are pseudonyms. It is difficult to say how far the titles represent work actually in existence or generally known to be in progress. The twenty-first title will suggest the somewhat satirical nature of the list:

Receueil des Questions inutiles, frivoles & dangereuses que le raffinement & l'abus de la Scholastique a introduit dans les Écoles, avec une Requête aux Puissances pour obtenir leur suppression ou leur banissement, par le Sieur Daniel Alibert de Villeneuve.

There is here no doubt an allusion that Baillet intended to be recognized. The last title is a disguised reference to Baillet's own dictionary of pseudonyms that was pub-

---

[94] Note, as examples, the books by Caspar Gottschling (*Einleitung zur Wissenschafft guter und meistentheils neuer Bücher*, Dresden, 1702) and C. G. Ludovici (*Bibliotheca nominalis curiosa*, Wittenberg, [1703]), cited by Petzholdt, pp. 74–75. His comment "Nichts mehr werth" is justified.

[95] I have used the edition in Bernard de la Monnaye, ed., Adrien Baillet, *Jugemens des savans* (17 vols., Amsterdam, 1725), VIA, 228–245.

lished in 1698 (see Taylor and Mosher, p. 10, n. 24). There
is therefore probably a foundation in fact for the twenty-
fifth bibliography that is described as follows:

Bibliothèque générale de matières sacrés & profanes, c'est-à-
dire, Théologiques, Juridiques, Historiques, Physiques, &c. qui
ont été traitées singulièrement par les Auteurs, & éxaminées à
fonds, par Antoine Tribler de la Ruë.

Perhaps readers in 1689 recognized Baillet's intention. I
cannot and am content to point out that Baillet is familiar
with the notion of a general subject-index and to hope
that someone may explain the allusion. This curious subject-index differed from most others in containing critical
comments and deserves notice as a criticism of the state
of bibliography at the time, but an adequate interpretation
must await another occasion and a competent hand.

SUBJECT-INDEXES OF MISCELLANIES
AND JOURNALS

During the seventeenth century the making of subject-
indexes developed rapidly and men perceived the need for
indexes of special kinds of publications that were not included in general indexes. Miscellanies, an ancient genre,
contained a variety of information that the compiler had
assembled from many sources but, lacking an index or any
clear arrangement of materials, they were difficult to consult. During the seventeenth century some important miscellanies were provided with indexes, but not all were so
fortunate. In the last years of the century men saw the
need for an index to them. Like miscellanies, journals
contain a variety of materials and call for an index. The
publication of journals in the modern sense begins with
the foundation of the *Journal des sçavans* in 1665, and an

index to it followed twenty-six years later. Although these indexes to miscellanies and journals that can be compared to modern indexes to journals and volumes of collected essays seem very useful to us, scholars of the late seventeenth century showed little interest in them.

J. G. Schiele(n), Bibliotheca enucleata (1679); the Bibliographies Announced by Cornelius à Beughem (c1683) and B. H. Wüsthoff (c1705)

The *Bibliotheca enucleata* by Johann Georg Schiele (or Schielen), whose name does not appear in the ordinary biobibliographical dictionaries, is virtually unknown and seems to have been unknown in its own day. D. G. Morhof does not know it and knowledge of it came late to Antoine Teissier, a bibliographer of bibliographies. Teissier does not cite it in a *Catalogus* published seven years after the appearance of the *Bibliotheca* in 1679 but includes it in the *Auctuarium* of 1705.[96] Teissier and Giusto Fontanini in the Imperiali catalogue, which I shall mention later, give the place of publication as Vienna. The Princeton University copy that I have used was published at Ulm. The *Bibliotheca enucleata* is a subject-index of miscellanies and is therefore comparable to the modern subject-indexes of collections of essays.[97] The frontispiece suggests its character very well: a man holds torches in both hands while miners in front of him are working with pick and shovel in an open-face mine. In an introductory section without

---

[96] The *Catalogus auctorum qui librorum catalogos, indices, bibliothecas, virorum litteratorum elogia, vitas, aut orationes funebres, scriptis consignarunt* (Geneva, 1686) is a bibliography of bibliographies based on an earlier work by Philip Labbé. The *Catalogi auctorum . . . auctuarium* (Geneva, 1705) is a supplement. For the reference to Schiele see p. 146.

[97] For bibliographies of essays see WBB, cols. 1306–1307.

a heading Augustinus Erath (1648–1719), who says that
he does not know Schiele personally, compares him to
Varro, to whom Caesar had erected a statue commemo-
rating his work in libraries. Erath thinks well of the book
and was a competent judge, for he later made an edition
of Filippo Picinelli, *Mundus symbolicus* (Augsburg, 1683).
The *Mundus* was a catalogue of themes used by writers of
emblem-books and was therefore a work somewhat similar in character to the *Bibliotheca enucleata*.

Schiele says (p. 19) that he owes the suggestion of his
book to Hieronymus Drexel, *Aurifodina* and characterizes
this successful guide in the art of making excerpts as "Lec-
tio sane omnibus studiosis necessaria, quam & nos in hoc
opere secuti." The *Aurifodina artium et scientiarum exer-
cependi solertia omnibus litterarum amantibus monstrata*
(Antwerp, 1639. The preface is dated at Munich in 1638)
is a detailed and practical guide, but it can have influenced
Schiele only in a general way. The three roughly equal
parts into which it is divided suggest its nature: Pars I,
Excerptorum necessitas, seu excerpendum esse; Pars II,
Excerptorum methodus, seu Quomodo excerpendum sit;
Pars III, Excerptorum diversus usus, seu Multiplex indus-
tria excerpendi.

Like their predecessors of the seventeenth century, the
bibliographers of the early eighteenth century pass Schiele
by without mention. I find him named only by Jacob F.
Reimmann, who owned a copy of the *Bibliotheca enucleata*.[98] Reimmann damns it briefly and effectively by
quoting Schiele's statement of his plan and then, as he

---

[98] *Bibliotheca historiae literariae critica* (2d ed.; Hildesheim,
1743), pp. 124–127. This is a catalogue of the bibliographical part of
Reimmann's private library and contains abundant criticisms of the
books included. Reimmann's concluding remark is an adaption of a
proverb quoted by Livy, 23. 47. 6: " 'Put the hack in the ditch,' he
said," i.e., "when it is useless."

says, judging the colossus by its first stone (ut ex primo statim lapide Colossum aestimare queas). The first stone or article in the *Bibliotheca* is the letter A, and Reimmann points out half a dozen serious errors in it. While Reimmann is correct enough in details, he has failed to see Schiele's purpose of offering an index of materials in miscellanies and not a critical account of them. He is therefore not judging the book for what it intends to be. He concludes, "Toties defecit Cantherius in porta. Quoties quaeso deficiet in via."

Schiele does not define his task very sharply, for he includes systematic treatises of a general sort on historical, geographical, and scientific subjects as well as miscellanies. He cites freely from the writings of Erasmus Francisci, G. P. Harsdörffer, Gaspar Schott, and Martin Zeiller. He makes much use of Simon Majoli, *Dierum canicularum tomi VII*, a classified collection of information that approaches an encyclopedia. Since Lipenius had cited only book titles, Schiele's *Bibliotheca* is more or less a complement to the *Bibliotheca realis*, although not by intention. Schiele does much the same thing as Fabianus Justinianus had done two generations earlier in Italy, but Justinianus's work has a pronounced theological coloring. Good as Schiele's idea was, he seems to have made no serious effort to identify the miscellany as a category and then to index examples. Many famous miscellanies escaped him. It is unfortunate that his example did not inspire someone to continue and improve upon his work.

The character and quality of Schiele's *Bibliotheca enucleata* can be easily shown by citing the first dozen headings: A, Abbas, Abbreviatura, ABCDarius, Abdomen, Abdicatio, Abies (a fruit), Abigeus (a legal term), Abitus (retreating as a military strategem), Ablactio (weaning), Ablutio (washing of hands), Abortus (in law and medi-

cine), Abstinentia. A few technical German terms like
Abtrag (indemnity for a wound) are used as headings,
but Latin headings are the rule. The article Academia fills
three pages, and Acus magneticum (magnetic needle) a
page and a half. An article like Clamor (outcry made on
the occasion of a crime, the German *Zetergeschrei*) might
have been useful to a modern scholar.[99] The fourteenth-
century *Ackermann aus Böhmen* begins with such an outcry that sets in motion the legal proceedings in the husband's complaint against Death for the loss of his wife.
There is no clear principle in the choice of proper names
as headings, but no doubt the material available determined it. Adam, Mahomet, and Nebuchadnezzar are present, and Judas and Noah are absent. Non-Biblical personal
names are of infrequent occurrence. The *Bibliotheca* is
not a dictionary of miscellaneous biographical information. Geographical names like Francofurtum, Münster, or
Nilus (Nile) seem to be more numerous than personal
names and reflect Schiele's interest in geography. He offers, for example, a list of names of straits under Fretum.
The articles Anglia, Gallia, Germania, Polonia, Hispania,
and Hungaria contain more geographical than historical
information. A few cities are mentioned, but London,
Paris, and Ulm are not present.

With the qualifications suggested, Schiele's interests
range widely. He gives a full page of references on Alea
(dice), two and a half on Angelus, a generous collection
under Aqua (water) with much concerning the ordeal of
ducking a witch under water (there are more in the article
Saga). He devotes three pages to Spectrum (ghost).

[99] L. L. Hammerich, *Clamor: eine rechtsgeschichtliche Studie*,
Det kgl. danske Videnskabernes Selskab, Historisk-filologiske
Mededelser, XX, no. I (1941).

These excerpts probably indicate Schiele's choice of headings sufficiently well. He gives perhaps more attention to theological subjects than I have indicated. Law, which is usually poorly represented in general subject indexes, and Medicine along with natural science, i.e., Physics, Botany and Zoology (note, for example, the headings Equus, Onager, Pavo, Tigrus), and Astronomy are generously represented. There are some curious omissions and oversights. Schiele promises (p. 470) references to the story of a female pope in a supplement, which seems never to have been published. He reserves Microscopum also for this supplement. Besterman estimates (WBB, cols. 464–465) that he cites 30,000 titles. The unsystematic and scanty choice of titles to be excerpted impairs the value of his work, but it deserved to be carried out methodically. It also needs a historical and critical account of miscellanies, but no one has yet written it.

A few years later Cornelius à Beughem, who was a competent bibliographer, saw the utility of a subject-index of miscellanies and announced his intention to make one, but nothing came of it.[100] Around 1700 the obscure B. H. Wüsthoff, about whom very little can be learned, also announced one, but seems not to have published it. Useful as such compilations might have been, they aroused no interest.

Cornelius à Beughem, La France sçavante (*1683*)

With his index of *La France sçavante* (Amsterdam, 1683. Pp. [xx], 694) Cornelius à Beughem, a bookseller at

---

[100] See his *La France sçavante* (Amsterdam, [1683], p. * 7. It was the sixth in a series of bibliographies and was entitled *Bibliotheca philologica, profana & miscellanea*. Struve-Jugler, I, 93, mentions Wüsthoff's plan; see below Ch. V, n. 1.

Emmerich about whom almost nothing is known, began the making of subject-indexes to journals. He had some local fame, for he subscribes himself in the dedication of his *Bibliotheca medica & physica* (Amsterdam, 1681. See WBB, col. 2496) as "Urbis Embricensis Tribunus Plebis." Theodore Besterman, who quotes this (*Beginnings*, p. 34), remarks, "In his prefaces he tells us a great deal about his bibliographical projects but little or nothing about himself."

The subtitle of *La France sçavante* describes the nature of the book at length:

Id est, Gallia erudita, critica et experimentalis novissima, Seu, Manuductio . . . non tam Scriptorium Operumque, quam Experimentorum, Observationum, aliarumque Rerum notatu dignarum cujusvis Facultatis, Artis, & Scientiae, quarum summaria in Ephemeridibus Eruditorum [i.e., Journal des sçavans] hujus celeberrimi Regni ab Ann. 1665, quo coeperunt, usque as Ann. 1681. recensentur.

It is, in other words, an index to almost two thousand reviews of books and other scholarly and scientific reports found in the *Journal* that was founded in 1665. Some bibliographers have loosely cited it as a bibliography. À Beughem made not only a chronological tabulation (pp. 3–231) but also an alphabetical tabulation (pp. 232–476) according to authors with anonymous writings listed separately (pp. 437–476) as well as a classified tabulation (pp. 477–694) in six sections: Theology, Law and Politics, Medicine, Philosophy, History and Geography, Literature and Miscellaneous, each arranged alphabetically by the names of authors.

This exhaustive index to the *Journal des sçavans* may have been useful in its day, for this journal of critical reviews enjoyed great prestige. D. G. Morhof objects to à Beughem's plan of merely listing the reviews without adding critical comment and says that the contents do not justify the title or meet the expectations of readers.[101] He seems to have neglected to read à Beughem's sub-title announcing the book to be only a list. No one could have written such criticisms of books in all fields as Morhof desires. It is clear that he fails to perceive the nature and use of a *Book Review Digest*.

In 1689 à Beughem began a more ambitious work of the same kind, now enlarged to include journals published in many countries. The first volume was entitled *Apparatus ad historiam litterariam novissimam* and with some changes in the title he continued the task to a fifth volume published in 1710 (see WBB, col. 3131).[102] Theodore Besterman comments, "The first volume of the Apparatus describes in 500 pages about 7,000 works, arranged in the alphabetical order of their authors, and the succeeding volumes are on a similar scale" (*Beginnings,* p. 37). Like *La France sçavante,* the *Apparatus* is a subject index to journals (virtually to reviews published in journals), but on an international scale. We shall not see another international subject-index to journals for more than a century. The *Apparatus,* being divided according to languages, is difficult to use. It is not easy to say how valuable it was to scholars around 1700. Contemporary bibliographers do not make many references to book reviews and the reviews that I see mentioned appear to have been noted by the bibliographers themselves and not to have been obtained from *La France sçavante* or the *Apparatus.*

[101] See *Polyhistor,* I, ch. xvi, § 45 (ed. 1747, I, 179). Adrien Baillet sees correctly what *La France sçavante* is but does not welcome it; see *Jugemens des savans* (nouv. éd., 13 vols. in 17, Amsterdam, 1725, IIA, pp. 59–60). Additional notices, especially Bayle's commendation, are collected in Struve-Jugler, I, 991–992.

[102] All five volumes are in the Newberry Library.

SUBJECT-INDEXES OF THE LAMOIGNON AND IMPERIALI LIBRARIES

In the last years of the seventeenth century, when enormous subject-indexes were being made in Germany and Italy, Adrien Baillet compiled a large subject-index of the library of Chrétien-François de Lamoignon and a few years later Giusto Fontanini catalogued Cardinal Giuseppe Renato Imperiali's books and added a subject-index. Before discussing these indexes, it will be helpful to say something about catalogues of private libraries, the rare subject-indexes to them, and their usefulness as subject bibliographies. Virtually all the early catalogues of private libraries—an exception is to be made chiefly for Italian catalogues—were classified, not alphabetical in arrangement. Catalogues made for the owner like the Des Cordes catalogue of 1643 made by Gabriel Naudé and the De Thou catalogue of 1679 or sale catalogues like the *Heinsiana* (1682), listing the books of Nicolaus Heinsius, and the Pedro Núñez de Guzmán catalogue (1677) made by José Maldonado y Pardo were readily consulted bibliographies and much sought after at the time.[103] Their value as bibliographies depends on several circumstances: the number and quality of the books, the care used by the maker of the catalogue, and the presence of an index of author's names. The general nature and the quality of the books can be inferred from the owner's profession and nationality: the *Carpzoviana* (1700), owned by a prominent German theologian, supplements the Núñez de Guzmán catalogue and more or less duplicates the *Ittigiana* (1711), the catalogue of Thomas Ittig's theological books.

---

[103] For references to these catalogues see my *Book catalogues*.

These catalogues have various handicaps to their usefulness as bibliographies. They are not always easy to obtain. Their arrangement is often awkward. They are careless about titles and other bibliographical details. They usually deal summarily with minor items that would not bring a good price at a sale. The large number of books listed under a general heading may occasionally make it necessary to read many pages for the desired information. The utility of catalogues was common knowledge in the late seventeenth and early eighteenth centuries, and several bibliographers compiled lists of the most useful examples.[104]

Only a few private libraries had both an author catalogue and a subject-index. We have already noted Liebniz's subject-index of Baron von Boineburg's library. Perhaps the most important example at this time is the Lamoignon index made by Adrien Baillet.[105] Guillaume de Lamoignon had assembled an important collection of books and bequeathed it to his son, Chrétien-François de Lamoignon. After Guillaume's death in 1677, the family steward M. de Hersant asked Baillet to take charge of the library. He warned him to adopt an agreeable manner and adjust himself to the metropolis. Baillet came in April, 1680 and was appointed librarian in the following month. He is said to have been cordial to patrons and to have proved successful and competent from the beginning. Something of his nature and the wisdom of M. de Hersant's advice may be inferred from the fact that he

[104] These early lists are combined into one in my *Book catalogues*, pp. 229–266.

[105] For these details see Gabriel Peignot, *Dictionnaire raisonné de bibliologie* (2 vols. and suppl., Paris, 1802–1804), I, 159; Giuseppe Fumagalli, *Cataloghi e indici* (Florence, 1887), p. 181; and my *Book catalogues*, p. 249.

was allowed Monday as a free day but preferred to stay in the library. He spent some months in arranging the books and then began an index that he completed in 1682. It is said to have been in two volumes. It was the basis of a larger work in thirty-five or thirty-two volumes folio [106] that perished in the burning of the municipal library of Paris in 1871. The books passed through the hands of several heirs and were listed in a rare and luxurious catalogue published in 1770 in fifteen copies. According to a manuscript note at the end of a copy in the Bibliothèque nationale, the catalogue was still being revised and enlarged in 1785. The history of the catalogue and its revision—there are several copies with manuscript notes in the Bibliothèque nationale—need study. Since the revisers used Baillet's subject-index in their work, we can perhaps learn more about it from such a study.

After 1700, when Baillet had probably finished his subject-index, Giusto Fontanini (1666–1736) compiled an index to the Giuseppe Renato Imperiali library. The two resembled each other in having difficult temperaments and being diligent workmen. Fontanini's catalogue lists some 20,000 volumes in alphabetical order with all the details required by modern technique. A classified subject-index (pp. 583–720) is followed by a table of contents (pp. 723–738). The typography is attractive and in every way the catalogue and the index are pleasant to use.

Cardinal Imperiali (1651–1737), who came from a distinguished Genoese family, became cardinal in 1690. He visited Spain as legate to Charles III, but his library does not contain many books acquired on this occasion. As might be expected, it is especially strong in ecclesiastical

---

[106] The figure varies; see *Dictionnaire de biographie française* (Paris, 1933–   ), IV, 1266–1268.

books. Those dealing with the saints, the religious orders, and canon law are numerous. The classifications of the last group seems to me to be perhaps useful. There are titles referring to the religious orders that I do not readily find in the *Enciclopedia italiana*. The books on Astronomy (p. 660) are rather few in number and seem unimportant. The Bibliographical books (pp. 700–701) are abundant and well-chosen. The cardinal even owned a copy of Schiele, *Bibliotheca enucleata* (see above), which occurs rarely even in German catalogues. The choice of such Catalogues of private libraries as the *Aprosiana, Slusiana, Telleriana, Thuana,* and the Johan de Witt catalogue (1701) (p. 531), which is esteemed but little-known, shows good judgment. Virtually no German catalogues were then available, and the cardinal would probably have had little desire to acquire them. Yet he did not limit himself to orthodox books, for writings on Pope Joan are present and duly listed in a special category (p. 612). More than eighty titles give a generous representation of English history (p. 696). The care shown in describing and classifying the books makes the Imperiali catalogue and its subject-index a good source of information about seventeenth-century books.

PLANS FOR SUBJECT-INDEXES COMPILED FROM LIBRARY CATALOGUES

Around 1700 three men in Germany and a bookseller in London conceived, apparently independently, the idea of assembling several library catalogues in a reference work. They do not mention Pierre Blanchot's proposed alphabetical index of 1631 as a predecessor but intended to produce a classified guide to scholarly books. The plan was altogether feasible, for good catalogues of public and private libraries were available. Most of those they intended to use were already classified and could be combined with little difficulty. Only the alphabetical Bodleian (1674), University of Leiden (1674), and Barberini (1682) catalogues would have required the making and classification of slips for the titles.[107] Scholars bought and used library catalogues for reference purposes, but only the wealthiest and most fortunate could hope to acquire a sufficient collection. It is clear now, and must have been clear then, that the conflation of catalogues would yield a very valuable scholarly aid. Nevertheless, nothing came of several proposals.

Philip Huselith, Bibliotheca contracta (1698)

Philip Huselith, a doctor of medicine, who is unknown to biographical dictionaries, announced a plan to make a *Bibliotheca contracta, seu, Catalogus bibliothecarum insigniorum Thuanae, Barberinae, Slusianae, Heinsianae, Tellerianae, aliarumque, collectus atque in justam ordinem dispositus* (Jena, 1698). We cannot draw many inferences from the brief record.[108] Since he has arranged the catalogues in chronological order, he was probably a systematic worker. Since he has chosen what are still regarded as the best catalogues of the time, he was a man of good judgment. Since his selection represents France

[107] For description and identification of the catalogues mentioned in this section see my *Book catalogues*. All of them are in the Newberry Library.

[108] All I know about Huselith and his plan is found in a bibliographical note in Antoine Teissier, *Catalogi auctorum qui librorum catalogos, indices, bibliothecas, virorum litteratorum elogias, vitas, aut orationes funebres, scriptis consignarunt auctuarium* (Geneva, 1705), p. 230. This is a supplement to Teissier's enlargement (1686) of Philip Labbé's bibliography of bibliographies.

(*Thuana, Helleriana*), Italy (*Barberina, Slusiana*), and the Netherlands (*Heinsiana*), he recognized the necessity of consulting catalogues from various countries. We can safely call him a judicious and well-informed bibliographer. He intended to produce a classified bibliography (in justam ordinem dispositus) and very likely limited himself to Latin works. This modest and practical proposal could have been completed in a few months and would have yielded a useful book. We hear no more of it, and bibliographers then or later rarely mention it.

John Hartley, Catalogus (1699, 1701)

The London bookseller John Hartley (fl. 1697–1707) went so far as to publish two volumes of excerpts collected from several catalogues and promise a subject index to accompany them. This anonymous *Catalogus universalis librorum* (2 vols., 1699) contains names excerpted from nine catalogues arranged in seven alphabets. There are of course many duplications. He promised a subject-index, but got no further than an index of authors published in 1701. The catalogues he used are the Bodleian, University of Leiden, and University of Utrecht institutional catalogues and the sale or owner's catalogues of the Barberini, Des Cordes, Nicolaus Heinsius, De Thou, Sluis, and Le Tellier collections. It might be possible to identify excerpts from each of these, but I can see no reason to undertake this laborious task. These were the best catalogues of the seventeenth century and could have been supplemented by the Pedro Núñez de Guzmán catalogue (1677), the Richard Smith catalogue (1682), and the German *Carpzoviana* (1700). From these he would have obtained many vernacular titles that would have altered somewhat the nature of his compilation. It is scarcely likely that he ever saw the Spanish and German catalogues, but his neglect of the English catalogue suggests that he was aiming to make a scholarly work that did not include vernacular materials. Since Hartley employed a rough alphabetical arrangement in the excerpts, he may have conceived the final work as an alphabetical rather than a classified catalogue. Hartley included the Des Cordes catalogue, which was famous in the seventeenth century, but it added rather few titles to those he obtained from the others he names. We cannot know whether Huselith omitted it intentionally or accidentally.

Valentin Ernst Loescher, Pandectae (*1700*)

With a young man's enthusiasm Valentin Ernst Loescher (1672–1749) announced in 1700 plans for many books largely bibliographical in nature that he never completed.[109] This became an occasion for embarrassment to him and resulted in a formal statement of his studies and endeavors and what he had accomplished. One of the books that he promised was subsequently called *Pandectae* and appears to have been a subject-index. His anonymously published *Breviarium continens Initia eruditionis, oder A. B. C. der Gelehrsamkeit, zum Nutzen der Trivial-Schulen aufgesetzt* (Leipzig, 1711), which I have not seen, is

---

[109] *Arcana literaria & alios XXX libros edendos Musis consecrat* (1700), cited from J. F. Reimmann, *Bibliotheca historiae litterariae* (2d ed.; Hildesheim, 1743), pp. 235–236. I have not been able to see or identify this. Theophil Georgi, *Allgemeines europäisches Bücher-Lexikon*, I, 414 cites *Arcanorum literariorum specimina* (Coburg, 1700). In the same year Loescher announced three theological bibliographies in the *Vorschlag dreyer höchst benöthigten Schrifften, als Phraseologiae Sacrae, Theologiae polemicae generalis, und Theologiae mysticae* (cited from Reimmann). Reimmann's comments on Loescher are harsh and those whom he quoted spoke with similar unkindness.

a result of his bibliographical studies, but can scarcely have fulfilled his brave promises.[110] Its anonymous appearance may imply that he did not regard it highly.

Loescher's activity as a Protestant theologian explains his failure to complete what he had undertaken. Soon after announcing his plans he accepted the editorship of a very important journal, *Altes und Neues aus dem Schatz theologischer Wissenschaft* ([Wittenberg, 1700] ff.), later called *Unschuldige Nachrichten von alten und neuen theologischen Sachen,* and did not relinquish it until 1722. It can be readily understood how sensitive he was to allusions to his failure to publish what he had promised. The language used in these allusions was severe: "thirty literary heroes would scarcely have accomplished such tasks."

In 1715 Loescher published a "Responsio de statu progressuque scriptorum a se promissorum" that amounts to an *amende honorable* of sorts for his vainglorious promises of 1700. It deserved a kinder reception from contemporary bibliographers than it received and was rarely mentioned later. Since it throws much light on both Loescher and contemporary bibliography, I venture to summarize it at some length. This "Responsio" is attached to Christian Feustelius, *Miscellanea sacra et erudita de phraseologia et emphasi biblica antiquitatum studio biographis elencho pontifico . . . accessit Loescheri Responsio* (Leipzig, 1715).[111] The *Miscellanea* is itself a curious work that would call for remark, if space permitted, and it is not clear why the "Responsio" was attached to it. The "Re-

---

[110] Cited from Lawätz (see below), no. 6352.

[111] I have used a copy in the Royal Library, Copenhagen. Feustelius's comments on books of ana have been overlooked by bibliographers. They are worth reading.

sponsio" is virtually an *Apologia pro vita sua* and fills pp. 671–775.

Before he was 16, Loescher says, he had made collectanea that he entitled *Athenographia* (p. 678), but this "crudum opusculum & puerile," which appears to have been a general bibliography, he threw away. In it he told what books he had read or consulted and at times gives the impression of being a name-dropper. About the same time he had also begun a list of historical names (i.e., a general biographical dictionary), and had done some work on Francisco Suarez (1548–1617), the author of *Quod nihil scitur*. These tasks he did not complete. Later, when he was 19, he was making a list of new stars (*Schediasmata de novis stellis*) and continuing his historical and geographical collectanea. He wrote an *Ecloga Vitruviana de Symmetris ordinibus,* "but I didn't finish it (sed no perfici)," as we shall hear many times. He also wrote a study in solid geometry, arranged his father's library, and wrote *De claris typographis* (Famous printers), to which he added in the next year *Clari correctores* (Famous proofreaders). This was not enough for a youth not yet 19. He found time for a bibliography of writers on the Trojan War (p. 684) and *Pandectae genealogicae* (pp. 684–685), a general account of family histories. The amazing variety of what he had already begun or accomplished did not satisfy his restless spirit. He adds:

Singulari praetera studio congessi Scriptores rei Nauticae, Anemologicae, Oneirocriticae, Cynegeticae, Ornithologicae, Hortensae, Rusticae, Ampelurgicae & Dendrologicae (i.e., naval affairs, the winds, dreams, swans, birds, gardening, country life, viticulture, and trees).

But, as all too often, "I did not carry this very far (neque vero hoc institutum pressi)." Nor was this all: he began a

Historia literarum renascentium, to which he devotes nearly two pages (pp. 690–691), and three studies in names.

At 20 he was teaching "honestos juvenes" at Wittenberg modern literary history. These lectures he undertook to revise along with studies in biblical apocrypha (p. 694), such learned families as the Bartholins and Estiennes, literary quarrels, and (at Jena) numismatics. He travelled widely, visiting Holland, Belgium, and Denmark. When he was 23, he began the *Pandectae bibliothecae theologicae, historicae, philosophicae & philologicae,* a subject-index embracing all ages, regions, sects, and languages and including a supplement to G. M. König, *Bibliotheca vetus et nova* (Altdorf, 1679), the standard universal bio-bibliographical dictionary of the time. He expresses regret that he did not continue work on this task (p. 700), but does not describe it in more detail. He need not have taken the trouble to complete and publish a *Historie des römischen Huren-Regiments,* but the hackneyed subject appealed to readers. He worked up some part (aliquam partem) of a *Lexicon elegantioris litteraturae* (p. 704), but we hear no more of it. At 27 he took up the *Pandectae* again and enlarged its scope. This sort of activity continued after he was firmly established in the theological profession. After twenty more pages, in which I find no mention of the *Pandectae,* he concludes, "This will be enough (Haec . . . sufficere potest, p. 704)." He has now realized (p. 742) that the plans of

Pandectarum eruditionis inferioris, Historiae Philosophiae recentioris, Systematis Antiquarii, Pandectarum Genealogicarum, Historiae litterariae universae, Notitiae librorum universalis, Lexicon Antiquarii, Aprocryphorum sacrorum & Fragmentorum

are beyond his strength and all the more so with the ob-
ligations he has assumed. He will do what incidental work
on them he can, but is ready to give his collectanea to
anyone who will carry on the enterprises. He then describe more precisely the state of various theological compendia and a historical handbook on which he is engaged
(pp. 743–756). There is some vanity in all this, but there
is also a lot of hard work. Loescher did not find the right
niche. He should have undertaken to make a new edition
of Lipenius.

Mauritius Huselitt, Cogitata (1710)

In a pamphlet entitled *Cogitata de bibliotheca materiarum ac auctorum moderno seculo conficienda ac usur-
panda per epistolam communicata* (Jena, 1710. Pp. 14)
Mauritius Huselitt, a doctor in the Pomeranian village of
Stargard, offered a somewhat more ambitious plan for a
subject-index. He intended to compile and classify the
contents of the best existing library catalogues (public
and private), publisher's lists, and the specialized bibliographies of various academic disciplines. He foresaw two
bibliographies as the results of his labors: one of authors
and one of subjects. He intended to list books, but expected to include some journal articles, especially those in
the *Acta eruditorum.* His emphasis was on current usefulness and consequently he did not plan to include many
old books. He had been working, he said, for three years
on a *Bibliotheca philosophica* and hoped to finish it in six
months. He expected to continue with a *Bibliotheca medica, Bibliotheca physica,* and *Bibliotheca mathematica,*
which might appear together, since their subjects were
closely related. He said nothing about law or theology.

Huselitt was a practical man aware of what he is undertaking to do and what has been done, but he was far from being as well-informed as Pierre Blanchot had been three generations earlier. He knew Gesner's *Bibliotheca*, although he did not make it clear that he was acquainted with the *Pandectae* and the *Partitiones*. If he had commented on them, we should have a better idea of his bibliographical judgment. In any case his emphasis on modern books would mean that Gesner did not offer him much duplication. He thought that the chance of finding the manuscript of Welschius, *Panglotta* was desperate, but intended nevertheless to make inquiries in Augsburg. It was not quite as desperate as he thought. He was also going to search for a manuscript index by G. J. Vossius (see above). By this he probably meant the material that Vossius had given to Welschius and other students in his endeavor to interest them in making a subject-index. Finally, he expressed once more the often-repeated complaint that Thomas Hyde never published the promised subject-index of the Bodleian catalogue (1674). Huselitt was informed about previous efforts to make a subject-index.

It is not surprising that Huselitt knew nothing about the plans of Raffaello Savonarola and Francesco Marucelli, who had published no more than title-pages, but his ignorance of Martin Lipenius, *Bibliotheca realis* (1679–1685) is incomprehensible. He says nothing about bibliographical guides for students and may have thought they did not call for mention. He does, however, cite D. G. Morhof, *Polyhistor* (first complete ed., 1708), which is similar to them. He has a firm grip on the task and, being both diligent and modest, may have given it up when he realized all its difficulties. Perhaps some books of historia litteraria seemed to him to be competitors. He says that a bookseller at Jena was urging him to proceed, but we hear nothing further of his plan.

Huselitt intended to arrange his materials according to the *Bibliotheca Telleriana* (1693). The decision shows his practical sense, for it was long regarded as a model and was actually used as a basis for library catalogues (see my *Book catalogues,* pp. 158–159). He must have made considerable progress with his work because he tells how many new subdivisions will be necessary. If he had only attempted something as modest as Huselith's combination of half a dozen catalogues, his energy and organizing ability would have quickly carried it through.

A LOOK BACK

The critical years of the seventeenth century, when modern notions of bibliography and of reference works generally were in the making, did not see the publication of a subject-index that might have been a model to be imitated or a generally accepted work calling for improvement and supplements. There are various explanations of this situation. Throughout the century bibliography, that is, the listing of books, was still conceived in terms of the men who wrote them and regarded as history. A work like Johannes Tritheim's fifteenth-century biobibliographical dictionary of German authors was a contribution to German history; an account of ecclesiastical writers was a contribution to church history. This tradition reaches back to early Christian bibliographers and beyond. In A.D. 392 St. Jerome had called his survey of Christian writers *De viris illustribus,* at the end of the fifteenth century Johannes Tritheim had used the same title for a biobibliographical dictionary of ecclesiastical writers. At the end of the sixteenth century Israel Spach called his bibliographies *Nomenclator scriptorum medicorum* and *Nomenclator scriptorum philosophicorum*, that is to say, lists of medical and philosophical authors and meant something more biographical than historical. The subtle distinction between a list of authors and a list of books is difficult to make because the books must be listed by the authors' names. It is nonetheless real and significant. The revolutionary title *Bibliotheca materiarum* (1618) that Johannes Molanus (d. 1585) or his anonymous editor adopted shows a clear notion of a list of subjects, but half a century later in the index to his bibliography of bibliographers Philip Labbé wavers between listing authors and listing subjects. Even at the end of the seventeenth century the notions of bibliography and of reference books as a category had not fully and clearly established themselves. Except for the editor of the *Bibliotheca materiarum,* makers of lists of subjects did not conceive their books as general reference works, although they might claim general usefulness for them in subtitles. They thought of them as reference works in particular fields. A list of materials on virtues, vices, and life in general—in other words, a collection of tales or exempla—was a preacher's handbook to be listed in theology with sermons. A list of themes like Ortensio Lando's *Sette libri di cathaloghi* or Johannes Ravisius Textor's *Officina* was intended for writers of belles lettres and to be listed with literature. While a few encyclopedic works might be recognized as general reference works, the subject-index did not establish itself among them.

Subject-indexes were made in the early years of the seventeenth century without being recognized for what they were and political, religious, and geographical boundaries hindered them from being appreciated. Even if the *Bib-*

liotheca materiarum by Johannes Molanus had reached
Protestant hands (it is safe to say that it rarely did), its
strongly confessional aspects would have prevented its
wide use. The overwhelming and yet obviously incomplete
Bibliotheca exotica with Georg Draud's companion bibliographies did not and could not suggest to readers outside
Germany the notion of complementary works because the
facilities for making them did not exist. There is no evidence that Fabianus Justinianus set a model to be imitated
by his *Index universalis alphabeticus.* These three bibliographies—I group the *Bibliotheca exotica* and Draud's
two books together—exemplify three ways of making a
subject-index: (1) the compilation of an individual's excerpts (Molanus); (2) the arrangement of publisher's lists
(the *Bibliotheca exotica* and Draud's books); and (3) the
enlargement and revision of a library shelf-list (Justinianus).

Discussion of subject-indexes and plans for making
them filled the middle years of the century and clarified
the problem, but resulted in nothing. Pierre Blanchot proposed a plan which might have been successful, if it had
been less ambitious. Great difficulties barred the way to
compiling in a single work both subject bibliographies and
library catalogues, but he was in the process of overcom-
ing them. His clear thinking and his sense of order would
have produced an invaluable reference work, but the time
was not ripe and circumstances were not propitious. Sir
William Petty's proposal with an emphasis on practical
utility had no success but recurs again after the lapse of
almost three centuries and it is again an Englishman's
proposal.

Three great subject-indexes made in the last years of
the seventeenth century failed of recognition. Lipenius's

Bibliotheca realis, which is the first that we know to have been made by a staff of workers and not an individual, got into print. It was too costly to circulate widely and too unsatisfactory in details to suggest revision and improvement (although this did happen to the volume for law and proved very successful). The indexes by Raffaello Savonarola and Francesco Marucelli remained in manuscript and did not affect the course of development except to conflict with each other and thus prevent either being published.

Independently John Hartly in England and Philip Huselith and Mauritius Huselitt in Germany hit upon Pierre Blanchot's plan of combining few well-chosen representative catalogues and thus they showed an admirable sense of what was feasible. Probably Valentin Ernst Loescher intended to restrict himself to contemporary writings. It is not altogether easy to see why these rather modest schemes failed. Hartly in London and Loescher, a university professor, were impractical in executing it. Huselith and Huselitt were resident in places where no large collections of books were available, but had judiciously cut their plans accordingly and could have carried them out. Their compilations would have been larger than any individual catalogue, but scarcely bulky enough to frighten an adventuresome publisher. The labor involved was not great and might have been reduced by clipping and pasting two copies of the catalogues used.

Had one of these compilations been published, it would have been a solid foundation for scholarly work and would, even today, be useful, but subject-indexes had fallen on evil days. In 1648 Mathias Prideaux had rejected them. In 1689 Adrien Baillet had satirized them. A few years later (1698), as Herbert Davis says, Charles Boyle

(1676–1731) scoffed "again and again at the learning that is derived from an Index or a Lexicon." [112] This passed to Dean Swift and ultimately to Alexander Pope, who summarized the temper of the age when he wrote in the *Dunciad* (ed. 1742, I, 279):

> Here Index-learning turns no student pale,
> Yet holds the eel of science by the tail.

[112] See his "Introduction" to Swift's *A tale of a tub* in *Prose works* (13 vols., Oxford, 1939–1959), I, p. xxiv, referring apparently to Section VII (pp. 91–93). The reference to Boyle is to *Dr. Bentley's dissertations on the Epistles of Phalaris and the Fables of Aesop* (3d ed., London, 1699), as cited by Davis, I, p. xvii (with the title *Dissertation* and the abbreviated title *Examination*). Boyle names no indexes or lexicons. Professors Mackie L. Jarrell, Francis Lee Utley, and John Harold Wilson have clarified these confusing references for me.

5

Subject-Indexes in the Eighteenth Century

FEW SUBJECT-INDEXES WERE MADE OR PROPOSED DURING THE eighteenth century. The notion of a general subject-index implies an interest in a great variety of miscellaneous facts and did not accord with the synthetic, historical, and interpretative temper of the new age. The miscellanies of the seventeenth century were, for example, replaced to a considerable extent by collections of personalia. The lack of interest in subject-indexes may also be explained by the rapid growth of encyclopedias that filled their place. The making of specialized subject-indexes prospered during the eighteenth century and obscured the need for a compilation of wider scope. This development is foreshadowed at the beginning of the century by bibliographers who made large bibliographies but preferred or were compelled by circumstances to print them in the form of small specialized studies. Around the middle of the century Camille Falconet left on his death collectanea that a few scholars have used as a subject-index. A little later J. C. Daehnert made a subject-index of the library of the University of Greifswald, and in 1790 two men compiled a good index of articles in German journals. Around the end of the century various scholars compiled large bibliographies that combined a historical purpose with a review of the best books in the several fields.

BARTHOLD HEINRICH WÜSTHOFF, *UNIVERSALIS BIBLIOTHECA* (1707)

An anonymous folio *Universalis bibliotheca, sistens omnium facultatum, ordine alphabetico, libros nov-antiquos, tam manu exaratos, quam typis impressos* (Frankfurt and Leipzig, 1707) by Barthold Heinrich Wüsthoff has dropped into oblivion. I know it only from Pie Namur's citation.[1] Petzholdt and Besterman do not mention it. Wüsthoff, who published juridico-political and theologico-political bibliographies in 1704 and 1705, is unknown to ordinary biographical dictionaries. The Swedish invasion of Saxony, a quarrel with his publisher Thomas Fritschius, and the lack of funds prevented him from going ahead with ambitious plans for eight more bibliographies that

[1] *Bibliographie paléographico-diplomatico-bibliologique générale* (2 vols., Liége, 1838), II, 11. Wilhelm Ernst Tentzel says he knew Wüsthoff well and expected his work to be better than the excellent *Bibliotheca Carpzoviana* (Leipzig, 1700), which is a large and valuable sale catalogue; see *Curieuse Bibliothec, I,* v (1704), pp. 472–473. Erik Dal of the Royal Library, Copenhagen, tells me that no Scandinavian, German, or Dutch library reports the possession of the *Universalis bibliotheca*. For references to the juridico-political and theologico-political bibliographies see Petzholdt, pp. 478, 612 and WBB, cols. 3180, 4028.

were to deal with virtually every academic subject. Three of particular interest that show his judgment as a bibliographer were accounts of miscellanies, academic disputations, and sermons for holidays, special occasions, and funerals. They filled gaps in contemporary bibliography; but seem not to have been printed. The title of his *Bibliotheca juridico-politica, ordine alphabetico distributa, edita a B. H. W. a vel auctione, vel privata venditione distrahenda* (Lipsiae, in aedibus Westhoffianis, 1704. See Petzholdt, p. 612) has more than a little the air of a sale-catalogue. Critics did not approve of his work. Struve-Jugler says briefly (I, 93), "As a matter of fact, the world of letters has suffered no great disaster from the loss of these [unpublished] bibliographies," and then qualifies the condemnation by adding that Wüsthoff was more careful than many other bibliographers. Petzholdt damns one of his books as worthless and makes the patronizing comment, "Not without value," on the other. Until a copy of the *Universalis bibliotheca* turns up, we can only say that it continues the seventeenth-century alphabetical tradition and is curious for a belated endeavor to include manuscripts.

CAMILLE FALCONET (d. 1762), *COLLECTANEA*

In his own hands a scholar's collectanea are a very valuable subject-index, but how far such materials serve others is more or less uncertain. No doubt most collections of notes and excerpts have disappeared on their maker's death, but one such collection seemed valuable enough for the maker to dispose of it in his will. Later scholars used it, and it has survived to the present day. The learned Camille Falconet (1671–1762), physician to Louis XV, had interests extending far beyond medicine. He was an active member of academies and societies and published articles on such subjects as the Assassins, the principles of French etymology, the first French translators of classical literature, and revised a translation of Erasmus, *Praise of Folly*. He bequeathed some 11,000 volumes chosen from his library to the Bibliothèque nationale. According to the catalogue made for the sale of his books in 1763,[2] he left his notes to a younger contemporary, Jean Baptiste de la Curne de Sainte Palaye (1697–1781), a bibliographer and a student of classical literature. Mlle Malclès says that Jean Antoine Rigoley de Juvigny (d. 1788) used them in writing a history of French literature (6 vols., Paris, 1772–1773).[3] My friend Lucien Gerschel has discovered them in the Bibliothèque nationale, Fonds français, nouv. acq. 5731. They amount to 66,039 slips, which are subdivided as follows:

1. Languages: Old French, Modern French, Greek, etc.
   Dictionaries, proverbs, dictionaries of rhymes, notes on Old French romances (in alphabetical order).
2. Political and literary history
   Dictionaries of weights and measures, geographical dictionaries, bibliographical dictionaries of famous men and scholars; alphabetical catalogue of their works; index of names and works cited in J. A. Fabricius, *Bibliotheca latina;* names of authors and books seen by Fabricius; mistakes and errors made by authors (books cited), painters, sculptors, and architects.
3. Sciences
   Dictionary of natural history; dictionary of medical Latin; medicine.

[2] See my *Book catalogues,* pp. 240–241; Gustave Brunet, *Dictionnaire,* col. 457.
[3] *La Bibliographie* (Paris, 1956), p. 32. For Rigoley de Juvigny's literary history see Petzholdt, p. 325.

4. Miscellaneous
Mythology, religion, philosophy in general, literature, obscenities; historical miscellany.
5. Varia
Unclassified slips. Many have been lost. They are very difficult to read and are "véritables feuilles de la Sybille."

These collectanea are Falconet's slips (*fiches*) and have on occasion been used as a subject-index. A devoted bibliographer might describe them at greater length and point out what is still useful in them or how an eighteenth-century scholar with varied interests worked.

RENEAUME, *PROJET* (1739)

A general subject-index that was proposed in the first half of the eighteenth century is known only from an anonymous prospectus entitled *Projet d'une bibliothèque universelle* (Paris, 1739. Pp. 8).[4] Michel Adanson, encyclopedist, member of the Académie, and former owner of the pamphlet, ascribes it in a manuscript note to Reneaume, "chanoine régulier, curé de Feuvy près Chartres," who died in 1749. He says that the author's library and manuscripts passed to the Maison des Chanoines-Réguliers de S. Jean à Chartres, citing as his authority Guillaume Doyen, *Histoire de la ville de Chartres* (Chartres, 1786). Since the proposed subject-index involved making a universal biobibliographical dictionary as the first step—and this was never completed—I have not pursued it further.

Reneaume was aware of what a general subject-index should be. He was inspired to undertake these tasks by

[4] For knowledge of this and two somewhat similar French proposals mentioned below I am indebted to the kindness of Dr. Stanley Pargellis and Mr. James M. Wells. Mr. Wells gave me xerox prints of the prospectuses in the Adanson Collection and additional information.

DuCange's remark in the preface to the *Glossarium mediae et infimae latinitatis*. DuCange had said that many had asked for information about the authors cited. Reneaume conceived his biobibliographical dictionary on a very grand scale to include texts, translations, criticisms, and excerpts from journals. With this "vaste dessein" we have little to do. A second part or work would include titles arranged according to subjects and would apparently be classified, but this is not clearly stated. He had conceived the idea thirty years earlier and had even begun work, but unfavorable circumstances hindered his progress. He was now (1739) taking it up again when friends urged him to do so and when he had more leisure. He began by saying that a similar task had been undertaken several times before, citing Naudé and Labbé, quoting Struve, and naming (among others) Blanchot and the *Idea* of 1631. He was therefore informed about the task and its difficulties. His rhetorical questions, "Aussi quelle multitude de Livres: combien de Mémoires, de Journaux littéraires à lire, à consulter, à feuilleter? Ajoutons de plus, quelles avances ne faut-il pas faire pour conduire un plan aussi vaste à son exécution?," raise no high hopes of his success. Since he recognized his situation was not well suited for the enterprise and he intended to employ reference works in his own library, we cannot regret that nothing came of the plan.

J. C. DAEHNERT, *REPERTORIUM REALE* (1776)

In the *Academiae Grypeswaldensis bibliotheca catalogo auctorum et repertorio reali universali descripta* (3 vols., Greifswald, 1775–1776) Johann Carl Daehnert (1719–

1785) [5] gave the scholarly world a useful account of a small university library. The author catalogue (vols. I and II) lists some 52,000 titles or perhaps 35,000 books and half as many dissertations, monographs, and journal articles. The appendix (II, 1005–1040) brings 780 additional titles received during the course of publication. The third volume entitled *Repertorium reale* lists books, minor publications, and journal articles according to subjects. At that time no such index was available and Daehnert's index is consequently valuable.

The arrangement of the *Repertorium* is alphabetical. For example, the various books of the Bible are headings under which both general commentaries and specific works (often sermons) referring to individual verses are listed. A historian finds information under place names like Stralsund (33 entries), Westphalia (16 entries), or Zürich (Tigurum, 6 entries) and notes the decline in the number of titles from the north to the south. Personal names used as headings show a similar variation that reflects their closeness to Greifswald and Pomerania: Jeanne d'Arc (4 entries), Cardinal Mazarin (9 entries), and Gustavus Adolphus, who ruled Pomerania (35 entries). A jurist might turn to Conjugium (two and a half pages) and Contractus (a page of references). A scientist finds sixty-five references to the Aurora borealis, three pages of references to Aqua (water) and almost as many to Aquae medicatae. References to Motus (motion, change), which concerns students of physics and philosophy, fill three pages. A literary student will perhaps more often consult the author catalogue, but he will find eleven references

[5] For biographical details see F. L. Hoffmann, *Serapeum*, XXX (1869), 373–345. See also M. Zobel von Zobeltitz, "Ein Schlagwortindex der Greifswalder Universitätsbibliothek von 1776," *Zentralblatt für Bibliothekswesen*, XLI (1924), 244–249.

to Horace (editions are cited in the author catalogue), six-teen to Virgil, and twenty-seven to Ars poetica (with a cross-reference to Poesis). In general, there is rather little on belles lettres. Such large categories as Poemata are difficult to use because these poetical works are listed according to languages without citing the authors' names. A bibliographer will not be dissatisfied with three pages on Bibliotheca (library, bibliography, catalogue). In brief, we have here a convenient index to eighteenth-century German learning.

There are of course limitations on the usefulness of Daehnert's catalogue and index. It deals only with books in a comparatively small library without many interna-tional connections. Founded in 1456, the University of Greifswald was never wealthy, and its library was never the recipient of important gifts. The city and the univer-sity suffered severely in the Thirty Years War. Conse-quently the library did not have many old or rare books. On the other hand, Daehnert was a competent librarian and made wise additions. The journals in particular repre-sent a judicious selection of those printed in the eighteenth century, and the excerpting of them adds much to the value of Daehnert's work. Finally, since Greifswald was for many years a Swedish, not a German, university, it acquired a considerable number of Swedish books that are not ordinarily indexed in German sources. With whatever reservations one may make, Daehnert has written a valu-able subject guide to eighteenth-century German books, journals, dissertations, and fugitive materials. Daehnert announced a continuation of the index but never pub-lished it. He was severely criticized for exceeding his budget and his authority to make book purchases was taken away. We may infer that the faculty did not wel-come his bibliographical efforts. The catalogue does not seem to be rare, for three copies have been in my hands in the last ten years. It is a forerunner of similar subject-indexes of institutional libraries.

[LE CHEVALIER DE POUGENS], *BIBLIOGRAPHIE ENCYCLOPÉDIQUE* (1780)

The subtitle of this work as given in a prospectus printed at Lyons in 1780 describes it at length: Dictionnaire raisonné et analytique des ouvrages intéressants, imprimés ou manuscrits, dans toutes langues et dans tous les genres, depuis le commencement des siècles jusqu'à nos jours; avec une biographie abrégée des auteurs. I take the author's name from the "Invitation," where it appears as the man to whom subscriptions are to be addressed. The prospectus is in the Adanson collection in the Newberry Library and I am indebted to Dr. Stanley Pargellis and Mr. James M. Wells for a xerox print. The bibliography is to consist of seventy or seventy-two quarto volumes in five series of twelve volumes each. Apparently the remaining ten or twelve volumes are reserved for contingencies of an unspecified nature. The bibliography, which was to include works in manuscript as well as Sanskrit and Pehlevi writings, is described in such general terms that one cannot come to grips with it. The brief summary of the titles and contents gives little notion of the work. Five volumes—one for each series—were to be published every eight months, beginning in December, 1781. The Société de gens de lettres that announced this ambitious plan quoted a motto from Horace on the titlepage of the prospectus: "Nil mortalibus arduum est" (Od. III. 5). It does not appear that the society had any success in this brave proposal.

[J. H. C. BEUTLER AND J. C. F. GUTSMUTH], *ALLGEMEINES SACHREGISTER ÜBER DIE WICHTIGSTEN DEUTSCHEN ZEIT- UND WOCHENSCHRIFTEN* (1790)

This little-known and, I am afraid, less-used index to eighteenth-century German journals is briefly mentioned here to suggest the novelty and independence of German bibliographical developments and a lack of continuity in the growth of bibliography. Theodore Besterman has caught it in the wide-flung net of his *World bibliography of bibliographies,* but most bibliographers do not know it. Although Cornelius à Beughem had begun the bibliography of journal articles a century earlier, there is no sign of a connection between his work and the *Sachregister.* Like Daehnert's subject-index to the University of Greifswald library, it is an independent venture. Being restricted to a single country and language, it calls for no lengthy comment. It begins (pp. 1–360) with an important list of German periodical publications before 1790 (see WBB, col. 3089) that might have been an aid to Carl Diesch in writing his *Bibliographie der germanistischen Zeitschriften* (Leipzig, 1927). It shows what a solid foundation the compilers laid for the *Sachregister.* The articles excerpted may number 11,500. My estimate is somewhat larger than Besterman's (see WBB, col. 3126). Though the utility of the *Sachregister* is obvious, I do not see it cited often by scholars writing on eighteenth-century German literature.[6]

[6] I have seen only the copy in the Newberry Library. It lacks one signature. F. L. Hoffmann, *Serapeum,* XXIX (1868), 371 credits it to J. S. Ersch, but the preface is signed "Die Verfasser (The authors)." Julius Petzholdt cites it as an anonymous work (see p. 298) and by failing to include it in the index makes it hard to find.

D'UNE NOUVELLE BIBLIOGRAPHIE (1796)

A third prospectus in the Adanson collection in the Newberry Library describes still another French subject-index that did not appear in print. The anonymous announcement ([Paris, 1795]. Pp. 8) might perhaps be traced to an author by the remark (p. 6, n. 1) that he had already published *Feuille de correspondance du libraire* in three volumes.[7] He seems to be a Parisian publisher and bookseller. The first seven pages were perhaps intended for later use as a preface; the eighth containing the subscription terms could be easily eliminated. The author complains eloquently and vaguely about the number and variety of existing bibliographies and the difficulty of using them and wishes to make it easier to collect information. He expects to publish twice a month three different bibliographies: (1) a list of new books, (2) an alphabetical dictionary of old books and all the new books, and (3) a generously conceived *Book review digest*. The first and third of these were to begin publication in 1796, and the second in 1797. The dictionary, which alone concerns us, was to appear in fascicles of thirty-two pages and would, when complete, fill two volumes, listing an estimated 64,000 titles. The figure awakens respect, but the citation of bibliographies by Maittaire, DeBure, Duclos, and Rive as sources to consult—worthy as they may be for the purposes intended by the authors—inspires no confidence in the compiler's knowledge of guides to subject matter. Adanson or another early owner found the prospectus interesting and annotated it freely. It is important here as

[7] See the article "Bibliographie" in *La grande encyclopédie* (Paris, n.d.), VI, 603 (first col.).

evidence of an interest in subject-indexes at the time of
the French Revolution.

THE PRINCE DE SOUBISE
CATALOGUE (c1780)

The scanty record does not make it clear whether a
manuscript catalogue in twenty-five folio volumes of the
Prince de Soubise library was an author or a subject catalogue. Its size justifies comparison with the contemporary
Lamoignon subject catalogue in more than thirty volumes,
and it is not easy to see how an author catalogue of perhaps twenty thousand volumes could fill twenty-five volumes. The Prince de Soubise library included the books
collected by J. A. de Thou in the seventeenth century and
listed in the *Bibliotheca Thuana* (Paris, 1679). The manuscript catalogue was presumably purchased by M. de
Lamy when the books were sold in 1789, but it is not mentioned in the sale catalogue. It appears as no. 6295 in the
*Catalogue des livres manuscripts et imprimés . . . du cabi-
net de L* [amy] (Paris: Renouard, 1807). The *Nouveau
manuel* (col. 705) quotes the description as "redigé par
ordre alphabétique, contient tous les livres qui étaient
dans la riche bibliothèque de Soubise. It avait été dressé
pour le service de cette bibliothèque, lorsqu'elle était
ouverte au public." Lucien Gerschel calls my attention to
a copy of the Lamy catalogue in the Bibliothèque nationale that contains the names of purchasers and the
prices at which the books changed hands. I have seen it.
The sale price of the Soubise catalogue, which Roger
Lecotté of the Bibliothèque nationale tells me was
"énorme," indicates that it was esteemed. The purchaser
was "Mayence," i.e., a dealer in Mainz. An effort to find

the catalogue in Germany has not been successful, but there is still a chance that it may turn up.

HISTORIA LITTERARIA

Historia litteraria,[8] which quickly established itself as the characteristic eighteenth-century German form of subject-index, is an account (historia) of the literature (litteraria) of subjects generally and not a history of belles lettres. The word literature is used as in the literature of chemistry. Historia litteraria names the books that are significant in the historical development of a subject, that are regarded as the best, and that are useful in academic studies. This information is presented in narrative fashion as a history and not as a list. It is neglectful of such bibliographical details as the date and place of publication, pagination, format, illustrations and the like and may even omit the title. It is bibliography because men of its own age accepted it as bibliography and after them Julius Petzholdt and Theodore Besterman have done so. Its origin has been the subject of dispute in books of historia litteraria itself and remains to be fully studied.

Burkhard Gotthelf Struve (1671–1738), *Introductio ad notitiam rei litterariae & usum bibliothecarum* (Jena,

[8] For suggestions of Baconian influences see such books as Hardin Craig, *The enchanted glass. The Elizabethan mind in literature* (New York, 1936) and Richard Foster Jones, *Ancients and moderns. A study of the background of the "Battle of the Books,"* Washington University Studies, 1936, Language and literature, 6. These authors mention only incidentally Bacon's bibliographical ideas. The best introduction to the beginnings of historia litteraria is now Rudolf Blum, "Bibliotheca Memmiana. Untersuchungen zu Gabriel Naudés 'Avis pour dresser une Bibliotheèque," *Bibliotheca docet. Festgabe für Carl Wehmer* (Amsterdam, 1963), pp. 209–232. I have used historia litteraria as a common noun without italics or quotation marks.

1704. See WBB, col. 469), which had at first a pronounced bibliographical and bibliothecal emphasis; Christoph August Heumann, *Conspectus reipublicae litterariae
sive via ad historiam litterariam juventuti studiosae aperta*
(Hannover, 1718), which seems least like a bibliography
because it usually cites no more than authors' names and
is not considered to be a bibliography by Besterman; and
Gottlieb Stolle, *Kurtze Anleitung zur Historie der Gelahrheit* (Halle, 1718. See WBB, col. 471) are three competing
surveys of learning that can be regarded as the founda-
tions of historia litteraria. Each of these enjoyed four or
more editions in the first half of the eighteenth century.
They differed somewhat in the method of presentation,
but contained virtually the same mass of information.
They were by intention histories of learning but developed quickly into bibliographies of learning and in the
latter use they can be regarded as subject-indexes. These
three books cited, according to Besterman, at most in their
latest editions not more than 7500 titles. It is evident that
these are primarily historical in nature, but on such foun-
dations later scholars erected much larger structures with
a bibliographical and not historical purpose. The earliest
examples are characteristically northern German and the
later developments are more widely distributed in the
German-speaking lands. The huge editions of Struve's
book that terminated its career: J. C. Fischer, *Introductio
. . .* (Frankfurt a.M., 1754) and with a new title, J. F.
Jugler, ed. *Bibliotheca historiae litterariae selecta* (3 v.,
Jena, 1754–1763, Suppl., 1785) with 7500 references or
more made such works much more valuable as subject-
indexes. In the development of historia litteraria we can
recognize a first period, primarily historical, that extended
to 1740, a second period that was primarily bibliographical

that includes the enlarged editions, a third period, after the middle of the century when it profited greatly by the more important place it won in the Prussian schools, and a final period which had a much wider success in central Europe when the size of the treatises increased enormously. This last period extended from the 1780's to 1860 and the appearance of J. G. T. Graesse's *Lehrbuch*. These works do not lend themselves easily to excerpting.

At the end of the century Carl-Joseph Bouginé (1735–1797) acknowledged his indebtedness to the tradition of historia litteraria and especially to Heumann's *Conspectus* in the *Handbuch der allgemeinen Litterargeschichte, nach Heumanns Grundriss* (5 vols., 1 vol. supplement in 2 pts., 1789–1802). Like Heumann, Bouginé arranges his work chronologically by epochs and then subdivides according to disciplines. He cites authors with few bibliographical details, and generally omits even titles. The whole is historical, critical, and selective, with much incidental comment. According to Besterman (WBB, col. 476), Bouginé cites 33,000 titles. The figure is generous, if we bear in mind that the estimated 8,000 references in the supplement concern a myriad of corrections and additions to the estimated 25,000 titles in the main work. Since the references concern largely eighteenth-century writings and therefore supplement those in earlier books of historia litteraria, they are likely to be useful, e.g., Bouginé's comment (V, 294–296) on the anonymous *De tribus impostoribus,* a famous scandalous book that calls Moses, Christ, and Mohammed imposters.[9] His footnote cites more eighteenth-century bibliographers and scholars

[9] There is a copy of this great rarity in the Newberry Library. See now J. Presser, *Das Buch "De tribus impostoribus"* (Dissertation; Amsterdam, 1926).

than I recall seeing mentioned elsewhere as critics of the book. He continues (pp. 296–298) with similar but less extensive comment on two or three books notorious for their obscenity. The table of contents is not a very helpful guide to the *Handbuch*, and the index (V, 395–718), which is very full, includes both authors' names and subject headings, the names greatly exceeding the headings in number. I cannot discover in the index references to the Lisbon earthquake of 1755, comets, or the three-field system of agriculture, subjects that were of great interest in the eighteenth century. On the other hand, there are such headings as the means to be used for the bite of mad Dogs (Biss toller Hunde, Mittel dagegen), the cultivation of Potatoes (Erdapfelbau), Magnetismus; and Sugar (Zucker). While Bouginé's *Handbuch* serves as a subject-index and will yield valuable references, its consultation is not easy.

Heinrich Wilhelm Lawätz (1748–1825) writes in the same tradition, but the title of his *Handbuch für Bücherfreunde und Bibliothekare* (7 vols., 3 suppl.; 1788–1794, see WBB, col. 476) shows him to be turning in a new direction with a less historical emphasis. His *Handbuch* listing almost 50,000 titles was left incomplete with an introductory first volume in five parts, two volumes of a biobibliographical dictionary, and the supplements. The first volume deals with bibliography and literary history, but the volume or volumes most useful for subject information never appeared. Lawätz was a careful workman and enlisted aid from England and Scandinavia. His failure to complete the *Handbuch* is regrettable.

For two generations after 1790 German bibliographers continued the work of Bouginé and Lawätz. Some write comprehensive bibliographies "from the beginning of the world down to the present time" and show themselves aware of the enlargement of scholarship by the inclusion of Sanskrit and Oriental writings. Others restrict themselves to German works published after 1750 with only casual glances at books in other languages. Each has his own purposes in view and differs in relatively minor details from his contemporaries, but produces in the end a work very little different from theirs. J. S. Ersch (1766–1828), J. F. L. Wachler (1767–1838), W. T. Krug (1770–1842), J. G. Eichhorn (1752–1827), and J. G. T. Graesse (1814–1885) display an astonishing diligence and learning.[10] Within a generation their bibliographies were forgotten. No one has bewailed this fantastic waste and few readers in our century have taken these dusty books off the shelves.

I characterize these bibliographies by citing a reference from one and describing two examples, the shortest and the last and largest. The description of Graesse's *Lehrbuch*, my second example, will appear later in this book. While

[10] Ersch, *Handbuch der deutschen Literatur seit der Mitte des achtzehnten Jahrhunderts bis auf die neueste Zeit* (2 vols.; Amsterdam, 1812–1814; 2d ed.; 8 vols.; 1822–1840. See WBB, cols. 1634–1635; F. L. Hoffmann, *Serapeum*, XXIX [1868], 369–372). Wachler, who began with a *Versuch* in 1793, was never satisfied with it. He published a revision entitled *Handbuch der allgemeinen literärischen Cultur* (2 vols.; Marburg, 1804–1805. See WBB, col. 477) and after enlarging and condensing it, concluded with a final edition called *Handbuch der Geschichte der Litteratur* (4 vols.; Leipzig, 1833. See WBB, col. 477) and a schoolbook entitled *Lehrbuch zum Gebrauche in höheren Unterrichtsanstalten* (5th ed.; Breslau, 1838). I have seen all or almost all of these in the New York Public Library. F. L. Hoffmann (*Serapeum*, XXX [1869], 353–365), Petzholdt, and Besterman (WBB, col. 5643) cite more of his historico-bibliographical works. For Krug see below. Eichhorn's encyclopedic *Geschichte der Literatur von ihrem Anfang bis auf die neuesten Zeiten* (12 vols.; Göttingen, 1805–1811. See WBB, col. 479) contains some 20,000 titles. The word *Literatur* in these titles does not mean belles lettres.

these books are useful for subject information, their primarily historical emphasis, their selectivity or other limitations exclude them from longer consideration here. An instance of what we can learn from them will suffice. In its second edition Ersch's *Handbuch* was quadrupled in size by other hands. It was then issued in a third edition in separate parts under the names of individual editors (see Petzholdt, pp. 290–291). One of these parts is Christian Anton Geissler, *Bibliographisches Handbuch der philosophischen Literatur der Deutschen von der Mitte des achtzehnten Jahrhunderts bis auf die neueste Zeit* (see Petzholdt, pp. 491–492; WWB, col. 3199). Petzholdt recommends it with wry comment that is not altogether fair. For Geissler "philosophy" includes what are now called Courtesy books. He mentions (col. 156) two curious books of worldly and religious counsel credited to Benjamin Franklin. On these follow an amazing list of etiquette books for women readers (col. 156, no. 1877[a]– col. 163, no. 1953) and lists of similar books for children, students, and officials of various kinds, all neatly set apart. A student of German social life in the first half of the nineteenth century will find them instructive. These forgotten bibliographies contain many similar collections, but few students open them.

For the characterization of late eighteenth-century historia litteraria I choose the shortest example: W. T. Krug, *Versuch einer systematischen Enzyklopädie der Wisssenschaften* (3 vols. in 10 pts.; 1796–1819) and disregard the first two separately numbered volumes of prefatory information that contain nothing bibliographical. The *Versuch* consists of the following volumes by Krug or, when indicated, by others (Besterman lists the parts separately according to authors).

I, i (1804). *Enzykopädisch-philologische Literatur* by Krug (WBB, col. 3180: 1000 titles).

A selective bibliography of general works on language and languages. There are, for example, ten titles on Pasigraphy or a script intended to be intelligible to speakers of any language (pp. 32–33 and seven more titles in the supplement, III, 13). Krug ranges widely, for he cites a Kurdish grammar published at Rome in 1787 (p. 53).

I, ii (1813). History and geography by K. H. L. Politz (WBB, col. 1888: 3000 titles). Although inadequate in comparison with Struve-Meusel and Lenglet du Fresnoy, it was written a generation and more later and contains some additional titles.

I, iii (1812). Mathematics and astronomy by E. F. Wrede (WBB, col. 2455: 3500 titles).

I, iv (1805). Philosophy (WBB, col. 3194: 600 titles). Krug cites almost exclusively eighteenth-century titles.

II, i (1806). Anthropology, i.e., sciences connected with man, e.g., physiognomy, aesthetics, natural law, and politics (WBB, col. 3279: 250 titles).

II, ii (1806). Physics, including meteorology, geology, botany, chemistry, zoology, and such practical arts as forestry by E. F. Wrede and F. B. Weber (apparently lacking in WBB). The section on hunting (pp. 213–215) includes books on the language of hunters.

II, iii (1806). Medicine by Immanuel Meyer (WBB, cols. 2499–2500: 1500 titles).

II, iv (1806). Law by K. S. Zachariä (WBB, col. 2270: 600 titles).

II, v (1806). Theology (WBB, col. 4035: 800 titles).

III (1819). Additions and corrections.

Krug's carefully made *Versuch* shows great success in obtaining accuracy and full citations of Christian names. The table of contents is rich and the book can be easily consulted. The article Agriculture (II, i, pp. 196–210 and supplement, III, 289–309) is richly documented. There are variations in the range of the bibliographies from volume to volume, and some volumes, especially that for theology, are selective. One notes unusual titles here and there, e.g., a book on teaching modern languages pub-

lished at Åbo in 1791 (I, i, p. 23) or a dictionary of Latin
rhetorical terms (I, i, p. 75).

A LOOK BACK

The lack of subject-indexes in the eighteenth century
offers a conspicuous contrast to their abundance in the
seventeenth century. Plans to make them were either abor-
tive or obviously ill-considered. Various proposals to combine judiciously chosen library catalogues in a subject-
index can perhaps be called a continuation of seventeenth-
century bibliography and its climax, but the time for such
a conflation had passed and the plans came to naught.
Giusto Fontanini's carefully made subject-index attached
to the Imperiali catalogue (1711) was not separately published or identified as anything more and different than
a useful appendix. Neither it nor the unpublished Lamoignon catalogue nor the lost Soubise catalogue could
create a tradition of subject-indexes. Nothing came of
various hastily made plans conceived in France during
the century. In its last quarter J. C. Daehnert's valuable
subject-index to the University of Greifswald library found
little approval and dropped out of sight. The *Allgemeines
Sachregister* neither continued nor established a tradition
of subject-indexes to journals.

There are various reasons for the disappearance of subject-indexes in the eighteenth century. The seventeenth
century had produced no example that called for imita-
tion and enlargement. The legal volume of Lipenius's *Bibliotheca realis* had, to be sure, found recognition and was
quickly and successfully improved for a century and a
half, but the notion of extending this labor to the other
volumes occurred to no one. Men were thinking in differ-

ent and more limited terms. Johann Albert Fabricius, who might have rewritten the volumes entitled *Philosophica,* went no further than to interleave his copy and make a few notes. He gave his energies to large bibliographies of Greek, classical Latin, and medieval Latin literature and a score of minor specialized books. At a time when his admirable bibliographies of lesser scope enjoyed great success he failed to see the value of a general work.

Political, religious, and social developments of the eighteenth century brought with them a new orientation in scholarly reference work. Men consulted the old reference works less frequently and were not tempted to continue in directions that they suggested. For example, the *Allgemeines historisches Lexikon* (5 vols.; Leipzig, 1709), compiled by C. G. Buder (1693–1768) and subsequently enlarged down to 1740 by other hands, disappeared from reference shelves. It was not a very satisfactory book and many complained of its defects and inaccuracies. But its disappearance is to be explained not by its faults but by the fact that men no longer thought in the international terms that it suggested. Another example is furnished by the miscellanies that we can regard as a characteristic sixteenth- and seventeenth-century genre. They ceased to be compiled in the old manner and books of ana with a much more personal emphasis and a preference for the anecdotal replaced them. Such examples may suggest why interest in subject-indexes that aimed to be miscellaneous and international in quality declined to the vanishing point.

A decisive event was the publication in 1751 of the *Encyclopédie* by D'Alembert and Diderot. This represented a new synthesis and became the typical reference work of the century. To it the subject-indexes of the preceding century made only a negligible contribution. The *Encyclopédie* and the large Germany encyclopedias that competed with it left no place for a general subject-index. Heinrich Zedler, *Grosses vollständiges Universal Lexikon aller Wissenschaften und Künste* (64 vols., 4 vols., supplement; Halle 1732–1754) with many bibliographical references and J. J. Krünitz, *Ökonomisch-technologische Encyclopädie* (242 vols.; Berlin, 1773–1858) with few bibliographical references complemented each other and satisfied the needs of most readers.

The discipline of historia litteraria was also a synthesis with a strong emphasis on the historical side. Especially in Germany works in this tradition contained much bibliographical information and to that extent made subject-indexes unnecessary. In Germany they developed into either texts for school use that gave particular attention to contemporary learning and science or, at the end of the eighteenth and continuing down to the middle of the nineteenth century, unwieldy bibliographies (Bouginé, Lawätz, and their successors) that surveyed literary and scientific studies with special regard to events since 1700. These were relatively complete for work done in northern and western Germany (where they flourished) and less full for other countries. In England, France, and Italy works of this sort brought very little bibliographical information. In Germany and elsewhere the emphasis was on synthesis, on the main lines of developments, and not on details. By their nature subject-indexes did not accord with the spirit of the century.

6

Subject-Indexes in the
Nineteenth Century

AS WE HAVE OFTEN SEEN, THE CHARACTERISTIC ASPECTS OF
the subject-indexes made in a particular century are likely
to appear clearly somewhat after the beginning of the century. In a general recognition of the convenience of an
alphabetical arrangement the nineteenth century resembles the seventeenth century. Compilers show the
familiar disinclination to profit by the labors of their
predecessors or avoid their mistakes. A few nineteenth-
century indexes are, like Gesner's *Pandectate* and *Partitiones*, limited only by the compiler's resources and
linguistic abilities; others are supplements to biobibliographical dictionaries or trade bibliographies and are
therefore national in scope or concerned with the writings
of a religious order; others list books in a single library;
others are lists made by publishing houses and confine

GENERAL SUBJECT-INDEXES

themselves to the books of a particular country; and still others index writings of a particular kind like collections of essays, articles in journals, or books having the arrangement of dictionaries. A rapidly increasing specialization and a restriction to current publications, often those written in one language or published in one country, is almost universal. The exceptions to these rules are either determined by the special nature of the index or are hasty and often injudicious efforts to broaden its scope. For all these reasons the utility of nineteenth-century subject-indexes varies greatly from instance to instance.

Although subject-indexes of many kinds were made after 1800, bibliographers do not regard them as a category of bibliographical writing. Handbooks like Georg Schneider, *Handbuch der Bibliographie;* Louise-Noëlle Malclès, *Les Sources du travail bibliographique;* Constance M. Winchell, *Guide to reference books;* or A. J. Walford, *Guide to reference material* do not assemble them in a group. They list subject-indexes to journals under journals and subject-indexes to books in a library under library catalogues without recognizing a common element in them. This bibliographical tradition is perhaps most readily seen in Theodore Besterman, *A world bibliography of bibliographies,* in which subject-indexes of books are mingled with trade lists and other varieties of national bibliographies and subject-indexes of journals with lists of journals.

In the last years of the eighteenth century a newly awakened interest in subject-indexes had expressed itself in a general index to journals (*Allgemeines Sachregister*) and in the continuation and enlargement of the tradition of historia litteraria (Bouginé, Lawätz, and others). Both of these varieties of bibliography developed after 1800: the usefulness of subject-indexes to journals was rather slow to be recognized but many were made after the middle of the century. General subject-bibliographies employing a chronologico-geographical arrangement reach a climax in Graesse's *Lehrbuch* (1837–1859). When Graesse began work the flood of general bibliographies had subsided and his book is a colossus left on the beach by a receding tide. In large measure these examples of historia litteraria were independent compilations and could have been indexed in a rather small book containing critical comment and additions. If someone had made such a book, the labors of half a dozen learned bibliographers would have been preserved for use even today. Graesse did not think of doing this and buried himself and his readers in details. The old tradition of an enormous alphabetical subject-index made by a single hand such as we have seen in the books of Spach, Bolduanus, Lipenius, Marucelli, and Savonarola is repeated in Watt's *Bibliotheca britannica* (1819–1824). Around the middle of the nineteenth century men proposed to enlist the aid of specialists in a cooperative enterprise, but found no helpers to join in the task. Only in the twentieth century do we see indexes brought to completion by a staff of specialists.

SUBJECT-INDEXES TO THE PUBLICATIONS OF LEARNED SOCIETIES: J. D. REUSS, *REPERTORIUM* (1801-1821); *CATALOGUE OF SCIENTIFIC PAPERS* (1867–1914).

We have already noted Cornelius à Beughem's subject-indexes of journals of the late seventeenth and the *Allgemeines Sachregister* of the late eighteenth century. The idea of such an index was slow to be accepted and shows specialization during the nineteenth century in regard to subject matter or the kinds of journals excerpted. In the first quarter of the nineteenth century J. D. Reuss (1750–1837) published an enormous *Repertorium commentationum a societatibus litterariis editarum secundum disciplinarum ordinem* (16 vols.; Göttingen, 1801–1821), listing and classifying publications of societies and academies in all fields down to 1800.[1] As Petzholdt remarked in 1866, the *Repertorium* was then being offered at considerably less than half its original price. It had found no ready market and the publisher wished to salvage what he could. Such neglect of laborious bibliographical compilations is only too familiar and a modern reprint (New York, 1961) does the *Repertorium* belated justice. The *Catalogue of scientific papers* (19 vols.; London and, in part, Cambridge, 1867–1914) published by the Royal Society continues Reuss's work but is restricted to scientific fields.[2] In this restriction we see a specialization characteristic of much nineteenth-century bibliography.

JACQUES-CHARLES BRUNET, *MANUEL DU LIBRAIRE*, *"TABLE MÉTHODIQUE"* (1810)

In the first edition of his *Manuel du libraire et de l'amateur des livres* (1810) Jacques-Charles Brunet (1780–1867) added a subject-index and thereby extended the purpose and usefulness of a catalogue of rare books in a new direction. Brunet's lifelong connection with the *Man-*

[1] For a lengthy collation see Petzholdt, p. 87. Besterman deals with the volumes separately according to subjects, but the set can be readily traced through the index (see WBB, col 5417). See also K. Geiger, "Jeremias David Reuss und seine Bibliothek," *Zentralblatt für Bibliothekswesen*, XXII (1905), 465–490, especially pp. 488–489, where attention is called to Reuss's own copy of the *Repertorium* at Göttingen.
[2] See WBB, col. 3731.

uel began with a *Supplément* (1802. See WBB, col. 539) to André Charles Cailleau and R. Duclos, *Dictionnaire bibliographique, historique et critique des livres rares, précieux, singuliers, curieux et recherchés qui n'ont aucum prix fixe . . . avec leur valeur réduite à une juste appréciation, suivant les prix auxquels ils ont été portés dans les ventes publiques, depuis le fin du XVIIe siècle jusqu'à présent* (3 vols.; Paris, 1790). The long title shows clearly and fully the intention that guided the compilers. This appraisal of rare, unusual, or sought-after books contained good bibliographical descriptions, and served primarily the French dealers who were selling books that came to their shelves as a result of the secularization of libraries in the eighteenth century or the disorders of the French Revolution. The *Dictionnaire* survives in an improved form in Brunet's *Manuel.*

It can be properly asked whether a subject-index was an altogether suitable addition to a book like the *Manuel.* Earlier, characteristically German catalogues of rare books had been typically lists of books primarily interesting to scholars and dealt chiefly with writings in theology and the classics and incidentally a few famous rarities. Being thus limited, they scarcely needed a subject-index. Like its predecessors Cailleau and Duclos or the earlier *Dictionnaire typographique* (2 vols.; Paris, 1768. See WBB, col. 538) by J. B. L. Osmont, Brunet's *Manuel* ranged more widely, using only rarity as a criterion. A subject-index to it was useful to both collectors and students. A man interested in the history of Paris, heraldry, or travels could learn what rare books to search for or to study.

Brunet saw clearly that students needed more than a subject-index to the titles in the *Manuel.* Although he added a subject-index in the first edition of 1810, I com-

ment only on the "Table méthodique" in the fifth edition
of 1860–1865 (see WBB, col. 540). In order to increase
its usefulness he cited modern scholarly works that did
not necessarily have a claim to rarity. The last edition of
the *Manuel* lists 31,872 titles, and the subject-index, according to Besterman's estimate, 47,500. Brunet has added
16,000 titles. He distributed them very unequally through
the Table méthodique and obviously took great pains in
this task. Theology received few additions. Those in Astronomy (cols. 481–494) are chiefly in the sections entitled Astronomical Observations, Astronomical Tables,
Celestial Atlases (cols. 488–491). He substantially enlarged Calendar (col. 493) by adding thirteen new titles.
Medicine (cols. 368–450) was greatly improved by citing
contemporary writings. Since it is conveniently subdivided, it may well be an elementary guide to the field as
it was in 1865. English History (cols. 1510–1552) was
generously brought up to date. On the other hand, he
added almost nothing to the books dealing with Turkish
history (cols. 1573–1577). Such variations reflect in part
the actual differences in advances in the respective fields
and in part Brunet's interests or his opportunities to obtain
information. Perhaps there was little that was new to be
cited in Turkish history, although the Crimean War had
directed attention to Turkey and the Near East generally.
A long list in Linguistics (cols. 637–721) looks valuable.
The sketchy article entitled Ana (cols. 991–992) shows
Brunet's unawareness of available bibliographies and implies a lack of interest. Emblems (cols. 992–995) also did
not interest him, although a few French titles may be
worth noting. Among subject-indexes Brunet's Table
méthodique has a special novelty in the attention given
to belles lettres. Conrad Gesner had made generous men-

tion of it in 1548 and such categories as the literary genres —drama (comedy and tragedy), eclogue, epigram—or handbooks of poetics occur in seventeenth-century subject-indexes. Later indexes are less generous. Except for the accounts of French and Neo-Latin writings, Brunet would have done well to omit it.

The Table méthodique is an amazing piece of work. The task of classifying nearly 50,000 titles, of which more than one-third had to be collected for the purpose, commands respect. Brunet's rather finely divided classification makes consultation easy. Although I have made no extensive verification of references, the whole leaves an impression of competence and accuracy. One might complain that works in foreign languages, except in sections dealing with the countries where these languages are spoken, are somewhat scantily represented. We cannot justly complain about this and the fault is easily remedied. One can profitably consult what Brunet has given us, but it is doubtful whether he would find us sufficiently grateful for the love and labor he lavished on the task. How many have consulted the Table méthodique? Nevertheless, Paul Deschamps and Gustave Brunet continue in the same manner in the *Supplément* (2 vols.; 1879, 1880), but their work (II, cols. 1081–1226) leaves me with a feeling that they had little interest in it.

GERMAN PUBLISHERS AS COMPILERS OF SUBJECT-INDEXES: T. C. F. ENSLIN AND WILHELM ENGELMANN

In the first half of the nineteenth century two German publishers compiled various specialized subject-indexes.

The work of either man, if taken as a whole, amounts virtually to a general subject-index of German books since 1750. In the choice of titles and in format and bibliographical style these compilations resemble one another and were obviously conceived as forming a series of a sort. Perhaps the previously mentioned bibliographies by W. T. Krug and J. S. Ersch, which were of a similar character, inspired their making. Publishers had now undertaken to do what professors had been doing a generation earlier. These widely used compilations often enjoyed second and third editions and were worn out by their readers. They were based on the national bibliographies by Heinsius and Kayser but included titles that did not appear in these lists for the booktrade. They have disappeared almost completely from the bibliographical scene. Bibliographers give no complete account of them, and they rarely occur in antiquarian catalogues. Libraries—even very large libraries—did not acquire or keep all of them or put them in reference collections. This neglect is easy to understand because their limitations made them easy to discard. They were intended to sell books rather than to serve scholarly uses and much of the information they contained could be found elsewhere in more "scientific" bibliographies. Although their limitations exclude them from any lengthy consideration, they may be mentioned briefly as forerunners of the increasing share that publishers have in nineteenth- and twentieth-century bibliography.

Theodor Christian Friedrich Enslin (1787–1851), head of a publishing house known especially for medical books, made a number of specialized bibliographies. Had he identified them as a series (this is implied by the similarity of their titles) or had he identified them in some way as a unit, bibliographers would have credited him

with the making of an important subject-index. In the form
in which they appeared, they fell into obscurity. The bibliographies listed only German publications since 1700 or,
more usually, 1750 and included many schoolbooks. They
were printed on paper of poor quality and were no doubt
worn out in use and thrown away. They are forerunners
of the subject-indexes attached to the comprehensive
tradelists of the German book trade, but are more convenient to use because it is not necessary to consult several
volumes of the tradelist in order to obtain all the titles in
a particular field.

During the first half of the nineteenth century Enslin
published at least seventeen specialized bibliographies.
Petzholdt cites fourteen of them (p. 892) and Besterman
fifteen, including three overlooked by Petzholdt (WBB,
col. 4796). Other bibliographers have shown little interest
in them. I list in alphabetical order their subjects: Architecture, Business, Classical literature, Economics, Forestry and Hunting, History and Geography, Law, Medicine and Surgery, Military science, Pedagogy, Philology,
"schöne Wissenschaften," i.e., the Arts and especially Literature, Theology, and Veterinary medicine. The natural
and physical sciences were not represented. Enslin was
honored by election to the presidency of the German
league of booksellers and publishers (Börsenverein) and
received an honorary degree from the university of Berlin.

Wilhelm Engelmann (1808–1878), the son of a Lemgo
bookseller and a friend of the historian Gervinus, revised
some Enslin bibliographies and made similar bibliographies for new fields, especially the natural sciences and
technology.· His *Bibliotheca philologica* (Leipzig, 1840),
an account of grammars, dictionaries, and kindred works
in Greek, Latin, and the Oriental languages, is announced

as a "second, completely revised" edition of Enslin's bibliography of 1826, and the third edition of 1853, which is
restricted to the classical languages, makes no mention of
Enslin. Some of Engelmann's bibliographies have main-
tained themselves successfully: an eighth edition by E.
Preuss of the *Bibliotheca scriptorum classicorum* (2 vols.;
Leipzig, 1880) was reprinted in 1959 [3] and a reprinting
of the *Bibliotheca medico-chirurgica et anatomico-physio-
logica* (2 vols., *Leipzig*, 1848–1868) is announced for 1962.
Engelmann compiled a *Bibliotheca historico-naturalis,
mechanico-technologica, pharmaceuto-chemica*, and *zoologica*.[4] The University of Jena gave him an honorary degree. Like Enslin's bibliographies, Engelmann's books are
accounts chiefly of German publications. They include dissertations that do not get into the trade as well as journal
articles. Since Enslin's and Engelmann's bibliographies are
not universal in scope, we need say no more about them.

ROBERT WATT,
BIBLIOTHECA BRITANNICA (1819–1824)

The first nineteenth-century general subject-index is the
Bibliotheca britannica by Robert Watt (1774–1819). It
has the subtitle: *A general index to British and foreign*

[3] See Petzholdt, pp. 687–688; WBB, col. 3181. For a list of Engelmann's bibliographies see Petzholdt, p. 892; WBB, col. 4794. For
additional details see Petzholdt, *Anzeiger*, 1854, pp. 342–343;
*Jubiläumskatalog der Verlagsbuchhandlung Wilhelm Engelmann in
Leipzig* (Leipzig, 1911), pp. 57–63. The firm also published various
specialized bibliographies to supplement those made by Engelmann
himself, e.g., H. Jolowicz, *Bibliotheca aegyptiaca* (Leipzig, 1858).

[4] The *Historico-naturalis* and the *Zoologica* with both a supplement and a continuation are cited in Petzholdt, pp. 547–548.
Petzholdt devotes fifteen lines to unqualified praise of the supplement and Mlle Malclès (*Les Sources*, III, 337) a line and a half to
the faults of the continuation.

literature.[5] The first two of its four volumes are a bio-bibliographical dictionary of more than 40,000 British and selected foreign authors. In addition, the names of British and important foreign publishers are cited and the titles of books they published. Also, the "more important periodical works on art and science have been minutely analyzed." The third and fourth volumes are a valuable and easily consulted subject-index. Each article contains citations in chronological order with references back to the author-dictionary. In thus associating a subject-index and an author-dictionary Watt did what Conrad Gesner had done somewhat less systematically almost four centuries before.

Robert Watt, a friend of the historian William Richardson, was a man of humble origin. As a young man he began to collect bibliographical information and in 1812 published a *Catalogue of medical books.* In 1817 he abandoned the practice of medicine in order to devote himself wholly to the *Bibliotheca.*[6] He did not live to see more

[5] Two generations later J. E. B. Mayor suggested a new edition with the elimination of classical authors and all foreign editions of foreign authors. The result would have been a work somewhat like the *Bibliotheca danica* (see above). He added some collectanea, and said he had more, but I have not traced them. He also made some comparisons to Allibone's dictionary; see *Notes and Queries,* 5th series, vi (1876), 342–343. His suggestion was not discussed in a somewhat unpleasant exchange of views that followed; see *Notes and Queries,* 5th series, viii (1877), 151, 178, 238, 296.

[6] According to Petzholdt, p. 349, the first fascicles were printed at Glasgow in 1819 and 1820. The remainder was printed at Edinburgh, and the book was completed in 1824. The manuscript in 69 volumes is said to be at Paisley. For further details see Thomas Mason, "A bibliographical martyr—Dr. Robert Watt, author of the Bibliotheca britannica," *The Library,* First Series, I (1889), 56–63; F. Cordasco, *A bibliography of Robert Watt, author of the 'Bibliotheca britannica,' with a facsimile edition of his 'Catalogue of medical books' and a preliminary essay on his works, a contribution to eighteenth century medical history* (New York, 1950); James Finlayson, *An account of the life and works of Dr. Robert Watt . . .* (London, 1897).

than the first pages in print, but left his collectanea in such good order that his son John could carry on the printing. John died in 1821 and a second son completed the task. Robert Watt concluded his "Preface" with the words, "If unmeasured care and indefatigable labor for nearly twenty years—if the sacrifice of a useful life in the cause—was all that was necessary to render the 'Bibliotheca Britannica' accurate and complete, there would now be little solicitude about its success." In these words one hears the echo of a doubt that was probably justified by events. I have not found references to the use of the *Bibliotheca britannica* in the nineteenth century. It is of more than curious interest that in 1910 one large university library bought for ten dollars the book that had been published at eleven guineas almost a century earlier. The low price and the fact that this library, which had been making very judicious additions to its collection of English bibliography, had not previously bought the *Bibliotheca* imply that it was little-esteemed. Times and the estimate of the book have changed. It is now eagerly sought after. My own copy, which was bought not twenty years ago, cost perhaps twenty-five dollars, but copies of the original or the reprint are now selling, when they can be found, for six times that figure.

It is difficult to characterize the contents of Watt's subject-index in a general way and all the more so because he does not indicate what sources he used. He cites many classical Greek and Latin authors with references of their works and mention of such English translations as were available. Sixteenth- and seventeenth-century writers are included in a fashion that suggests the use of early bio-bibliographical dictionaries. Although a test is difficult to make, he seems less generous with minor eighteenth-century figures. Watt does not intend to offer more than a selection of foreign authors, but nevertheless includes many, especially French, writers of obscure fame. The headings for French, Italian, Spanish, and German authors are in a descending order of frequency that probably satisfied the needs and interests of his readers. Each subject heading contains citations in chronological order with references back to the author-index. It is therefore virtually a skeleton history of the subject in question. Some but not all the very long headings are broken down in subdivisions. In citing the names of men born in particular cities Watt is aware that he is going somewhat beyond what might be expected of a subject-index.

The *Bibliotheca britannica* cannot be easily characterized by describing the headings Astronomy and Medicine that I have ordinarily used as measuring sticks. These long lists—Astronomy fills five and a half and Medicine almost fifteen closely printed quarto columns—include so many titles of minor importance that one cannot see the woods for the trees. Short articles will more readily suggest the usefulness of Watt's work. For example, the three articles Garden, Gardener, and Gardening give an excellent notion of eighteenth-century writings on that subject. The article Memory is by no means complete, but serves very well as an introduction. The article Electricity illustrates the value of the *Bibliotheca* for studies in the history of science. As I have already said, Watt gives much information about subjects readily identified from book titles and less about subjects that are not equally obvious. For example, the article Epigram is very rich and Jest, Jests only a little less so because characteristic words appear in titles. The article Epic is scant, for few authors have chosen to use the word *epic* in the titles of their poems. Watt does not mention Ercilla's Renaissance epic *La Araucana* and gives no adequate notion of later epics. For the same reason Madrigal is not particularly informative. The collections under such proper names as Juliet, Lucretia, Rosamond, and Sophonisba can be helpful to a student of comparative literature. Watt's choice of such headings is somewhat unusual in a subject-index. He includes even Cobbett, William as a subject entry and names some interesting writings about him.

His choice of titles identified by a significant word means that the reader must make his own cross-references. The student of courtesy books (a modern term, I believe) will find only three titles under Courtesy and must not fail to turn to Courtier, Duty, Gallantry, Gentleman, Gentlewoman, Honesty, Honour, Living, and Manners. His dependence on a word in the title means that the collections can at times be more amusing than helpful: Dwarf lists medical observations on abnormally small people, Sir Walter Scott's novel *The Black Dwarf*, an old treatise on dwarfs and giants, and *The Black Dwarf*, a London weekly. The article Mint concerns both coinage and the plant, and Stone both geology and medicine. When the catchword has a single well-established meaning, as is usually the case in science, no difficulties arise.

The articles in the *Bibliotheca* are often incomplete, even in terms of the information in Watt's hands or easily within his reach. This is not at all surprising when we remember the thousands of references in the book. For example, Adrien Baillet, *Auteurs déguisez* (Paris, 1690), one of the earliest treatises on pseudonyms, does not appear in the article Pseudonymous Authors and works. Watt knows it and cites it under Baillet in the author-index. It is idle to call attention to such deficiencies. We might well be grateful for finding an enormous amount of information in a convenient form.

Many unwieldy articles are subdivided. The thoughtful elaboration of the rather brief article Bibliography shows a genuine affection for the subject and good understanding. The long article Bible is skillfully analyzed. In Spain and elsewhere under the names of countries the citations are neatly subdivided. We can readily pardon a failure to break down some headings. The chronological arrangement of hundreds of titles in the article Soul is more confusing than helpful, but I cannot suggest an improvement. A satisfactory critical analysis and arrangement of such difficult articles as this would have required him to possess or acquire competence in many wholly unrelated disciplines.

The *Bibliotheca britannica* is especially strong in such scientific fields as botany, chemistry, medicine, and physics. Here Watts's training aided him. The references to articles in important British journals are welcome because they cannot be easily found elsewhere. For foreign countries he might have cited Reuss's *Repertorium* (see above). Social and economic themes are generously dealt with: see Penitentiary, Police, the Poor, Prison, Prosperity, Revenue, and the like. The articles Earthquake and Lisbon might be used for studying the impact of the disaster at Lisbon on November 1, 1755 in English thought. With whatever deductions and criticisms one cares to make, the *Bibliotheca britannica* remains an amazingly rich source of information.

G.-F.-A. THOURET, *COLLECTANEA*

While Watt was still collecting materials for the *Bibliotheca Britannica*, Guillaume-François-Antoine Thouret (1782–1832) was engaged in a similar task. Thouret had held various posts as a lawyer, but retired from public life with the reorganization of 1815 and the return of the Bourbons. Whatever his competence in the legal profession may have been, the larger task of a subject-index was beyond his abilities. His work has been described in the following terms: "He conceived the plan of a bibliographical encyclopedia containing references for every subject. He is believed to have made more than a hundred thousand slips. The article 'Droit' is said to have been much more complete than the treatise of Camus and Dupin." [7] J.-M. Quérard, a bibliographer himself and a severe critic of his colleagues, knew Thouret's collections and expressed no hearty approval of them, saying that Thouret rejected suggestions that he might better limit himself to jurisprudence. Quérard refers to the collectanea as an uncritical listing of titles in all fields. Even with deductions for Quérard's somewhat uncertain temper, one can probably see here what he called "une manie de catalogographie." [8] We have one more example of a man who was scarcely qualified for the task undertaking the compilation of a subject-index. A hundred thousand slips is no surprising figure in such an enterprise. No one appears to have made quotations by which we might judge their quality. No doubt they contained what we might expect: some unusual items, a mass of readily obtainable information, and some conspicuous gaps. Thouret's heirs gave the slips to the municipal library of Paris, where they appear to have perished during the Commune.

[7] See Joseph Hoefer, ed., *Nouvelle biographie universelle,* XLV (Paris, 1846), col. 269 and the obituary by A. Tellandier, *Mémoires et dissertations sur les antiquités nationales et étrangères de la Société des antiquaires,* X (1834), pp. lx-lxv.
[8] *La France littéraire,* IX (12 vols., Paris, 1827–1864), 462–463.

J. G. T. GRAESSE, *LEHRBUCH* (1837-1859)

One who looks at J. G. T. Graesse, *Lehrbuch einer allge-meinen Literärgeschichte aller bekannten Völker der Welt, von der ältesten bis auf die neuere Zeit* (4 vols. in 17, Leipzig, 1837-1859. See WBB, col. 462) for the first time will be struck by various emotions. He will feel amazement at the enormous mass of information collected and arranged by one man. He will find it confusing to get into the work and discover the information that he seeks. He will feel regret that so much labor has been expended on a book that men have appreciated so little. The title clearly indicates Graesse's purpose of writing a historical survey of learning and technology from the earliest times in all countries from the earliest times to the middle of the nine-teenth century. This is the tradition of eighteenth-century historia litteraria and the *Lehrbuch* is its belated climax. Graesse adopted the pattern employed by Christoph A. Heumann in the *Conspectus* of 1718 and continued in C.-J. Bouginé's *Handbuch* of 1789–1802. He divided history into epochs and subdivided it according to displines and fields. The general table of contents offers some help in getting at what one seeks and the indexes of names and subjects, especially the former, offer more, but use of the *Lehrbuch* is by no means easy. Since Graesse was a li-brarian, the references are abundant and accurate in de-tails, although there are many in Heumann's abbreviated style of citation by names only. The typographical arrange-ment makes the book hard to consult.

The score of years that Graesse lavished on the *Lehr-buch* won him little appreciation. In 1866, when the *Lehr-buch* had been completed for seven years, Julius Petzholdt remarked (*Bibliotheca,* pp. 93-94) that the published price had been 50 thaler, but the book was selling for half that sum. This is a perhaps unnecessary observation since he usually says little about the prices of books. He makes the further comment that it is filled with materials of inferior bibliographical value. His savage criticism is still more unkind when we recall that Petzholdt was Graesse's chief in the Royal Library at Dresden. He could surely have found something more pleasant to say about a book that gives, according to Besterman, 170,000 references. Graesse realized that the *Lehrbuch* was both costly and unwieldy and made a condensed edition entitled *Handbuch der allgemeinen Literaturgeschichte aller bekannten Völker der Welt* (4 vols.; 1845–1850). The first three volumes of this were reprinted in 1850.

The most important general criticism of the *Lehrbuch* is that Graesse did not use the many specialized bibliographies within his reach to reduce the bulk of his work and to make more available what was novel in it. He cited them, but the suggested reduction would have conflicted with his intention to be comprehensive. It is difficult to pick out easily, unless one is familiar with a subject, what is new in a welter of references. The long accounts of the sciences may be useful to historians. The similar accounts of literature were superseded almost immediately and can at best be useful for little-studied subjects. A bibliography of Astrology (II, ii, 827–840; III, i, 936–944) that concludes with a closely printed page of references to Nostradamus may approach being exhaustive. There is a strange list of poems in which every line begins with the same letter or in which no word containing a particular letter is used (III, i, 95–100). On this follows a list (pp. 101–114) of satirical Encomia like the praises of fleas or gout. It is likely that these lists are more nearly complete than any others. The section on Neo-Latin literature (III, i, 326–375) is helpful in a field poorly provided with bibliographical aids. Graesse's exploration of remote corners appears in an account of western studies of the Turkish language (III, ii, 902–904).

Graesse's decision to follow the already outmoded tradition of historia litteraria and to combine the history of the study of a subject with bibliographical collectanea makes the *Lehrbuch* unusable. The day of historia litteraria was long since past. The highly selective eighteenth-century manuals had come to emphasize more and more the recent developments in history, science, and technology. Graesse failed to see that this pattern did not lend itself to indefinite expansion. Robert Watt had already chosen the only satisfactory method of dealing with the enormous collectanea Graesse had assembled. An alphabetical subject-index lists the material conveniently, and a chronological arrangement within the articles gives enough direction for historical interpretation. Graesse dismisses Watt with the devastating comment, "All wrong! (ein verfehltes Werk)," see II, ii, 1693.

Brief criticism of Graesse's collections for Medicine, Astronomy, and English history will characterize the *Lehrbuch* sufficiently for our purposes. His brief introductory historical comments on medical history seem judicious. He points out a new attitude in the sixteenth century toward classical writers, especially Pliny, who deal with Medicine (III, i, 1018–1053). He complicates matters by adopting somewhat different subdivisions for the seventeenth century (III, ii, 671–706). His references are abundant; see, for example, those concerning William Harvey (III, ii, 672–673, n. 2). Shortly after Graesse published his first volumes and long before he reached this point in medical history, Ludwig Choulant had collected a large part of this information and had arranged it in a more convenient manner.[9] Perhaps the richly documented account of eighteenth- and early nineteenth-century medicine, which has attracted somewhat less attention from historians of science than medicine in earlier centuries, may be useful (III, iii, pt. 2, pp. 1307–1422). Graesse's account of the history and bibliography of Astronomy resembles that of medicine, with the difference that the treatment of the latest period seems hasty and uninformative (see III, i, 925–936 [sixteenth century]; III, ii, 596–617 [seventeenth century]; III, iii, pt. 2, pp. 1100–1130) [eighteenth and early nineteenth centuries]). His collectanea for English history are love's labor lost; he need not have duplicated Lenglet du Fresnoy and Struve-Meusel. A conscientious reader might pick up the rich notes on Bayle or Leibniz (III, ii, 723–727) with citations of contemporary criticism, but his patience will be tried before he finds what he can use.

One lays the *Lehrbuch* aside with a sigh of regret. I can compare it only to N. H. Gundling's *Vollständige Historie der Gelahrheit* (5 vols. and suppl., Frankfurt a.M., 1734–1746), of which someone has said, "Useful to one who has a nose for bibliography."

SUBJECT-INDEXES TO JOURNALS

For convenience and because of its historical importance we may choose W. F. Poole, *An alphabetical index to subjects, treated in the reviews and other periodicals*

[9] *Bibliotheca medico-historica sive Catalogus librorum historicorum de re medica et scientia naturali systematicus* (Leipzig, 1842, with supplements by Julius Rosenbaum). See WBB, cols. 2489–2490.

... (1848 and later editions. See WBB, col. 3131) as a peg on which to hang a few historical and critical remarks about subject-indexes to journals. The remarks will be brief because these indexes have not always been recognized for what they are and because they are limited to a particular kind of publication and usually to a single country and therefore do not fall within the scope of this study. A rare bibliographer to deal sympathetically with such indexes is Mlle Louise-Noëlle Malclès.[10] We have already touched on subject-indexes of journals made by Cornelius à Beughem, [J. H. C. Beutler and J. C. F. Gutsmuth], and J. D. Reuss that found little understanding or appreciation when they appeared. Around the middle of the nineteenth century the climate changed and subject-indexes of journals have since been compiled in ever-increasing numbers. The modern examples deal characteristically with journals appealing to the "general reader." Many of them have been short-lived and I feel some doubt

---

[10] See Malclès, Les sources, I, 265–276. Additional titles can be gleaned from WBB, cols. 2991–3151; Schneider, pp. 369–407; Leroy H. Linder, The rise of complete national bibliography (New York, 1959), pp. 226–254; The John Crerar Library, A list of bibliographies of special subjects (Chicago, 1902), pp. 16–21; and Norma Olin Ireland, An index to indexes, Useful reference series, 67 (Boston, 1942), pp. 52–53. The last cites, for example, the Index to early American periodical literature, 1728–1870 (New York, 1940) that bibliographers often overlook. I do not see that anyone cites An index to current literature; comprising a reference to author and subject of every book in the English language, and to articles in literature, science and art in serial publications. 1859, 1860, 1861 (London, 1862). It is general bibliographical practice to mingle lists of journals and lists of subject-indexes.

François Joseph Nizet (d. 1899), who was qualified by his training in the social and political sciences and his position in charge of the subject catalogue of the Royal Library at Brussels, is occasionally mentioned in connection with subject-indexes. He participated in discussions at congresses and published a couple of brochures (Brussels, 1888, 1891) on a proposed periodical index. I have not found references to any interest in a general subject-index.

about their usefulness. I have beaten the dust off even the best of them—the *Internationale Bibliographie der Zeitschriftenliteratur* (1897–), when I have consulted it.

First published in 1848, Poole's *Index* rapidly increased in size and in the number of journals indexed, but was always restricted to those published in English. In the second edition of 1853 the number of articles indexed had more than quadrupled and in the third edition of 1882 it was more than tripled, reaching an estimated total of 175,000. It was continued by three supplements, each with an average 50,000 items, down to 1908. Such success implies it met a need and similar compilations were founded in many countries. They exist for almost all north European countries: France, Great Britain (with a special index of Welsh journals), Holland, and Scandinavia. Spanish and Latin-American examples are few. Schneider cites two Russian examples, and it would be possible to find others in countries that I have not named. While a historical and critical review of subject-indexes to journals would be desirable, it would exceed the scope of this study. Their popularity implies a rapid increase in interest in subject matter and in the creation of means to satisfy it.

APPLETON'S LIBRARY MANUAL (1847)

In the first sentences of the Preface *Appleton's library manual; containing a catalogue raisonné of upwards of twelve thousand of the most important works in every department of knowledge* (New York: D. Appleton & Co., 1847. Pp. xvi, 434) is declared to be a selective subject-index.[11] The last sentence of the following quotation is worthy of note:

[11] See WBB, col. 482. I have not seen the later edition (1852–1854) cited there.

The object of the Publishers of the following pages has been to present, in a collected form, indications of the most important works in every department of literature, arranged in such a manner as admits of the most easy reference. . . . What has been chiefly attempted is, to exhibit under each head the extent of its literature, so far as might serve the purpose of the general reader; to the Student, whose aim is exhaustive, the Bibliography of each subject, when known, being given, will direct him to sources where he may supply the deficiencies that must necessarily exist in a work of limited extent, like the present. Whenever a question of omission has occurred, the unknown work has been retained in preference to the well known.

The titles listed are almost exclusively in English. The contents may be illustrated by a few examples. The eighteen titles cited under "Affghanistan.—Cabul" with cross-references to more under other headings imply a contemporary interest in northwestern India and the adjoining territory. Agriculture receives a page and a half with a special section on Agricultural instruments. A dozen books written between 1821 and 1845 deal with the Albigenses. Thirteen editions of the Arabian Nights' Entertainments —some in French, one in Spanish, and a partial edition of two hundred nights in Arabic—are named. The generous treatment of Ballads is worthy of remark. After a list of twenty or more English collections that are no longer esteemed because they do not give oral tradition accurately there follows a listing of collections according to languages: German, Servian, . . . , French, . . . , Romaic (Modern Greek), . . . Persian. This is the background of F. J. Child's scholarly *English and Scottish Popular Ballads* (8 vols., Cambridge, Mass., 1857–1859). As a source of subject information the *Library Manual* has little value today, but it may serve to illustrate the cultural resources and interests of 1847.

NOUVEAU MANUEL
DE BIBLIOGRAPHIE UNIVERSELLE (1857)

A generation after Watt's *Bibliotheca britannica* had been completed, three Frenchmen undertook the task of making a comprehensive subject-index. Their *Nouveau manuel de bibliographie universelle* (Paris, 1857. Pp. xi, 706) is quite independent of its predecessors, being limited chiefly to writings in French. It does not clearly appear from the "Préface" what earlier work justified the adjective "nouveau" in the title and it may mean only "on a new plan." These three men differ from almost all others who made subject-indexes in possessing competence for the task, and they had the good fortune to reside in Paris and to be associated with a great library there. Ferdinand [Jean] Denis, "conservateur à la bibliothèque Sante-Geneviève," Pierre Pinçon, "bibliothécaire" in the same library, and Guillaume François de Martonne, "ancien magistrat,"[12] displayed extraordinary diligence in collecting and classifying 125,000 titles (the figure is Besterman's). The result of their labor deserves a better fate than it has enjoyed. The only review that I have found is well worth reading, but cannot be called sympathetic.[13] It gives no adequate idea of the considerable merits of the *Nouveau*

[12] The identification of these authors is slightly confusing. Ferdinand [Jean] Denis is sometimes cited as [Jean] Ferdinand Denis. Guillaume François de Martonne (b. 1791), who was a magistrate at the beginning of the second restoration and became bureau chief, is replaced, in the British Museum catalogue under "Pinçon," by his son Louis-Georges-Alfred (b. 1820), author, archivist, and archaeologist. See also the *Grand dictionnaire universel du XIXe siècle* under these names. My friend Donald F. Bond has given me good counsel here.

[13] See *Bibliothèque de l'école des chartes*, 4th Ser., IV (1858), 199–201.

manuel. Julius Petzholdt's condemnation (p. 97) may have contributed to the obscurity into which the book has fallen. The countrywoman of the authors, the noted bibliographer Mlle L.-N. Malclès, does not mention it in *Les sources,* probably because it is only valuable for historical purposes. Like all subject-indexes, it became obsolete on the day it was published. Nevertheless, it is a respectable piece of work and will often yield useful information.

The *Nouveau manuel* is a thick book printed in triple columns and contains many headings arranged alphabetically.[14] The more important headings—Angleterre, France, Médecine, for example—are conveniently subdivided. The titles cited have been judiciously chosen and are arranged chronologically to give a historical survey. They may include, as in Paradis, pertinent bibliographies. There are occasional critical or historical comments.

Many unusual headings deserve notice. For example, the article Tables (pp. 532–538) includes both mathematical tables and indexes to books. It would have been useful to H. B. Wheatley in writing his instructive *How to make an index* (London, 1877) [15] and is in some regards a parallel to Norma Olin Ireland's work.[16] The article Statues equestres (pp. 520–521) lists many examples, cites books about them, and gives the titles of orations delivered on

[14] A duodecimo edition of the same year contains only the subject-index and lacks the additional materials mentioned below. The references here are to the octavo edition.

[15] Read this edition and not the reprint that omits the valuable footnotes.

[16] *An index of indexes. A subject bibliography of published indexes* (Useful reference series, 67. Boston, 1942. Pp. 107) and *Local indexes in American libraries. A union list of unpublished indexes* (Useful reference series, 73. Boston, 1947. Pp. [xxxv], 221). These and other subject-indexes "in the second degree" cite places to look for information but do not give references to individual books. They are not included in this study.

the occasions of their dedication. I do not readily see the usefulness of this labor of love, but the example will show how a subject-index may be helpful for information about a subject likely to be difficult to investigate.

The categories of ordinary occurrence in subject-indexes are generously dealt with. The article Linguistique (pp. 271–272) brings references to writings about the origin of languages and the idea of a universal language. A handy bibliography of Catalogues of manuscripts (pp. 289–294) is obviously incomplete, but has the merit of including critical comments. The article on Encyclopedias (pp. 94–99) is worth reading. Such an article can easily be an introduction to a subject one intends to investigate and will suggest its bibliographical difficulties. Articles on minor subjects like systems of memorizing (Mnémonique et Mnémotechnie, pp. 313–314) are usually competent chronological surveys. In general, the articles on scientific and technological subjects seem to be better than those on literary subjects. Those on historical subjects are naturally better for subjects of interest in France and somewhat less useful for others. The article Café (coffee, p. 43) evidently interested its author. A historian of science may find useful the articles on Lithographie (p. 273) and Télégraphie (p. 545), which were rather recent inventions in 1857. The treatment of medical subjects seems excellent; see Strabisme (p. 522). The accounts of subjects that were interesting a century ago and are now little-studied promise to be valuable: Somnabulisme (pp. 513–514) or Tables tournantes (p. 538).

As makers of subject-indexes often do, Denis, Pinçon, and De Martonne give some additional information that one does not expect to find in a subject-index. An appendix to the "Préface" (pp. viii-xi) is a list of schemes for classi-

fying books that Petzholdt could have profitably consulted
(See Bibliotheca, pp. 26–65). In conclusion to the *Nouveau
manuel* the authors offer several more lists having no close
connection with a subject-index. The lists deal with such
subjects as the titles of books in various important collections of classical authors like the collection "ad usum Del-
phini" or of books printed by various early printers or a
very valuable list of public and private library catalogues
(pp. 693–706) that contains much helpful criticism and
comment.

Useful as the *Nouveau manuel* is, there are some qualifications of its merits that may explain why it has been
neglected. It is printed in type so small that a reading
glass is necessary. One shudders to think of the labors of
the men in the composing room and of the proofreaders.
A modern reader is likely to turn away from the book
without learning to appreciate it. The strong emphasis on
French sources with consequent neglect of English, German, or Italian authorities naturally reduces the value of
the book for readers outside France. The choice of catchwords is awkward at times. Cross-references are often
lacking: the article Savants (pp. 488–489) has cross-references to Institut and Philosophes, but not to Érudits.
Books are occasionally incorrectly classified: several titles
in the article Livres rares (p. 276) should have been put
in another category. Misprints are, I believe, few, but note
Hilienthal for Lilienthal in the article Ana (p. 10). These
are all minor faults. More serious objections are the stress
on classical authors, the hasty treatment of subjects in
literary history, and the neglect of obsolete ideas. Information about the editions of classical authors was readily
available in such works as Edward Harwood, *A view of
the various editions of the Greek and Roman classics*

(London, 1775 and many subsequent editions and translations)[17] and many subsequent bibliographies like it. The
listing of editions of works by Lord Byron, Cervantes,
Dante, and Dryden was scarcely useful in 1857 and has
no value now. General headings in literary history get very
short shrift; see Comédie, Epigrammes (a cross-reference
to Anthologie), but Satires et Invectives is useful for a
good number of French titles. The article Théatre does
not repair the lack of attention given to the genres, but
contains some useful references to historical and bibliographical works. Perhaps the unsatisfactory quality of the
bibliographical articles—Bibliographie générale, Bibliophile et Bibliomane, Bibliothèque—may explain the dis-
satisfaction of bibliographers with the *Nouveau manuel*.
For example, the first of these is a strange chronological
farrago of books about books, general bibliographies,
schemes for classifying a library (p. 29, No. 2 Trefler),
local biobibliographies that should have been listed according to the places concerned, handbooks for students
that have little bibliographical quality (p. 29, No. 8 Fi-
chet), Theophil Raynaud's discussion of objectionable
books (No. 10), Louis Jacob's biobibliographical dictionary of the Carmelites (No. 11), and so on. All this should
have been reorganized. Some books are cited according to
titles without examining the contents: Paul Boyer, *Dictionnaire servant de bibliothèque universelle* is not a bibliography but a dictionary of rhymes; the omission of "ad
artem obstetricam spectantium" in No. 54 Schweikhard
is grievous (it should have been cited under Accouche-
ment); the Van Goens catalogue (no. 46) is a sale catalogue. These random samples show a surprising neglect of

---

[17] See Petzholdt, p. 683 for these editions and translations and the
following pages for many later similar works.

a user's needs and an equally surprising haste on the part of the two authors who were librarians. While my criticisms are severe and might be extended, the *Nouveau manuel* seems to me to be better than these samples might suggest.

The emphasis of the authors on subjects likely to interest the contemporary student of natural or physical science is obvious. It is characteristic generally of nineteenth-century subject-indexes. The authors find, for example no space for such creatures as the salamander that lives in fire or the unicorn. The references to Dwarfs (Nains) concern, with one exception, actual dwarfs, although strangely enough the article Giants (Géants) deals chiefly with traditional giants. On the whole, one can justly say that the *Nouveau manuel* is a comprehensive and well-organized account of learning, science, and the arts in 1857 that gives much more attention to older books and ideas than nineteenth-century bibliographers are likely to give.

JAMES DARLING, CYCLOPAEDIA BIBLIOGRAPHICA (1854, 1859)

Only two volumes of a *Cyclopaedia bibliographica: a library manual of theological and general literature, and guide to books for authors, preachers, students, and literary men. Analytical, bibliographical, and biographical* (1854, 1859). See WBB, col. 4038 by James Darling (1797–1862) were published. The author's death explains why it was not continued. Darling intended to make a similar work for all the divisions of knowledge, but completed only the one for theology (see above). He had obviously not examined works having a similar purpose, for he writes (*Cyclopaedia*, 1859), p. [iii]):

In first announcing the design of a Bibliographical Cyclopaedia, the compiler was under the impression that one volume would comprehend both an Alphabet of Authors, with an account of their works, and a systematic arrangement of Subjects, with references to the best authors who have written on them . . . In commencing the publication of the Subjects, the extent to which the work ought to be carried in order to its design being satisfactorily carried out, became still more apparent, and therefore the compiler determined to bring it out in divisions, each division forming a volume complete in itself, so that the purchaser might have a complete book, without being under the necessity to take more than one, if inconvenient.

The volume of 1859 devoted to the Holy Scriptures is, accordingly, the first division. He did not indicate what the other divisions may have been. A cross-reference to Literature under the heading General Bibliography (1859, p. 1) probably implies that one division was to be Literature, which I take to mean scholarly treatises rather than belles lettres. Although Darling carefully subdivides this heading, he does not have a sub-division for subject bibliographies. This omission explains why he was unaware of the extent of the task that he was undertaking. It is curious that he is equally unaware of the many bibliographies that list the materials found in his second volume. He describes his purpose as follows:

The great aim in this volume is to point out the authors who have written illustration of any or all of the books, chapters, and verses of the Holy Scriptures. It is limited to no sect; the contributions of all denominations will be found here referred to. It is limited to no nation; English, French, Italian, German, and other nations are, to a greater or less degree, here represented; nor is it limited to any time, authors from the earliest to the latest period are here ranged under each head in chronological order.

Concerning his further intentions he writes (pp. [iii-iv]):

As it is contemplated that books in the whole range of human knowledge may be ultimately embraced in the work now commenced, the volume is initiated by a short account of the Bibliography, Dictionaries and Encyclopaedias of Universal Knowledge, enumerating them to a very limited extent, and introducing them chiefly to show that in exact bibliography they cannot be placed under any subordinate head, inasmuch as they comprehend all. In compliance, however, with general custom, an article will be appropriated to these heads should the work be so fortunate as to proceed so far, where these subjects will be treated more at length.

Such a biobibliographical dictionary and subject-index as Darling proposed to make was no undertaking to be begun at the age of 57. We must praise what he accomplished in five years. Since the second volume or subject-index to the Bible deals with a limited field, I shall not attempt to criticize it here. It is worth saying, however, that much can be learned from it about the intellectual temper of England in the nineteenth century. Darling's linguistic attainments did not permit him to go farther.

XAVIER HEUSCHLING, *PLAN* (1873)

The *Nouveau manuel* suggested a very ambitious expansion to the Belgian Xavier Heuschling (1802–1883).[18] He was also aware of collectanea made by John Locke, Albrecht von Haller, and Condorcet but it does not appear that he had any firsthand acquaintance with these materials. A sample consisting of 55 articles in the first part of "A" gives an idea of the book Heuschling proposed to compile. As he points out, they are much more numerous than the seven in the corresponding portion of the alphabet in the *Nouveau manuel*. The comparison is not entirely fair,

[18] "Plan d'un dictionnaire universelle," *Le Bibliophile belge*, VIII (1873) 45–52.

for Heuschling's predecessors had not recognized the titles of poems or paintings as suitable headings. He does not say what progress he has made in his enterprise, and it is not heard of again. It is one of many brave contemporary plans to survey a large field. A general catalogue of French manuscripts was already being made. Enrico Nerucci (1823–1893) proposed a union catalogue of Italian libraries. In the same spirit is Ferdinand Bonnange's suggestion of a universal catalogue (1874) based on the use of library cards. This inchoate proposal suggests its value for finding references to subject-matter, but does not go into details about this aspect.[19] Twenty-two years later Bonnange renewed his proposal and thought it might be completed for the international exposition of 1900. Nothing seems to have come of this.

[J. A. CROSS?], NOTES OF A PROPOSAL (1875)

Two years after Heuschling published his plan for a comprehensive subject-index an anonymous author in London suggested an even more ambitious undertaking of the same kind. In its suggestion of governmental and institutional cooperation and in its proposal to establish a center or bureau to keep and organize materials and answer questions it resembles Sir William Petty's plan of the 1660's (see above). The prospectus entitled *Notes of a*

[19] *Le Bilan de l'esprit humain. Projet d'un catalogue universel des productions intellectuelles. Mémoire sur les moyens à employer pour dresser repidement des catalogues exacts et complets des richesses renfermées dans les bibliothèques* (Paris, 1874); *Projet d'un catalogue général unique et perpétuel des imprimés compris dans les bibliothèques nationales et les bibliothèques municipales. Mémoire explicatif des moyens à employer pour accomplir ce grand oeuvre, l'imprimer et le mettre au jour dès l'ouverture de l'exposition universelle de 1900* (Corbeil, 1896. Not seen).

Proposal to Make a Universal Index to Literature (London, [1875]) is now a very rare pamphlet. Julius Petzholdt cited the copy received by the *Neuer Anzeiger für Bibliothekswissenschaft* [20] at the time of publication, but after this it disappeared from sight. In 1893 Richard Garnett, keeper of the books in the British Museum, sought for it in vain, and five years later Fritz Milkau could not turn up a copy.[21] Fortunately, however, a copy given to Harvard University Library by John Fiske, then Assistant Librarian, has survived. According to a manuscript note in it he received it as a gift from one W. I. The manuscript note identifies "J. A. Cross (an American)" as the deviser of the scheme. At the end of the pamphlet J. Ashton Cross declares his readiness to receive, at a London address, any suggestions or promises of support. Some who refer to the pamphlet credit the authorship to E. C. Thomas (1850–1892), the translator of Richard de Bury's *Philobiblon*, but I do not know what the grounds for the ascription may be.[22]

The eight pages of the *Notes* list and briefly describe reference works that might be used in making a universal subject-index. (The word "literature" in the title is to be understood as referring to scholarly writings of any kind and not to belles lettres.) These works are "Miscellaneous Indexes,... drawn up both by libraries and by individuals,"

[20] 1876, p. 369.
[21] See *The Library*, 1st Ser., V (1893), 93; *Zentralblatt für Bibliothekswesen*, Beiheft 20 (Leipzig, 1898), pp. 49–50.
[22] It is not mentioned in the obituary and bibligraphy in *The Library*, 1st Ser., IV (1892), 73–80. Leroy H. Linder ascribes it to Thomas; see *The rise of current complete national bibliography* (New York, 1950), pp. 107, 124. In this context (pp. 106–109) he mentioned various proposals between 1810 and 1878 to compile a universal catalogue, but it does not appear that any concerned a subject-index.

special indexes to various branches, and bibliographical
and library journals. The author has no very clear idea of
the extent, number, and nature of these resources, for he
often cites the names of institutions and individuals without the titles of the books intended. The institutions to
which he refers are the London Library; the Royal Institution with the date 1857 (this evidently means B. Vincent, ed., *A new classified catalogue of the Library of the
Royal Institution of Great Britain* [London, 1857]); the
Advocates' Library, which he says is "half done"; the
Bodleian Library, which he says is "very imperfect; scattered through the Alphabetical Catalogue"; [23] the Birming-
ham Free Public Library ("ditto"); the Manchester Free
Public Library; the Melbourne Library; the Library of
New York State, 1872, with the remark that the subject-
index fills 651 double-columned pages; and the British
Museum (Royal Library only). Such a list as this is not
very encouraging evidence of the author's acquaintance
with the nature and difficulty of the enterprise that he
proposes. The catalogue of the Advocates' Library (7 vols.,
Edinburgh, 1863–1879) is, for example, alphabetical and
is not a subject-index at all. The list of individuals includes
alphabetical catalogues of private libraries, such roughly
classified sale catalogues as the huge Thott catalogue,[24]
and the antiquarian catalogues issued by Bohn and Quar-
itch. The most interesting item in the list, and the most
interesting item in the whole pamphlet, may be quoted in
the author's words: "Thouret (Project—left 100,000 titles
of books and 30 quarto vols. of MSS., now in Town Library
at Paris)." This was, as I have said above, burned in 1871.

[23] Subject entries in the Bodleian catalogue concern only works
published anonymously. Can the author have failed to preceive this
fact?
[24] See my *Book catalogues,* pp. 120–121, 264.

The reference to manuscripts indicates that he had either made inquiries or had access to some description of Thouret's materials that I have not seen, for I have not found a reference to manuscripts. The author has no adequate international view of his task. His list of fifteen subjects —art, music, mathematics, political economy, etc., in this order—for which special bibliographies already exist shows no competence in the field of specialized subject bibliography and no talent for arranging materials. A disorderly and inadequate list of journals to be consulted is equally discouraging. It cites bibliographical journals, national trade lists, the Smithsonian Reports, and a "Year Book," whatever it may be. More interesting than the inadequacy of his account of books to be consulted is his suggestion of the establishment of a central office to combine the "now isolated fragments and to carry them out still further." This is in more than one regard Sir William Petty's seventeenth-century plan and a predecessor of the suggestion made by the Belgian Institut de documentation two generations ago. He would induce each library, learned society, and publisher to continue its present work of indexing and to complete it by going back to their beginnings as institutions. Finally, he wishes to see the work undertaken locally and its parts assigned to particular local libraries. He estimates that a "Central Office" might be established and the local agencies set to work for a sum between £600 and £1000 a year. Such a sum, even in 1875, seems fantastically small for the purpose. It is not surprising that nothing came of this inchoate plan. A general enthusiasm of a similar sort prevails through much of the nineteenth century and appears in the improvement of library organization and services that marks the age.

ULYSSE CHEVALIER, *REPERTOIRE DES SOURCES...*, *TOPO-BIBLIOGRAPHIE*
(1894–1909)

A work which in many ways accomplished what Heuschling had planned in 1873 was published a few years later. It is the *Répertoire des sources pour l'histoire du moyen âge* by Ulysse Chevalier (1841–1923). Like Heuschling, Chevalier was a Belgian, but it does not appear that he was influenced by Heuschling's proposal. Chevalier published the first part of his book with the subtitle *Bio-bibliographie* (Paris, 1877–1886, Supplément, 1888), but with this and its second edition (2 vols., Paris, 1905–1907) we are not concerned. The second part entitled *Topo-bibliographie* (1894–1909) contains far more than a bibliography of places or a bibliography solely for the medievalist. As he says, "Le sous-titre Topo-bibliographie n'a été adopté que faute d'un terme plus comprehensif pour désigner *tout* ce qui n'est pas personnages: il offre la bibliographie de l'universalité des sujets sous lesquels peut être classée alphabétiquement l'histoire médiévale dans ses moindres détails." [25] He did not go quite as far as Heuschling in admitting headings taken from literature and chose very few from the plastic arts.

Since no completely clear principle is apparent in the choice of headings, one never knows what one may find in the *Topo-bibliographie*. And, although Chevalier's emphasis is on the Middle Ages, he brings much that is useful for more recent times. There are, for example, bibliogra-

[25] Quoted from the Avertissement (prospectus) in Ch. -V. Langlois, *Manuel de bibliographie historique* (Paris, 1901–1904), p. 135, n. 1.

phies of the mythical Gargantua (col. 1268), the Old
Norse Sagas (col. 2656), a medieval poem like Huon de
Bordeaux (col. 1474), Sacred Oil (col. 1472), the Hu-
miliati, a Lombard religious order (cols. 1472–1473),
Hymns (cols. 1476–1482), Guillaume Libri, "Bibliophile
indélicat" (cols. 1674–1675), and Book-binding (cols.
2531–2532). The rich article Bible is conveniently subdivided (cols. 391–396). That on Biographie (cols. 404–
415) might easily be a basis for a historical account of
biographical dictionaries. The article Manuscrits (cols.
1836–1838) cites many interesting and important general
works and offers a good list of catalogues of manuscripts.
In the headings place names, and especially French place
names, predominate, but even under them one finds materials not immediately concerned with geography or history. Under Paris, for example, there are paragraphs of
bibliographical references dealing with libraries, liturgy,
law, printing, and the University of Paris. One finds something surprising at every turn: there are rich collections
on Botany (col. 454), collective editions of Papal Bulls
(col. 528), the Calendar (cols. 548–550), the Cistercians
(cols. 718–721), Hunting (Chasse, cols. 666–667), the
Imitatio Christi (cols. 1490–1495), and Theology (cols.
3088–3092). I cannot easily cite another place to find the
information contained in the articles on the cry "Haro!"
(col. 1392), the Christian symbol of the Fish (col. 1559),
and Ordeals ("Jugements de Dieu," cols. 1580–1581).
Chevalier limits himself to subjects having some connection with medieval life, but is nevertheless very inclusive.
The articles on bibliography (Bibliographie, cols. 397–403
and Bibliothèques, cols. 404–405) are hard, but informative reading. For all this one should be very grateful.
Langlois calls the book indispensable to a medievalist

(aucun médiéviste ne saurait se dispenser de l'avoir con-
stamment sous la main), but thinks that one must learn
to use it. It is not, he thinks, a work to which the inexperienced should be referred.

Much that Chevalier brings can be found more readily
and more conveniently in other sources. Information about
the religious orders and religious ideas generally can, for
example, be obtained more easily from religious encyclopedias—Wetzer-Welte, for example—and the great French
encyclopedias of the Benedictines. To be sure, the latter
were not available when Chevalier was writing. Nevertheless, he could have greatly reduced the bulk of his collections by appropriate references to Wetzer-Welte for religious subjects and to the *Histoire littéraire de la France*
and Gröber's *Grundriss der romanischen Philologie* for
literary subjects. If he had shown greater familiarity with
reference works, literary histories, and the like, he could
have substantially condensed his *Répertoire* without loss.
Nevertheless, Chevalier is likely to cite, even in the articles
dealing with church history and literary history, a title
that might escape a specialist. There are many subjects
for which he is the most convenient source of information.
He chose to cite titles alphabetically in the various articles.
This procedure is not usual in subject-indexes and has
some disadvantages. Chevalier's *Topo-bibliographie* has
a somewhat limited usefulness as a general subject-index,
and is far more extensive than its title might suggest.

PAUL OTLET AND HENRI LA FONTAINE, INSTITUT INTERNATIONAL DE BIBLIOGRAPHIE (1895–   )

The largest of all modern subject-indexes was never
published and appears to have been intended to be a man-

uscript file of references compiled for scholars. For various reasons general bibliographies rarely mention it and are disappointingly uninformative about details. After surviving two world wars and other disasters that touched it even more closely the Institut international de bibliographie (since 1931, Institut de documentation) is still in existence and can be visited at the address Parc Léopold, 3, rue de Maelbeek, Brussels 4. Its director is M. G. Lorphevre. This Institut founded in 1895 by Paul Otlet (1868–1941) and Henri La Fontaine (1854–1943) set to work at once on two enormous tasks, an international author-index of books and an international subject-index of books and periodicals. Nor was this all it undertook. It occupied itself with a revision of the decimal classification that was much discussed and was adopted by some European libraries. It compiled a list of more than 700,000 periodical or serial publications and made a union catalogue of the holdings of more than a hundred Belgian libraries. These amazing achievements do not concern us. We shall limit the following remarks to the subject-index.[26]

The subject-index consisted some forty years ago of more than seven million slips drawn from various unspecified sources. It is not clear how they are arranged nor

[26] For general references to the Institut see such guides to bibliography as A. D. Roberts (3d ed., London, [1956]), p. 83; Malclès, Les sources, I, 34; Josefa Emilia Sabor, Manuel, p. 112 (with a bibliography). Such books have little to say about the subject-index. Le Mundaneum, a mimeographed brochure published by the Institut, that M. Lorphevre kindly sent me is the richest source of information I have found. Oskar Thyregod, Die Kulturfunktion der Bibliothek (The Hague, 1936) pp. 184–189 gives some additional information about the classification sponsored by the Institut and the impact of the Institut on congresses of librarians. I have consulted friends in Belgium and elsewhere to very little avail. One of them who visited it at my request in search of references to proverb literature found the collections disordered, incomplete, and marred by errors.

whether additions continue to be made to the file. The withdrawal of state funds naturally was a severe blow that virtually destroyed it as a going concern. I have not been able to learn much from those who have visited the Institut about its present situation. According to a newspaper article cited later, an Englishman visited it and obtained valuable references for his study in the history of Belgian railways. The Institut made a valiant effort to demonstrate its usefulness by compiling bibliographies of Esperanto and Richard Wagner (Not seen and not mentioned in WBB). A distressing article in *Le Peuple* (Brussels), Dec. 16, 1964, p. 5 may be the most recent report on the Institut and its collections. It is illustrated by a photograph of a building something like a greenhouse. Many panes are broken; the shelves, halls, and steps are covered with dust and trash. There is some current discussion about razing the building in order to use the land for other purposes. The Royal Library has shown no interest in the collection. Neither public nor private support has been offered to save it and the pittance on which it exists is altogether insufficient.

ALFRED COTGREAVE,
A CONTENTS-SUBJECT INDEX (1900)

Subject-indexes to periodicals have been only briefly mentioned in this study. An exception may be made for Alfred Cotgreave (1849–1911), *A contents-subject index to general and periodical literature* (London, 1900. Pp. xii, 744), which has a wider scope and purpose than other indexes of this sort. As the author, who was Chief Librarian at West Ham, London, says, it "is not an index to works devoted entirely to particular subjects, but is intended to supply a pressing want by indexing under subject headings important articles and references from the *contents* of works which would otherwise remain practically unknown and valueless. . . . The chief aim of the work is not to give everything which appears in a select number of works on a few selected subjects, but rather to cover as many subjects as possible and give a few references to each one. The requirements of the many readers rather than those of the few has [*sic*] been the guiding rule." [27]

The author has achieved his purpose, but one can ask whether it was worth achieving. His index to contemporary semi-popular periodicals and books, often chapters in books, has some similarity to Fabianus Justinianus's *Index universalis alphabeticus* of the books in the Vallicelliana, but the selection of titles and headings is on a lower scholarly level. It may also be compared to Schiele's *Bibliotheca enucleata* of 1679 as an index to miscellaneous information. Like both of these, it is an index to contemporary writings that goes beyond the titles to the contents and is limited, in the earlier instances, to books in Latin and the vernacular and, in this later instance, to books in English. More than half the references are to journal articles. Cotgreave is aware that he is duplicating the general indexes to journals, but believes that they are too expensive to be generally available. In other words, he has given us a Poor man's reader's guide. There may be some doubt about the number of readers to whom it could appeal.

Few subject-indexes, large or small, have so many head-

[27] In his commentary, "An Index to the contents of general and periodical literature," *The Library*, 1st ser., IX (1899), 270–275, Cotgreave suggests continuing and enlarging his work as a co-operative enterprise.

ings. In this small octavo volume (pp. xii, 744) Besterman counts 40,000 references! The headings range widely
in Art, Education, Literature, Science, and Technology.
A typical sample (pp. 398–399) is: Mice, Michaelmas,
Michel (Louise, French anarchist), Michelangelo, Miche-
let (Jules, French historian), Michelham Priory (Sussex),
Michigan, Microbes, Micrometer, Microphone, Microscope, and Middelburg. Since Cotgreave restricts himself
to books and articles in English, his *Index* serves only the
general reader in a public reference library with rather
limited resources. He intends to write a book of this scope.
A few brief articles quoted entire will show how he went
about his task:

> Pernambuco, Brazil.—Atchison's Winter Cruise, 1891.
> Condor's Modern Traveler, vol. 30, 1830. Vincent's
> Around and About South America, 1890.

> Perpetual Motion, Attempts to Discover Perpetual Mo-
> tion.—Burnley's Romance of Invention, 1886. Nature,
> vol. 37, 1887–8. Penny Mag., vol. 3, 1834.

> Pestalozzi (J. Henri, Swiss Philanthropist and Educa-
> tionalist, died 1827). Views of Teaching.—Leitch's
> Practical Educationalists, 1876.—General.—Macmil-
> lan's Magazine, vol. 64, 1891.

> Petronius (Titus, a licentious Roman author, who lived
> at the court of Nero, died A.D. 66). New Review, vol.
> 15, 1896.

While Cotgreave's book is, as these extracts show, intended for the "general reader," it may on occasion serve
a more serious student, especially one interested in the
life and ideas of Victorian England. It exemplifies what
that age found interesting or important. More than one

article contains information that would be troublesome to assemble. For example, the dozen articles on Etiquette (p. 211) cited from journals of the 80's and 90's would be useful to a student of Courtesy books and social life. The two pages of references to Evolution (pp. 213–214) suggest the tremendous impact of Darwin's ideas. A dozen or more references to Genius (p. 247) show the influence of Sir Francis Galton's book. While Cotgreave's *Index* has outlived its usefulness as a general reference work because the citations have an altogether popular quality, it is just for that reason a summary of its age. The forty thousand citations (see WBB, col. 3145) are a cross-section of what the middle class read and need only diligence and imagination to yield an interpretation of Victorian life and thought.

A LOOK BACK

In the nineteenth century the making of subject-indexes passes from professional hands into those of publishers and librarians. The indexes repeat curiously enough the same sequence of the patterns already identified in their earlier history. Like the sixteenth-century indexes, the "Table méthodique" (1810) in Brunet's *Manuel* is classified. Watt's *Bibliotheca britannica* (1819–1824), the *Nouveau manuel* (1857), and later subject-indexes generally employ the alphabetical arrangement characteristic of seventeenth-century works. In his *Lehrbuch* (1839–1857) Graesse continues the historico-chronological manner of eighteenth-century historia litteraria and represents an outworn tradition. Had anyone seen all this clearly by recognizing subject-indexes as a bibliographical category, he might have been wise enough to build on the foundation laid by the *Bibliotheca britannica*. A continuing tradition appears, for example, in F. K. Beilstein, *Handbuch der organischen Chemie* (2 vols., Hamburg, 1881–1883. See Malclès, *Les sources*, III, 178). In this book everything written on the subject is assembled and reference back to the beginnings is readly possible from the current fourth edition (Berlin, 1918–   ). It is greatly to be regretted that nothing of the sort occurred in the history of general subject-indexes. It did not come to pass because bibliographers did not set them apart and did not fully appreciate their nature. The treatment of Gesner's *Bibliotheca,* which is almost the only generally known comprehensive subject-index, illustrates the situation. Bibliographers recognize the first volume, which is a biobibliographical dictionary, for what it is and neglect the subject-index in the *Pandectae* and *Partitiones.* The various historical accounts and lists of national bibliographies pay little attention to them as subject-indexes. Bibliographies of journals usually do not separate lists from subject-indexes and are likely to neglect the latter category. Cooperation, which becomes possible to an extent not previously imagined, is called for in the second half of the nineteenth century. This and the use of technical improvements in printing and photography would have greatly facilitated the making of widely ranging subject-indexes. Except to the degree that proposals for cooperative enterprises envisage a comprehensive general subject-index, efforts to make one ceased by the middle of the century. The subsequent development occurs in more limited directions: subject-indexes of journals, the books in particular libraries, the best books, and the books in particular languages. Activities with this practical emphasis have continued down to the present time.

7

Subject-Indexes in the Twentieth Century

IN THE TWENTIETH CENTURY THE HISTORICAL PATTERN WE
have learned to know repeats itself once more: an old manner of writing a subject-index continues for a brief time,
and a new one arises: In the *Register of national bibliography* W. P. Courtney lists books and articles on all subjects
from all periods of time, but naturally does not achieve
completeness. Gesner, Lipenius, Watt, and the *Nouveau
manuel* had done this before him. With Courtney's emphasis on relatively recent writings and largely those in English, the *Register* belongs to the modern age and bridges a
gap between the old and the new. The new manner of
subject-indexes is seen in compilations of intentionally
limited scope. The limitations are of many kinds. In the
Subject-index of the London Library there are limitations
to books in a single library, to relatively modern books (be-

cause the library was founded in 1840), and books chiefly
in English. Its immediate forerunner, the *Subject index of
the modern works added to the library of the British Museum in the years 1881–1900*, is intentionally limited to
current publications. This is also true of other modern indexes of library holdings or accessions. In a proposal of
1926 H. G. Wells stresses modern books and approaches
the notion of a list of best books without being aware of
what he is doing. In the 1940s Hirshberg and Murphey are
wholly practical and choose modern, almost exclusively
English titles with very little attention to the historical
aspects of subjects. In many of these works, and especially
Schuder, *Universitas litterarum* (1955), the emphasis falls
on technology and science. A subject-index containing
references to classical, medieval, and Renaissance authors
like Adler, *The Great Ideas* aims to provide materials for
modern thinking rather than historical study. The characteristics of the most recent subject-indexes are (1) selec-
tiveness that is dictated by either circumstances or
intention, (2) a particular regard for the needs and interests of the modern age, (3) a predominating but not ex-
clusive restriction to a single language, (4) an emphasis
on technology, the physical and biological sciences, and
social sciences in that order with perhaps less attention to
history (except post-Napoleonic history and geography)
and literary history, and (5) a growing interest in art and
music. Zischka's anomalous list of works that adopt a lexicographical plan of arrangement lists many books that do
not deal with subject matter and is a curious misapprehen-
sion of bibliographical method.

W. P. COURTNEY, *REGISTER*
OF NATIONAL BIBLIOGRAPHY (1905–1912)

With an estimated 30,000 references Courtney's *Register* illustrates in a striking fashion the good and bad qualities of subject-indexes generally.[1] This compilation of bibliographical notes on a great variety of subjects is entirely independent of its predecessors and can usually be consulted with profit. A convenient alphabetical arrangement makes it easy to use, and it is available in most American libraries. Long articles like America are neatly subdivided, and cross-references are numerous. Frequent citations of bibliographies in specialized treatises, journal articles, and government publications—three categories often neglected in subject bibliographies—offer welcome information not otherwise easy to come by. Yet, the faults of the *Register* are many and grievous. Although Courtney spent twenty years on the task and did little else in the last four, he seems not to have studied any similar work to learn its difficulties and problems. He names no predecessors, although Robert Watt, *Bibliotheca britannica* cannot have escaped his notice. He says the *Manuel de bibliographie générale* by Henri Stein suggested making the *Register* to him, and he commends it for references to "Slavonic" authorities. Although Stein cites them, they are neither numerous nor particularly significant. Courtney is aware of criticisms of the *Manuel* but does not appear to have profited from them.

When Courtney had assembled the materials for the first two volumes, he found it necessary to reduce their quantity. He omitted sale-catalogues, bibliographies of

[1] London, 1905–1912. Pp. viii, 314; iv, 315–631; v, 340.

manuscripts, maps, and charts, and catalogues of free libraries. We cannot object to his decision, but fortunately
he did not carry it out strictly. Three sale-catalogues are
cited under Alsace. He is aware that special bibliographies
contain much for which he can find no space and points
out bibliographies of Geology and India as examples. He
might have dealt more systematically with this difficulty.
There is an awkward supplement (II, 538–559) to the first
two volumes, the whole third volume is a supplement, and
it, too, has a supplement (III, 287–292). In other words,
one must consult four alphabets.

The very miscellaneous contents of the *Register* include
articles on cities, places, and countries like Aberdeen,
Bradford, Liverpool, London, Strawberry Hill, and Tas-
mania. The collectanea dealing with foreign cities concern
those particularly interesting to an English reader (Berlin,
Florence, Geneva, Madrid, Munich, Paris, Rome, Vienna)
or important in the history of printing (Lo, Saint; Olmütz;
Tarragona). The articles are often conveniently subdivided in a manner like that used by Robert Watt and
Ulysse Chevalier. Courtney's collectanea on the history of
printing largely duplicate information readily obtainable
from other sources. For such a general work as he was
writing the treatment of the sciences, medicine, and technology is probably adequate: see Algae, Anatomy, Echino-
dermata, Optics, Sponges. It seems amusingly unnecessary
to cite a note of three pages on the Tapeworms of hares
and rabbits. Like cultured Englishmen of the time, Courtney has an active interest in the Archaeology of Greece,
Rome, and the Near East. Here he could have saved space
by referring to the British Museum *Subject Index* or a
similar work. He gives generous notice to John Ruskin
and a few other authors and critics. A clearer realization

of what readers could easily find for themselves would have aided him greatly. He might, for example, have omitted citations of editions of classical authors or Beowulf for the bibliographies in their prefaces. He thanks G. L. Apperson, a widely read antiquarian, and Robert Alexander Peddie, himself the compiler of a subject-index (see below), for collectanea.

The *Register* contains unusual and therefore useful information. There are, as random examples, a good account of Angling, some curious notes on Anagrams, five titles on Suicide, and many on Water (especially drinking water). The titles dealing with Frosts on the Thames (I, 205) will serve for a note on the children's rhyme, "Three children sliding on the ice." [2] In quality, quantity, and organization of citations the Register compares unfavorably with the *Bibliotheca britannica* or the *Nouveau manuel.* Currently quoted prices of $150.00 for the *Bibliotheca* and $90.00 for the *Register* are a fantastic over-valuation of the latter that can be explained only by the fact that it cites recent books. It is curious that Mlle Malclès omits the *Nouveau manuel* and includes the *Register* (*Les sources*, I, 29).

H. G. WELLS, *IDEA* (1936)

In *The Idea of a World Encyclopedia* H. G. Wells made an ambitious proposal that involved the incidental compilation of a master bibliography of subjects.[3] This subject-index he thought might be the first step to be taken after the formation of an Encyclopedia Society. He writes:

[2] Iona and Peter Opie did not use the *Register* for a note on the rhyme; see *The Oxford Dictionary of Nursery Rhymes* (Oxford, [1951]), pp. 118–119. Add *Frostiana, or a history of the river Thames, in a frozen state* (London, 1814).

[3] Day to Day Pamphlets, 25 (London, 1936, Pp. 32). The passage quoted will be found on p. 26.

And next this society of promoters will have to survey the available material. For most of the material for a modern Encyclopedia exists already—though in a state of impotent diffusion. In all the various departments with which an Encyclopedia should deal, groups of authoritative men might be induced to prepare a comprehensive list of primary and leading books, articles, statements which taken together would give the best, clearest and most quintessential renderings of what is known in their departments. This would make a sort of key bibliography for a World Bibliography to the thought and knowledge of the world. My friend Sir Richard Gregory has suggested that such a key bibliography for a World Encyclopedia would itself be a very worthwhile thing to evoke. I agree with him. I imagine something on the scale of ten or twenty thousand items. I don't know.

Possibly our Encyclopedia Society would find that just such a key bibliography was in itself a not unprofitable publication, but that is a comment by the way.

This proposal is but one more illustration of what we have so often seen in the history of subject-indexes. Its author is a man wholly unfamiliar with the task and quite unaware of what had already been done; he gives no thought to the difficulty of finding a publisher ready to risk funds in such a work. Bibliographies already existed that gave virtually all that Wells called for: W. Swan Sonnenschein, *The Best Books* [4] or F. C. Tweney, *Standard books. An annotated and classified guide to the best books in all departments of literature.* [5] If he were to object that they employed a classified rather than an alphabetical arrangement, an answer was easy to find. His secretary could convert them into an alphabetical subject-index at

[4] 2d ed.; 2 vols.; London, 1891, 1895. This lists 75,000 titles and is perhaps as large a book as Wells wished. A third edition contains 150,000 titles and probably exceeds the limit he had in mind. For references see WBB, col. 485 and below.

[5] 4 vols.; London, [1911]. It cites an estimated 20,000 titles. There was a revision (1912–1915?) of many pages in this book. See WBB, col. 486.

a cost less than a year's royalty from *Mr. Britling sees it through*. If a critic were to object to the scarcity of foreign authorities, suitable foreign reference works could be easily found and excerpted. These compilations are akin to selective lists of books recommended for public libraries. In the early years of this century the influence of the so-called Carnegie List was very considerable. Its more recent parallel, Dorothy H. West and Estelle A. Fidell, comps., *Standard catalog for public libraries; a classified & annotated list of 7,610 non-fiction books recommended for public & college libraries, with a full analytical index* (4th ed.; New York, 1959. Pp. 1639) is, curiously enough, only half as large as the edition of 1950. The selective quality of these lists and the lack of titles in foreign languages exclude them from further consideration here.

There are many such problems that Wells should have met and solved and he needed no committee of scholars to help him in the task. For example, he is altogether unaware of the fact that summarizing articles that he desired already existed. In the professorial trade they are called articles on the "Stand der Forschung." Diligent reading in the bibliographies of individual disciplines would yield examples. Inquiries addressed to specialists in various fields would yield references to more. There is no royal road to their discovery. We often hear that a survey of what had been accomplished in a particular discipline with indications of what might yet be done is a worthy enterprise. Ever since the end of the seventeenth century men had made such surveys, and I do not see clearly what the result of them has been.[6] It might be instructive for a

---

[6] The only bibliography of such surveys that I know is Johann Justus von Einem, *Commentariolus historico-litterarius de fatis eruditorum apud potiores orbis gentes* (Magdeburg, 1735. Not seen).

scholar familiar with a particular field to examine an account of what might be done and determine how much of what had been suggested had been accomplished and what influence the account may have had on the course of investigation. For example, Georg Heinrich Welschius, *Somnium Vindiciani* (Augsbury, 1676. Not seen) is said to mention medical subjects calling for study. Medicine has, to be sure, advanced far beyond the stage it had reached in 1676 and the book has no practical value today. A historian may ask what value it had when it was published and what influence it may have exerted.

A problem that Mr. Wells or any maker of a subject index should face is to determine how fine a network of headings he wishes to use. No one seems to have discussed this problem, and yet the choice of headings has much to do with the usefulness of a subject-index or an encyclopedia, which are especially in this regard kindred reference works. Had he made an index to Sonnenschein's *Best Books*, the network would have been rather coarse. If he preferred, as would probably be the case, a somewhat finer network, he would do well to choose some list of subject headings made for library use. It would be difficult to find any other tabulation that would give him a relatively equal treatment of such subjects as astronomy, economics, agriculture, and medicine. He could not profitably call in the help of specialists, as he proposed to do, because it would be extremely difficult to get them to adopt a single

There is a copy in the library of the University of Tübingen. Around 1700 surveys of this sort were usually entitles "De fatis . . ." For the reference I am indebted to Dr. Rudolf Blum of the Deutsche Bibliothek, Frankfurt a.M. A later and famous example of a survey of a field of research is J. A. Ernesti, *Archaeologia literaria* (Leipzig, 1768) that reviews what had been accomplished in the study of archaeology and related subjects like writing, sculpture, cameos, metals, books, inscriptions, numismatics, painting, and architecture.

basis for choosing catchwords. If he did not insist on using the advice of specialists, he might have obtained from them the titles of the best handbook in each of their fields and have then instructed his secretary to compile a list of headings from the tables of contents or the indexes of these handbooks. Further advice from specialists at this early stage in carrying out his plan would, I think, have proved more confusing than helpful. Probably a list of headings made from textbooks would not be much different from a list used by a librarian. With this in hand he could readily compile from the card catalogues of any large American library a very satisfactory subject dictionary. If he wished to ensure its completeness for historical studies in the various fields, it would be an easy task to go through the earlier subject-indexes and transfer titles from the categories used in them to the categories he was using. Such a dictionary as he wished could have been made by a competent director and a staff of four or five workers in two or three years at no extravagant cost. He could then have called in specialists to read and enlarge the compilation.

One difficulty that Mr. Wells did not face and settle arises from the many demands made on any subject bibliography. It can be easily illustrated by comparing a subject-index of a specialized field with the one that his proposed committee of specialists might have made. Take, for example, an excellent subject-index of folklore—R. A. Beitl, *Wörterbuch der deutschen Volkskunde* (2d ed., Stuttgart, 1955), in which we find such headings as Eel (Aal), the Eucharist (Abendmahl), and Abortion (Abtreibung) with bibliographical references useful to a folklorist. I cannot imagine that a zoologist, theologian, or doctor would have contributed them. A mathematician who contributed articles dealing with numbers would not, in all likelihood, cite anything on the symbolism or magic use of the number three. For this reason subject-indexes like Watt's *Bibliotheca britannica* that collect references to the word without attention to its various meanings are often serviceable. Such a book as Wells proposed to make would almost necessarily be limited to the primary meanings of the catchwords. We need not regret that nothing came of his proposal. A subject bibliography of the sort that he suggested is to be seen in Werner Schuder, *Universitas litterarum* (1955) that is discussed a few pages later.

ROBERT ALEXANDER PEDDIE, *SUBJECT INDEX OF BOOKS PUBLISHED BEFORE 1880* (1933–1948)

In a *Subject index of books published before 1880* (Second series: *up to and including 1880*) Robert Alexander Peddie (1869–1951) showed an amazing diligence (4 vols., 1933–1948) by collecting and classifying at least 175,000 books.[7] His work complements the *Subject index* by George K. Fortescue and successors that lists books published after 1880 and owned by the British Museum. Since Peddie does not limit himself to books in the British Museum, I deal with it separately. In zeal Peddie, who is said to have spent thirty years in the reading room of the

---

[7] The following collation is too bulky to include in the text: First Series, 1933, pp. xi, 746; Second Series, 1935, pp. xvi, 858; Third Series, 1939, pp. xvi, 945; New (Fourth) Series, pp. vii, 872. See WBB, col. 487. According to Besterman, Peddie lists 40,000, 50,000, and 40,000 titles respectively in the first three series. The last volume, which Besterman overlooks, contains as many titles as its predecessors and the whole therefore contains at least 175,000 titles.

British Museum, can be compared with C. T. Hagberg Wright and his helpers, who made the *Subject-index* of the London Library (see below).

In the Preface to the First Series Peddie briefly states his purpose as follows (p. xiii):

It may be worth while to state that the main principle of selection of titles has been with the object of throwing as much light as possible on the smaller and more obscure subjects. Therefore less stress has been laid on the great general divisions of History, Geography, Literature and Religion on which subject information is always available. On the other hand works on the smaller industries, histories of towns and villages in Europe and America, books on out of the way subjects such as the Golden Rose or the Iron Mask, Lace Patterns or Type Specimens (to mention a few topics at random) will be found in most cases to be effectively dealt with.

He carries out his purpose very well. We cannot therefore characterize his work justly by commenting on his collections for Astronomy, Bibliography, English history, or Medicine. Much curious information about such headings can be gleaned by consulting the smaller headings that belong to these "general divisions," but we are not led to them by cross-references in any convenient way. Except for articles on Printing and closely related subjects, Bibliography, a field in which Peddie was especially competent and in which the bookshop with which he was connected specialized, is rather scantily represented. For example, the list of books of Type-specimens in the New (Fourth) series recapitulates lists in earlier volumes and includes additional titles. It was obviously of special interest to him and is a result of his experience as librarian of the St. Bride Foundation Typographical Library and his authorship of bibliographies of incunabula. Yet he does not cite here or in other articles pertinent bibliographies that he must have known or could have easily discovered. Thus, he makes collections of books of Ana in the Third and Fourth (New) Series and names unusual titles, but gives no references to bibliographies of them (see WBB, cols. 190–191). English history and geography is represented by many articles for counties, towns, and villages, but again pertinent bibliographies are not cited. This omission is typical of subject-indexes generally and Peddie follows the custom. In accordance with his "main principle of selection" we find curious specialized articles that may be serviceable to a historian of medicine: Brunonianism (an old medical theory), Phrenology, Spiritualism, Theriac (a medieval specific), and Women's Diseases. Peddie's interest in Technology is particularly important and characteristic. He had compiled a bibliography of engineering and metallurgy that may have drawn his attention to technological bibliography. We may also see here a reflection of the rapid development of technology since the Industrial Revolution and might compare Robert Watt's and Peddie's treatment of it. His collections for Agriculture (see also Potato), Alchemy, and Astrology are rich. Like Besterman (see WBB, I, p. xv and cols. 5328–5336), Peddie consulted the Classified subject catalogue of the Patent Office Library and chose subject headings from it. See also Microscope, Telescope, and Windmills for good examples of his work. He did not limit himself to modern technology.

In the Second series one notes twelve titles from 1847–1848 that deal with Ether (the anaesthetic), five sixteenth- and three seventeenth-century titles that deal with Chocolate, and generous numbers of titles on Horseshoeing (see also the Third series), Sailing, and Salmon. Peddie's treatment of literary subjects is not generous. Titles of books of Anecdotes and Jests, which might be called a minor category, are not numerous. There are scarcely any books on Enigmas, also a minor category. The articles on Proverbs are somewhat richer, and some of the titles are unusual. There are twelve Utopias in the New (Fourth) series and some bear titles that do not immediately indicate their nature. Peddie is a careful bibliographer. The long list of editions of the Edda (Fourth series) might have been assembled by consulting such obvious sources as histories of Icelandic literature.

The few bibliographers who commented on the *Subject index* have not judged Peddie's work fairly. Even the two obituaries that I have found show scant sympathy with what he was trying to do.[8] In one obituary we read: "he certainly enabled librarians to have for reference nearly complete author and subject indexes of the [nineteenth] century's books." With Quintin Waddington Peddie completed the English author catalogue with a volume for the years 1801–1836 (see WBB, col. 1251). This is something altogether different from the *Subject index* and should not be grouped with it. The emphasis of the *Subject index* is by no means on nineteenth-century books. It may appear to be so to a hasty reader because Peddie deals with many minor subjects in English geography and history, technology, and medicine, but such an article as Monsters represents his intentions and his success in carrying them out. It contains a generous number of books written before 1800 and a good account of continental writings. It should have been obvious to the most hasty bibliographer that the *Subject index* was, as its title suggests, intended to complement Fortescue's *Subject index of books in the British Museum published after 1880.*

[8] E. A. S., *The library association record,* LIII (1951), 102–103; *The library world,* LIII (1951), 190–191.

W. SWAN SONNENSCHEIN,
THE BEST BOOKS (1887)

The nature of Peddie's *Subject index* appears more clearly when we set it beside an index published some years earlier and another published some twenty years ago. W. Swan Sonnenschein, *The best books. A reader's guide and literary reference book. Being a contribution towards systematic bibliography* (1887; 2d ed. [reprinted several times and provided with a supplement], 1895; 3d ed.; 6 vols.; 1910–1935. See WBB, col. 485) and Peddie's *Subject index* are selective subject-indexes by a single hand that reject journal articles, minor publications, government publications, and dissertations. In its last edition Sonnenschein's 150,000 titles are comparable to Peddie's 175,000. Except for these details they have nothing in common. Peddie elects to deal with the "small and more obscure subjects" and avoids general categories; Sonnenschein prefers general categories and rejects minor headings. Peddie lists books for an inquirer to consult in a very large library; Sonnenschein chooses books that a reader might acquire for his own library or that, taken as a whole, might constitute a modern public library, Peddie includes books in Latin and western European languages generally before 1880; Sonnenschein names primarily modern books written in English. Peddie arranges his *Subject index* alphabetically; Sonnenschein employs a classification. Peddie had but one edition; Sonnenschein has had three steadily enlarged editions with several revisions of the second. This comparison suggests the problems that the maker of a subject-index must face and the decisions that he must make. A detailed characterization

of *The best books* seems unnecessary. It is as good a collection of well-selected books as can be made and is representative of many such collections.[9]

COLLECTANEA OF ALFRED ELA
AND GEORGE S. LOANE

Two files of notes on subjects may be mentioned briefly.
Both have disappeared and can be no longer traced in the
libraries which once had them. Alfred Ela, a frequent con-
tributor to *Notes and Queries,* bequeathed his Index-cata-
logue file to the Andover-Harvard Theological Library
sometime before 1940.[10] One can infer from the nature of
his notes in that journal that his collectanea dealt chiefly
with the humanities. The file is referred to as "very large."
James Tanis, the librarian, has looked very carefully for it
and cannot find anything remotely related to it. He has
also inquired to the Andover-Newton Library with a simi-

[9] Thanks to the kindness of the interlibrary loan services at the
Universities of California and Kansas I have seen Luís Nueda, *Mil
libros (Recuerdos bibliográficos). Reseñas claras y fieles del con-
tenido de más de un miliar de voluménes de ciencias, filosofía,
religión, litteratura: ensayos, novelas, teatro, etc. (414 autores, 1,148
obras). Las doctrinas e hipótesis más transcendentales en diversas
materias, los pensiamentos más bellos y profundos de los hombres
más eminentes de todos los tiempos* (8th ed.; Barcelona, 1956. Pp.
35, 1424). First published in 1940, it was enlarged in later editions
and received substantial additions in 1956, four years after its
author's death. In general, the books summarized have been accepted as important in intellectual history, but many, like Jules
Verne's novels, represent Nueda's choice. The arrangement is alphabetical according to authors. The classified index of subjects (pp.
1385–1406), which are conceived in very general terms, is obviously
scanty. It lists books by titles without specific references and will not
be very helpful. It is mentioned here for the sake of the subtitle and
because it is difficult to find in this country.

[10] *Notes and Queries,* CLVIII (1940), 324. I am indebted to William A. Jackson of the Houghton Library for aid and counsel in the
search.

lar result. George S. Loane (d. May 17, 1945) left his "copious array of MS notes" to be preserved in Dr. Williams's Library in Gordon Square and it, too, has vanished.[11] Arthur Hudd of the British Museum, who made inquiry for me, enlisted the aid of the librarian and conducted a diligent search for the file but discovered nothing. It is idle to conjecture whether we should bewail the loss of these materials. The neglect of the Falconet collectanea in the Bibliothèque nationale (see above) suggests that later workers might not have profited from them.

HERBERT S. HIRSHBERG, *SUBJECT GUIDE TO REFERENCE BOOKS* (1942)

Guides to reference books are subject-indexes to a particular kind of books and are furthermore usually restricted chiefly to contemporary works. For such reasons they have not in general been included in this study. By their titles Constance M. Winchell, *Guide to reference books* (6th ed., Chicago, 1951; suppl., 1954, 1956, 1960); John Minto, *Reference books* (London, 1929; suppl., 1931), which has not been entirely superseded by A. J. Walford, *Guide to reference material* (London, 1959); and similar works identify themselves at once as examples of a special category of bibliography.[12] They ordinarily classify the titles cited according to bibliographical rather than subject headings and thus guide the user only indirectly to subject matter. They naturally include many titles not concerned with subject matter and are usually limited, with some obvious exceptions, to works in one language. They are

[11] *Notes and Queries*, CLXXXVIII (1945), 264.
[12] See below. For other guides see WBB, cols. 3552–3557.

almost without exception very careful about the bibliographical details of the works cited.

A *Subject guide to reference books* (Chicago, 1942. Pp. xvi, 260) by Herbert S. Hirshberg, dean of the School of Library Science, Western Reserve University, sets itself apart by both title and contents from other guides to reference works. It approaches them from the point of view of their subject matter and not through a classification based on the categories of library science. In other words, it is an alphabetical list of subjects with citations of pertinent titles. Cross-references from one heading to another are numerous. These headings "correspond in general with those conventionally used in card catalogs, with some [unspecified] variations" (p. v). The choice of headings "was based in the first place upon a review and analysis of reference inquiries" at the information desk in various Ohio libraries and "was further influenced by the existence or nonexistence of reference books in the field". The category of nonexistent reference works might well have been an occasion for an instructive listing and discussion. Experience led Hirshberg to cite more than 350 titles [13] additional to those in Isadore G. Mudge, *Guide to reference works,* the forerunner of Constance M. Winchell's book mentioned above. Perhaps many of them could not have been appropriately included in the *Guide,* but their number suggests the difference in results obtained by proceeding from the opposite side of the reference desk.

Hirshberg's very practical book contains some 3000 references. It is planned with the inquirer's needs in mind. This appears in the fact that the same book may be cited under more than one heading. Thus, standard English dictionaries are named under both Abbreviations and under

[13] For the list of these see Hirshberg, pp. 219–231.

Dictionaries and Etymology. The variety of titles in the article Abbreviations offers a good example of what Hirshberg learned by studying inquiries for information. Here he names almanacs, biographical yearbooks, dictionaries of English and foreign languages, handbooks of literary history, and many more kinds of books, including Whitaker's *Peerage* (p. 4). Appropriate journals are found under such headings as Accounting, Advertising, Anthropology, Architectural Terms and Topics, and do not need to be searched for in a list of serials. The articles Astronomy, Bibliography, English History, and Medicine that I have ordinarily used in estimating the strength and weakness of a subject-index give no satisfactory idea of Hirshberg's *Subject guide* and are in fact rather inferior to many other articles in quality.

By way of commentary and with the intention of illustrating the variety of information assembled by Hirshberg, I note that Concordances (p. 190) might have a heading of its own. Mottoes (p. 144–145) is a heading but lacks cross references. Slogans (pp. 200–201) is also a heading and lacks a cross-reference to collections of proverbs or quotations, which often include slogans. Games and Sports (p. 104) are seen only from a school playground and consequently such works of historial and critical importance as W. W. Newell, *Games and songs of American children* (new and enl. ed., New York, [1911]), which has recently (1963) been reprinted by Carl Withers, and Alice B. Gomme, *The traditional games of England, Scotland, and Ireland* (2 vols.; London, 1894, 1898) are lacking. The article about Money (p. 143) concerns tables of exchange rate and books about coins, but does not lead to books on economic theory. I note two books new to me that list the

Last Words of famous men (pp. 127–128). These may serve as examples of the value of consulting every well-made reference guide to subject matter. The books cited are almost exclusively in English. The *Internationale Bibliographie des Buch- und Bibliothekwesens* (p. 27 is an exception that proves the rule. While one cannot reasonably object to the rule as Hirshberg applies it, a non-English title that is more useful than its English counterpart will often occur to a thoughtful reader.

Hirshberg's *Subject guide* illustrates well the characteristic method of a subject-index as well as the merits and defects of one limited to modern works in a single language. Its particular strength—and this has not been fully appreciated—lies in what it offers to John Q. Public in the United States. Note, as examples, the abundant references to books and journals dealing with Business: Consumer Education (p. 73), Convention Dates (p. 74), Cost of Living (p. 76); Technology generally; and the American aspects of political and other general subjects like Education, Government Publications, Political Platforms.

In this history of subject-indexes Hirshberg's *Subject guide* exemplifies once more the independence of their compilers. Since it did not have a second edition (which Hirshberg was ready to make), we may infer that librarians did not find it useful. He set his standard too low, accepted all too readily what he collected by questionnaires, and failed to dominate his materials. Had he compiled the book in his own way and had he then enlarged, corrected it in the light of the questionnaires, the result would have been altogether different. The success of Courtney's *Register of national bibliography* and the failure of Hirshberg's *Subject guide* give point to these criticisms.

WHO KNOWS—AND WHAT (1949)

This reference book is both a *Who's Who* and a subject-index. Compiled by Marquis—Who's Who, a Chicago publishing house that has for many years published *Who's who* in all its varieties, it describes itself by its title: *Who knows—and what, among authorities—experts—and the specially informed* (1949. Pp. lvii, 796). This listing of 35,000 men was successful enough to enjoy an enlarged edition (pp. 907, including 76 pp. of indexes) in 1954. It is a listing of men rather than books (which are often but not systematically cited) and is provided with a classified index. It does not undertake to name all who know about a subject or to list all subjects. Legal and medical subjects are generally excluded, although historical aspects of these fields are admitted. Subjects that the editors do not regard as "exposed to general reference enquiry" are excluded. The list of specialized collections and libraries (2d ed., pp. 851–859) is worth noting as a supplement to surveys of American library resources. Useful as it is, *Who knows —and what* is not a subject-index in a strict sense as I have used the term. It is a practical illustration of the advice often given in seventeenth-century guides to scholarship to consult libraries and scholars and engage in learned conversation. The advice has rarely been accompanied by definite recommendations.

MORTIMER J. ADLER, *THE GREAT IDEAS. A SYNTOPICON OF THE GREAT BOOKS OF THE WESTERN WORLD* (1952)

This reference work by Mortimer J. Adler (1902–   ), which I shall refer to as the *Syntopicon,* is a topical index of passages selected for their importance in intellectual, political, or social history. It differs from them in being merely an index and in endeavoring to reduce the number of headings to a minimum. The arrangement is alphabetical in 102 headings ranging from Angel to World. They are analyzed minutely with citations of pertinent references and are supplemented by bibliographies of pertinent books. It does not appear from the long and instructive discussion of the making of the *Syntopicon* (II, 1219–1299) that the compiler and his staff consulted any predecessors, although the subject matter and the choice of sources is very similar in many dictionaries of quotations. The references to Hegel, Nietzsche, and Freud and to belles lettres are a valuable extension of the sources ordinarily used.

The *Syntopicon* (2 vols., pp. ll, 1082; xxvi, 1346) deals only with what may be called "philosophical" ideas, that is to say, ideas discussed in Philosophy in its modern sense, Theology, Economics, Political Science, and Sociology. The articles Astronomy and Medicine, which concern only general ideas, may perhaps be the easiest means for a reader to form an idea of the method of the book and its utility to him. They mention nothing specific like comets or cancer. The book is blessed with a very carefully made index (II, 1303–1345) of terms used. It has the great merit of being a fresh survey of standard and influential works. While it is helpful with references for a general discussion of war, it will not—and is not intended to—inform the reader about books on Waterloo, its military strategy, its economic importance, its consequences in political and social life, or allusions to it in belles lettres.

WERNER SCHUDER, ED.,
UNIVERSITAS LITTERARUM (1955)

In perhaps every respect but the manner of its making the *Universitas litterarum. Handbuch der Wissenschaftskunde* (Berlin, 1955. Pp. xx, 819), edited by Werner Schuder, is a contrast to Adler's *Syntopicon*. Both were compiled by a staff of workers under the direction of a general editor. Beyond that resemblance they have nothing in common. Schuder's term "litterae" (letters, literature), like eighteenth-century historia litteraria, embraces all learning, science, and technology but does not include belles lettres. As he says (p. v), "May this first attempt at a complete survey of the sciences help men to perceive the task and the field of scholarly activity." The *Universitas litterarum* is a classified compilation of more than 15,000 treatises and bibliographies. It is not, as historia litteraria ordinarily was, an interpretative historical account by a single hand but a compilation of bibliographical references introduced by a brief explanatory preface, in other words, virtually an encyclopedia. What is not currently useful is rarely mentioned. The prefaces are often oversimplified. The references are usually limited to modern works with a predominance of German titles. These works are ordinarily much too technical to help a layman, even if he could easily get access to them. The result—and perhaps it is unavoidable—is that readers do not get a sound understanding of the subject discussed. The preface is likely to consist of obvious generalizations and a handful of undefined technical terms that cannot be found in ordinary dictionaries. The subjects mentioned number more than 4,000. Since the emphasis of the *Universitas litter-*

arum is strongly technological, a translation of the brief
section (p. 363) on Refrigeration (Kühl- und Kältetech-
nik), which I choose quite at random, will illustrate these
criticisms:

Technology of Refrigeration
If it is not essential to reach zero, cold air and cold water can
often produce a sufficient degree of refrigeration. For lower
temperatures cold-producing machines are used that produce a
reduction of temperature either by mechanical means (com-
pression engines) or by dissolving and expelling a gas from a
liquid (absorption machines) and utilize it for refrigeration. For
the lowest temperatures and the liquefaction of gases ap-
paratuses are used that employ the Linde-technique.

A bibliography of five German handbooks dealing with
refrigeration is appended (all the works cited were published between 1947 and 1952) and a second paragraph
names five German journals (all founded in 1949 and
1950) devoted to the subject.

It is idle for a layman to criticize this survey of refrigeration for its competence. Any defects it may have are
to be explained by the editor's choice of a collaborator
and need not concern us. The criticism that might be
offered is of an entirely different kind. An intelligent layman gains an incomplete notion from these seven lines of
the nature of refrigerating machines, for the "Linde-technique" is left undefined. He learns nothing of the historical
and practical significance of refrigeration. Refrigeration
remains in a scientific and technological vacuum. With a
passionate desire for information a layman might pursue
the subject further with the aid of the handbooks cited in
the bibliography and perhaps obtain in this way what he
wants. For many reasons he is not likely to do so. Whether
it would be possible to write a different account and

whether it would be worthwhile to make the effort are difficult questions to answer.

The fate of the *Universitas litterarum* in one library under my observation is instructive and bears out what has just been said. Received by the University of California Library in August, 1955, it was catalogued and put on the shelves of the general library, not in the reference room. In the two years and a half since that time it has been taken out of the library by only two readers. Although others may have consulted it without taking it out of the library, it is still as fresh in appearance as it was on the day it came from a bookdealer. It does not stand among reference books in the library stacks, but among books on the "classification of knowledge," where I am afraid few searchers for a general reference book will find it. Although it obviously contains useful information, it will (I conjecture) share the dusty fate of eighteenth-century historia litteraria.

Since the editor of the *Universitas litterarum* no doubt used all possible diligence to obtain the best collaborators, it seems unnecessary to make a formal and systematic survey of their remarks on astronomy, English history, and medicine. I can be brief and choose only the sections for linguistic and literary studies (pp. 542–587) and bibliography (pp. 739–751). The remarks about literary and linguistic studies do not, it seems to me, give any adequate account of recent developments in these fields. Such remarks as these about a very sophisticated discipline are altogether inadequate: "Finno-Ugric linguistics has likewise gained greatly in importance in eastern and western Europe. For this reason [and] especially very recently, many treatises [based on] Slavic investigations in comparative linguistics and comparative literature have become available" (p. 584). This cannot be called helpful, and the suggestion that Slavic studies have had a large role in the development of Finno-Ugric studies is doubtful. The failure to include the *Finno-ugrische Forschungen* and *Studia fennica* among the three bibliographical references is unfortunate, for these journals contain good international bibliographies. The section devoted to bibliography in general seems to me to be little, if any better than the one just described. Twelve pages cannot possibly be sufficient to name and describe the modern developments. Enough of such criticism. The *Universitas litterarum* contains a great deal of information in a convenient arrangement. It is especially useful in scientific and technological fields, where it offers a non-specialist an introduction, often written in very technical terms, to subjects about which he cannot inform himself easily.

NATIONAL SUBJECT CATALOGUES OF PUBLICATIONS: CARL GEORG AND LEOPOLD OST, *SCHLAGWORTKATALOG* (1889–1913); *SUBJECT GUIDE TO BOOKS IN PRINT* (1957–)

Indexes of books according to subjects, when they are restricted in their scope according to time, place, or matter, have not in general been included in this study. The earlier lists for the booktrade are characteristically classified lists and are therefore subject-indexes of a sort. With the general adoption of an alphabetical arrangement in such lists subject-indexes became necessary. These we shall not consider here except to note that the German national list was provided with an index of subjects during the course of the nineteenth century. The *Catalogue gén-*

éral de la librairie française (1867–   ), which is often called "Lorenz," also has an index of subjects in the later volumes. It is not always easy to learn from the many bibliographies of current national publications whether an index of subjects is present.

Two publications separate from a national bibliography may be mentioned because they are subject-indexes. Carl Georg and Leopold Ost, *Schlagwort-Katalog. Verzeichnis der im deutschen Buchhandel erschienenen Bücher und Landkarten in sachlicher Anordnung* (7 vols.; Leipzig, 1889–1913. See WBB, cols. 1648–1649) is a rearrangement of the national bibliography according to subjects. The *Subject guide to books in print. An index to the Publisher's trade list annual* (New York, 1957. 2d ed.; 1958), which is issued by R. R. Bowker Co., a firm closely associated with bibliography and the book trade, is, as its title indicates, severely restricted in its choice of titles. Such compilations as these are primarily intended for booksellers but can also serve scholarly purposes. Their limitations exclude them from more than mention here.

ROBERT W. MURPHEY, *HOW AND WHERE TO LOOK IT UP. A GUIDE TO STANDARD SOURCES OF INFORMATION* (1958)

In this book we see an unslackened interest in guides to information. It has a refreshingly novel approach and a considerable number of new titles. With the first sentences of his "Preface" (p. vii) one can readily agree: "Previously published general guides to reference sources have been designed almost exclusively either to meet the needs of professional librarians or to train professional librarians. These guides have been organized in patterns largely familiar only to the trained librarian and have assumed knowledge that few laymen possess." In saying this, he has, to be sure, overlooked Hirshberg's *Subject guide* (see above), but it is the exception that proves the rule. He continues with remarks of a somewhat more doubtful quality:

The extensive use of reference sources, however, is by no means limited to the librarian. On the contrary, only a small percentage of the reference works published each year are sold to libraries. The remainder are brought for school use, for home libraries, for consultation in offices, laboratories, and factories. Even those works bought by libraries are used far more frequently by laymen untrained in their use than they are by librarians.

On such beliefs as these Murphey bases his book.

How and where to look it up is based on a library formerly owned by Fact Research Service, Inc., of Chicago, to which Murphey added a thousand books of his own choice. He says that he has preferred to analyze a small number of books that are commonly available, that deal with subjects of general interest, and that are reasonably up-to-date, especially in "fields where up-to-dateness is an important consideration." All this means that few books printed before 1945 or in languages other than English are mentioned. He cites briefly (pp. 80–83) encyclopedias in foreign languages.

In his introductory remarks Murphey prepares us for a novel classification of materials that consists in the subdivisions: (1) "How to Find Out About People," pp. 212–258; (2) "How to Find Out About Places," pp. 259–310; and (3) "How to Find Out About Things," pp. 311–649. Within these large subdivisions the arrangement of headings is alphabetical. As the word "Things" might suggest, the third category deals abundantly with concrete subjects and less generously with ideas. A selection of headings in the third category will characterize the book: Address, Forms of (primarily with Reference to British nobility); Business Machines; Cactus; Copyright; Etiquette; Knitting; Nature Study; Weightlifting. The references are rather elementary in quality, and many, especially those found under "Do-It-Yourself," are to books telling "how to do it." The article Bazaars gives references to books on how to organize them but none on their history. Some headings are a bit surprising: Coptics, i.e., Coptic language and literature; Dinosaurs. Even when subject bibliographies could be easily cited, Murphey avoids them. The article Chess names several books on how to play the game but no bibliography. All this is in keeping with his declared purpose. He has, within his chosen limits, been generally successful.

The fields in which *How and where to look it up* is weak and often wholly unsatisfactory may have already suggested themselves. The account of Theology (p. 625), citing seven titles, will answer hardly any questions. In a book of this sort it can be called a serious fault when Proverbs is uncritical: standard English collections are lacking and only a Chinese collection, two miscellaneous international collections of indifferent merit, and David Kim's strange *Dictionary of American proverbs* are present. Can Murphey have looked at the last of these? Burton E. Stevenson's invaluable *Home book of English proverbs, maxims and familiar phrases* turns up under Quotations, to which there is no cross-reference. One can find little to praise in Specialized Books about Words (p. 111) where the books by J. T. Shipley and Edwin Radford are of doubtful value and Eric Partridge's *Dictionary of slang* is cited in an obsolete edition.

The Fact Research Service, Inc., that published this book was the library and research branch of the Spencer Press, Inc., owned by Sears Roebuck. The press published the *American Peoples encyclopedia* and other reference works. The enterprise was sold in August, 1961, to the Grolier Company, publisher of the *Encyclopedia Americana*. The library consisting of about ten thousand volumes was shipped to New York and was presumably dispersed. The *Encyclopedia Americana* does not maintain a research library. R. W. Murphey is now editor of the *Encyclopaedia Britannica yearbook*.

G. A. ZISCHKA, *INDEX LEXICORUM* (1959)

In what may well be the most recent subject-index, the *Index lexicorum. Bibliographie der lexikalischen Nachschlagewerke* (1959), Gert A. Zischka adopts a principle rarely used for selecting titles. As he uses the word, a "lexicon' is a reference work arranged like a dictionary and usually in alphabetical order. He intends to exclude dictionaries of languages, whether of one or more, because Wilhelm Zaunmüller was compiling the *Bibliographisches Handbuch der Sprachwörterbücher* (Stuttgart, 1958) at the same time. This wise decision prevents duplication and might have been extended to dictionaries of the vocabulary used by freemasons (p. 77), international botanical nomenclature, and many other specialized vocabularies. There are advantages and disadvantages attached to any principle of selection, and for the present purpose Zischka's choice does not recommend itself. Two centuries before him [J. B. Durey de Noinville] had employed it in a very careless and unsatisfactory *Table alphabétique des dictionnaires en toutes sortes de langues & sur toutes sortes de sources & d'arts* (Paris, 1758. Pp. iv, 290. See WBB, col. 3189). The contents justify the title, but are almost exclusively dictionaries of languages. A *List of cyclopedias and dictionaries, with a list of directories* (Chicago, 1904. Pp. vi, 272. See WBB, cols. 1028, 1228, 3190) shows greater accuracy in details, cites more recent works, and does not range quite so widely. The former includes rather few works in languages other than French, and the latter only books then in the John Crerar Library, Chicago. Neither of them needs discussion here as a subject-index.

Zischka's *Index* is a work of motley contents, held together by the common characteristic of their similarity to a dictionary. It includes general encyclopedias, encyclopedians of particular disciplines or fields, collections of proverbs, quotations, and mottoes (but not inscriptions on tombstones), lists of place names, lists of painters, sculptors, and musicians, biographical dictionaries of all sorts, lists of coats of arms, flags, and abbreviations, dictionaries of anonyma and pseudonyma, anthologies of wit and humor, and many more subjects that admit of lexicographical treatment. An amazing variety of reference works, many of which I have neither seen nor heard of, is spread before us, but there is no index of the subjects with which they deal. One must find a desired title with such help as Zischka's table of contents can offer. Here are titles with answers to seemingly insoluble difficulties and categories in which the most obvious works are lacking. An altogether inadequate account of dictionaries of Anonyma and pseudonyma could easily have been improved. The *Index* is not a bibliography of bibliographies nor is it, in the strictest sense, a subject-index, but its greatest usefulness is in the latter category.

The *Index* ranges widely and cites a surprising variety

of unusual books. Where else will one find a reference to
N. Slonimsky, *Lexicon of musical invective. Critical as-
saults on composers since Beethoven's time* (New York,
1953. Not seen), cited on p. 167? A long list of dictionaries
of quotations, catchwords and slogans, proverbs, and
anecdotes (pp. 153–157) is divided according to languages, but not otherwise. It contains many curious titles,
including among others, dictionaries of Arabic, Persian,
and even Chinese quotations. I cannot easily find references to these elsewhere.[14] On the other hand, there is a
Greek collection here that was published in 1497 and is
much more easily available in recent editions that are not
cited. One is forced to say regretfully that the collections
are incomplete and disappointing. The classification leaves
something to be desired. Collections of Jests and Anecdotes
will be found in the section just described, but a book of
Bavarian jests is in Folklore (p. 92) and dictionaries of
stories and tales as well as a dictionary of similes appear
in the section for literature, authors, and scholars (pp. 132–
133). Since access to the contents is only through the
table of contents, such conflicts in classification are confusing. The *Index lexicorum* is a strange book and will on
occasion yield an unexpected bit of information.

SUBJECT-INDEXES
OF INSTITUTIONAL LIBRARIES

In his *Index universalis alphabeticus* (1612) Justinianus
offered a subject-index based largely on the holdings of a
single library (see above), but it was not recognized at

---

[14] See a good list in Norma Olin Ireland, *An index to indexes. A
subject bibliography of published indexes,* Useful reference series,
67 (Boston, 1942), pp. 58–61.

the time for what it was and set no model for later bibliographers to imitate. The large subject-indexes of the Imperiali, Lamoignon, and Soubise libraries that were made in the eighteenth century concern private libraries but had in contemporary practice a wider use than they might have today, but only the first of them was printed and we see no beginnings of a bibliographical tradition. J. C. Daehnert's subject-index of the University of Greifswald library (1775–1776. See above,) enjoyed no success. In Greifswald and elsewhere the local manuscript catalogues for users of the library gave all the subject information that readers desired. Few saw the utility of a printed subject catalogue that cited books under more than one heading or served scholars who might never come to the library.

For various reasons the value of a printed subject catalogue came to be perceived in the 1880's. Many alphabetical institutional catalogues had been published in France and the United States.[15] These rarely aimed to give subject information, although the need for it was obvious. Furthermore, the development of cataloguing, especially in the United States, brought with it a generous treatment of subject matter and emphasized its usefulness. G. K. Fortescue (1847–1912), Assistant Keeper of Books in the library of the British Museum, does not clearly say what motives led him to compile the *Subject index of modern works added to the library of the British Museum since 1880* (19 vols., 1886–   ), but we see in it a start in a new direction. A generation later Robert Alexander Peddie (1869–1951) made a complement to it in his *Subject index of books published before 1880* (4 vols., 1933–

[15] For a list of these see Henri Stein, *Manuel de bibliographie générale* (Paris, 1897), Appendice III. Répertoire des catalogues d'imprimés des principales bibliothèques du monde entier, pp. 711–768.

1948), paying special attention to minor and neglected subjects. Although generally similar in plan and execution, the *Subject-index of the London Library* (4 vols., 1909–1955) met a need somewhat different from that met by Fortescue's and Peddie's compilations. The London Library lends many books to readers outside London and for them the *Subject-index* is a convenient guide. In an essay "Meditations on El Greco" Aldous Huxley says that, when he was ready to visit Spain, he would go to the London Library and look up Spain in the subject-index.

Only in the last few years do we see signs that the usefulness of subject-indexes are beginning to be appreciated outside the walls of the institutions whose stores are listed in them. This appreciation finds a very practical expression in publishing them, when in manuscript, or in reprinting them, when they have been published. For example, G. K. Hall & Co., Boston, Mass., has recently published the *Library Catalogue* (i.e., subject catalogue) *of the Warburg Institute, University of London.* It is discussed below. This publishing house is also issuing the *Botany Subject Index* of the U.S. Department of Agriculture (15 vols., pp. 15, 040), the *Catalogue of the Ayer collection* (American and American Indians) in the Newberry Library (16 vols., pp. 8, 062), the *Catalogue of the Hispanic Society of America* (10 vols., pp. 10,000), the *Dictionary Catalogue, Oriental Collection, New York Public Library,* (16 vols., pp. 15, 166), and others. Such catalogues as these are not, in general, included in Theodore Besterman, *A World Bibliography of bibliographies* (see I, p. xvi).

The great value of these subject-indexes does not need to be stressed. Apart from their general usefulness, which depends on the size of the library, the nature of the collection, and the care with which the books have been catalogued, they tell where a desired book can be found. Their limitations are as obvious as their merits. They list only the books in a particular library and are necessarily incomplete. They are likely to show limitations in respect to the countries where the books were printed and the languages in which they were written. In the British Museum *Subject index* books printed outside Great Britain and books in languages not generally read are, as we might expect, less generously represented than books received in the Museum's capacity as a depository library. Four subject-indexes—two of general quality, a subject-index of older books, and a specialized subject-index—will be commented on here.

Subject index of the modern works added to the Library of the British Museum (1886–　); *Subject-Index of the London Library* (1909–　); *Library of Congress catalog. Books: subjects* (1955–　)

The titles and the circumstances of publication make the nature of these institutional subject-indexes sufficiently clear and a critical examination of them seems pedantic. Let me present them in a fashion entirely different from any used before in this study. The lightheartedness and brevity of my comments should not disguise their great value and my admiration for them.

No one who has lived in the company of catalogues and especially subject catalogues can fail to feel them as personalities. The *Subject-index* of the Library of the British Museum [16] is a conscientious civil servant trained in the universities of Oxford or Cambridge in letters or history.

[16] For some interesting details about the making of this catalogue see Henry Jennes's obituary of G. K. Fortescue, *The Library*, 3d Ser., IV (1913), 1–45, especially pp. 35 ff. Beginning in 1961, this index is published in a new format from the original library cards.

He reads widely and with good judgment. He takes good care of all put in his charge and enlarges it judiciously. He looks in the directions that might be expected and somewhat further and more deeply than the lady of the London Library does. He is interested in British history and literature, Africa, Australia, Canada, India, and the Commonwealth generally, and the United States, but gives less attention to Indochina, Java, and South America. He reads seriously in politics, economics, theology, and the classics. On a vacation in the Middle East he may have visited an archaeological "dig." The *Subject-Index of the London Library* (which I describe later in a conventional manner) is a charming, competent British lady who manages well her townhouse and her country estate. She provides reading and books for study for her husband in politics, current affairs, economics, theology, and the classics. He may be a squire with fields, a justice of the peace, perhaps even a member of Parliament, and is likely to be active in the parish. For vacations he and his wife travel abroad, and when they are in London, they visit the theatre. She looks after the household, takes the table seriously, and collects jade, jewelry, furniture, or pottery and china. The *Library of Congress catalog. Books: Subjects* (1955–   ) is an "organization man," efficient but caught in a tremendous machine. Insofar as his materials do not come to him automatically, he collects them according to the best obtainable advice. A specialist in "area studies" recommends a book on Tibet and someone in the Department of Agriculture one on onions. The grande dame of the *Catalogue* of the Bibliothèque nationale does not offer herself to the public in a subject catalogue. An admirable self-discipline in her author catalogue rejects such disorderly children as

anonymous and pseudonymous works.[17] We find her household neatly kept and abundantly furnished. I speak in the
warmest terms about all these friends of long standing.
Each commands respect and often awakens our love. With
his own individuality each has a characteristic share in our
community.

The *Subject-Index of the London Library* (1909–1955)

The *Subject-Index of the London Library* (4 vols.; 1909,
1923, 1936, 1955) compiled by the secretary and librarian
C. T. Hagberg Wright (1862–1940) and his successors is
rightly esteemed as a well-planned and carefully made
reference work of great value.[18] The "Preface" to the first
volume tells its history and gives much information of
general usefulness to anyone interested in subject-indexes.
"A library," Wright says, "without a Subject-Index is to
the unlearned reader what an unmapped country is to the
ordinary traveller, and is practically useless for his re-
searches. . . . Books unfortunately do not admit tabulation
and arrangement like objects in a museum. It is true that
attempts at classification on the shelves have been made
in all great libraries, but these attempts fall far short of
perfection, and can only be useful to those who are able
personally to visit the book-stores." Sir Leslie Stephen
(1832–1904), the president of the library in 1893, felt
keenly the need for a subject-index." 'The Library can
never be really useful,' he was wont to say, 'now that it

[17] It is perhaps worth saying that a copy of the catalogue of anonymous and pseudonymous works in the Bibliothèque nationale can be
consulted in the New York Public Library.

[18] Z.'s instructive review of the first volumes of the author catalogue is worth reading; see *The Library*, 2d Ser., IV (1903), 200–
206. Incidentally, the catalogue is valuable for the identification of
anonyma and pseudonyma.

has grown to its present size, until we have a Subject-Index. Books have increased so that the scholar even forgets what has been written on his own subject and requires a reminder.'" Sir Leslie lived to see the first volume of the *Subject-Index* in the stage of plans.

Wright found the London Library especially well adapted to a subject-index. "It was of the right size and of the right quality. A vast miscellaneous Library like the British Museum is too big to be analyzed and indexed except in sections, and that is useless to the ordinary reader. A library should not, it is suggested, contain more than a quarter of a million books, if the intention is to publish either an Author Catalogue or a Subject-Index of manageable size. The London Library fulfils this important condition.

"The peculiar merit of the London Library lies in the fact that since its foundation in 1841 it has been governed by committees of literary experts who in succession have devoted much of their leisure to its service, and during the seventy years have helped to bring together a collection of standard works in every subject."

From these remarks we see that Wright conceived his subject-index to be a guide for the general reader to a rather large and well-chosen collection of currently useful standard works, chiefly in English. While books of minor importance are generally lacking, the *Subject-Index* cites many journal articles. They were excerpted because they either were unusually long and informative or fell outside the usual limits of the journal in which they appeared and could therefore be easily overlooked.

The compilation of the *Subject-Index* was begun in May, 1905 and was completed in January, 1909. It was accomplished by the librarian, the assistant librarian, four junior

assistants (of whom two were typists), one boy clerk, and
one porter. It is nothing less than amazing that so few
workers could do so much in so little time in a room
seventy-four steps above the issue and reading rooms.
"Roughly 200,000 volumes—quartos, folios, octavos, and
the rest—have been laboriously carried there, partly by
lift and partly by hand, at the rate of about 200 a day."

Criticism and interpretation of this standard work is
probably unnecessary. It gives a general reader the information that it was intended to give. Wright and the subsequent editors have taken pains to use many headings
and to subdivide the larger ones in a convenient manner.
Cross-references are numerous. The *Subject-Index* is a
pleasure to use and is the port of first call for most English
readers and students. Other subject-indexes will be easier
to consult after one has become familiar with it. Its limitations are readily understood. There are here more references to Nigeria, a former British colony, than to Laos, a
former French colony. Books on ancient Scandinavian
religion are less abundant than those on the religions of
Rome, Greece, India, and China. Books on Economics,
Geography (especially Travels), History, and the Christian Religion are numerous; those on Technology are relatively few, except for writings on Aviation, Radium, and
like subjects of current interest. The books on legal and
medical subjects have a general rather than a specialized
character.

According to Wright the systematic enlargement of the
library began with its foundation in 1841. It would appear
from the dates of the titles in the *Subject-Index* of 1910
that funds became more abundant in the 1870s or 1880s.
Large and judicious purchases since then have given the
library its present character. It surveys admirably the

interests and tastes of cultured Englishmen during the last century, roughly since the Crimean War. The collection of books on that war is noteworthy and additions to it appear in the latest volume of 1955. In addition to well-chosen English titles the library contains a good representation of important French and German works, fewer in Italian and Spanish, and occasional books in the Scandinavian languages, Russian, and other languages.

The choice of headings is, as Wright says in the preface to the first volume, based on the American Library Association List of headings with some modifications that I have not attempted to discover. The article Bibliography with many cross-references offers a good review of modern writings and would deserve study as a definition. Particularly interesting is its recognition of subject-indexes as a category of bibliography. They are not, as is generally the case, scattered among such categories as general bibliography, library catalogues, journals, and so on. The subdividing of headings and the cross-references are admirable. Astronomy is subdivided into Atlases & Maps, Bibliography, Biographical Collections, Biographies, Dictionaries, History (Ancient & Medieval), History (General & Mod.), Miscellaneous Works (subdivided in five periods), Observations (subdivided according to regions: Africa, America, Arctic Regions, Asia, etc.), Observatories, Oriental, and Periodicals. Twenty-seven cross-references are appended.

The general emphasis is strongly historical with special regard to Social Life and Civilization. There is usually a subheading Social Life for the large geographical or political areas. Many headings are place names or personal names. Towns and counties in Great Britain are presumably almost completely represented, and those of countries ruled or visited by Englishmen, especially India, are favored headings. Patrons of the London Library have a strong interest in Religion—Church of England, Roman Catholicism, and Protestant sects—as well non-Christian religions like Hinduism. They call for books on Gardens, Housing, Metal-Work (with many cross-references), Sport (a separate heading for Cricket), and the economic problems of Victorian and modern England like the Poor. The generous attention paid to Ballads and Songs, Birds, Cookery, Coronations is to be expected. At first sight Convents and Nuns seems surprisingly rich, but the first title under this heading in the last volume of the *Subject-Index* is Monica Baldwin, *I leap over the wall* and this may explain it. Such headings as Hypnotism, Suggestion (Mental), the Supernatural, Telepathy, and those suggested by cross-references recall the interests of the later Conan Doyle that no doubt many shared. Literature is represented by critical works and anthologies; individual dramatists, novelists, and poets and criticisms of them are referred to the Author Catalogue. The article Wit and Humour gives a good account of both critical writings and collections, especially jest-books. The collection of Sagas is larger than one might expect. Few subject-indexes see the task more clearly and accomplish it more successfully.

The *Library catalog of the Warburg Institute* (1952)

The following description of this *Library catalog* is limited to what can be learned from a prospectus issued by the publisher G. K. Hall & Co., Boston, Mass., and calls for no change after having seen the reprinted catalogue. This company is reproducing a manuscript copy made for the Michigan State University. We are told that "the reproduction represents the state of the library as it was in 1952. Since that time the library has expanded and the sections of the catalog have been supplemented by new titles and distinguished by more sub-divisions. However, these amplifications are small in comparison with the whole list of the library." Since the scope of the Warburg Institute is limited, comment on this reproduction is brief and is intended rather to suggest the novelty of the idea. "The Warburg Institute of the University of London provides research on the survival and revival of classical antiquity in European civilization. It is concerned with the questions of what antiquity signified in different epochs, cultural centers and fields of human activity. Central to the development of the collection is the idea that the history of art should be studied in its interaction with other branches of learning, which in turn demand the same elaboration. . . . The 100,000 volumes are divided into the following main sections: 1) Religion, Natural Science and Philosophy; 2) Language and Literature, 3) Fine Arts and 4) Social and Political Life." In the later somewhat more detailed account of the contents of the *Library catalog* Astronomy and Medicine appear in section I, Bibliography in section II, and English History in section IV, under the sub-division "History of Social and Political Institutions in Southern and Northern Europe." The novelty of this classification calls for no comment here. The program of the institute has no place for technology or the vernacular literatures, except to the extent that they may appear as survivals or continuations of classical antiquity. We have in this *Library catalog* a gratifying recognition of the importance of the subject catalogue, to which the subject-index is a closely allied reference aid.

THE SCENE CHANGES

In the 1870s men proposed to use new developments in photography and the art of printing in subject bibliographies of various kinds, but the time was not ripe. About the same time modern cooperative techniques that had been the ideals of Pierre Blanchot and Sir William Petty two centuries before became practical with the rise of library science. The advances in more recent years have been in various directions. I have just touched on the reproductions of subject-indexes, chiefly library catalogues. Fremont Rider's microcards may render subject-indexes unnecessary in some fields by making it possible to assemble all the needed reference material in a compact form; see *The scholar and the future of the research library. A problem and its solution* (New York, 1944). Such ideas as these deal, however, with using information already classified and not with discovering and assembling it.

The modern development of bibliography known as "documentation" [19] and general subject-indexes have the same function: "Documenter c'est réunir, classer et distribuer les documents de tout genre dans tous les domaines de l'activité humaine" or, in the terms of library science, "the canalization of graphic records to all users, for all purposes and at all levels (of use) in such a way as to maximize the social utilization of recorded human experience." These definitions are enough for our purposes. Al-

[19] For orientation I have used a modest and well-informed book with a generous bibliography (pp. 166–182): Th. P. Loosjes, *Dokumentatie van wetenschappelijke literatuur* (Amsterdam, 1957. Pp. xvi, 184). The definitions quoted above will be found in Loosjes, on p. 9. Fernand Terron, *L'information* (Que sais-je?, 1000, [Paris, 1962]) deals rather with disseminating than collecting or classifying information.

though documentation may yield the results to be hoped for and may replace the comprehensive subject-indexes we have studied, it is a procedure and not a finished product. The procedure and examples cited by Loosjes are almost exclusively concerned with recent publications in the fields of the natural and biological sciences. Loosjes points out (pp. 9, 75, and elsewhere) the considerable difference between these fields and the humanities, with the social sciences perhaps occupying a middle position or inclining more to the former. He remarks (p. 76) that documentation in the modern sense begins in the nineteenth century. It is altogether likely that its techniques will find increasing use in the humanities. See an extremely interesting development that looks in this direction in Bengt Holbek's technique for classifying fables.[20] Documentation means compiling information that exists in various forms and places, but it does not create comprehensive subject-indexes such as have been described in the preceding pages.

A LONG LOOK BACK, A GLANCE AHEAD, AND FAREWELL

With almost astronomical regularity a new conception of the subject-index as a form of bibliography has arisen at the end of a century. The old pattern may persist into the new century for a few years; the new pattern may come into being in the last years of the old century. These minor variations need not prevent us from taking the end of a century as a convenient landmark. The classified subject-index of the sixteenth century—Gesner's *Pandectae* and *Partitiones*, Spach's *Nomenclator*, and Mareschal's *Guide*

[20] "The use of punch cards," *Arv*, XVI (1960), 156–161.

—did not survive into the next century. The new alphabetical subject-index that was forecast in the *Bibliotheca materiarum* by Molanus, who died in 1585, appeared in Draud's *Bibliotheca classica* of 1611 and Justinianus's *Index* of 1612. The *Bibliotheca materiarum* itself was not published until 1618. The atrophy of subject-indexes was already to be seen in unsuccessful proposals made by Hartley, Huselith, Loescher, and Huselitt immediately before and after 1700 and continued through Reneaume's *Projet* of 1839 to Le Chevalier de Pougens's *Bibliographie encyclopédique* of 1780. Future developments were in the making in Daehnert's subject-index of the University of Greifswald library and a subject-index of German journals. In some ways the nineteenth century recapitulated what had gone before. The comprehensive subject-index awoke again in Robert Watt's *Bibliotheca britannica,* continued in the *Nouveau manuel,* and in a somewhat novel manner in Brunet's *Table méthodique* that he enlarged by a selection of modern books. How far comprehensive national lists of manuscripts (which were partly realized) and comprehensive national bibliographies (which were not) encouraged somewhat similar proposals of subject-indexes that were made in the latter half of the nineteenth century seems doubtful. Opportunities to work on a grand scale were supported by advances in printing (the use of slugs in stereotyping) and library technique (the use of movable cards). It still seemed somehow possible to control all that had been written and printed. The new and characteristic emphases of the nineteenth century appeared in developments contrary to those just suggested. Bibliography in general and subject-indexes in particular became selective and adapted themselves to contemporary needs and interests. Bibliography passed from scholarly hands into the hands of librarians and then into the hands of publishing firms. The emphasis shifted from comprehensiveness to contemporary usefulness. Petzholdt, *Bibliotheca bibliographica* (1866), wavered now in one direction and now in the other. The selective subject-index limited in some characteristic manner became typical. Its choice of titles was determined by the ownership of the books listed, the manner in which the references were published, the quality of the books as authorities, or their availability according to the language in which they were written. Subject-indexes of the great libraries naturally ranged more widely and held to these limitations less strictly than subject-indexes of other kinds did. The emphasis was on modernity and accessibility, in the matters of location and language. Without a moment's hesitation Wells in his proposal of 1936, Hirshberg and Murphey in the 1940s, Schuder and Adler in the 1950s plumped for usefulness to a modern reader and cited recently published books or, only when none is available, an old one. The *Syntopicon* might seem to run contrary to the trend, but Adler has chosen only those fundamental ideas from the past that he believes to be essential for modern times. Zischka's *Index lexicorum* with a purely formal basis of selection and a classified arrangement is an anomaly.

A remarkable faith has inspired men to make subject-indexes for more than four centuries, from Gesner to Zischka. It is, I think, well-founded, but various circumstances explain why their work has not found the appreciation it deserves. In the first place, the makers of subject-indexes have not had an adequate command of bibliography generally to see the nature of the task. They are not familiar enough with reference works to establish a place for the subject-index among them. This failure appears in the previously mentioned neglect of bibliographers to recognize general subject-indexes as a category.[21] The makers of subject-indexes fail all too often to see that their work need not and should not duplicate other reference works. They include useful references along with references readily obtainable elsewhere. This criticism applies only in part to Gesner's *Pandectae* and *Partitiones,* which cite encyclopedic works in appropriate places, and concerns a fault that becomes more and more serious in the course of time. Even by the end of the sixteenth century specialized bibliographies had increased in number and made the task of making a subject-index correspondingly easier. Israel Spach saw this in 1598 when he said that he would not cite general works under specialized headings but would expect his reader to be aware of the general heading. If Robert Watt had perceived that information about the editions of a classical author was already available, he could have contented himself with appropriate citations of Harwood's or Fabricius's bibliographies. Ulysse Chevalier and W. P. Courtney could have made a similar economy by referring to a few standard historical bibliographies, literary histories, and encyclopedias. The substantial reduction in the size of their subject-indexes that would have resulted would have meant no sacrifice of information.

A general fault of subject-indexes has been often referred to in this study. The compilers have not consulted their predecessors and show little awareness of the special problems and value of a subject-index. There is no con-

[21] Louis Shores, *Basic Reference Sources* (Chicago, 1954), p. 239, recognizes "special indexes" but makes no mention of general subject-indexes. R. W. Murphey (see above) does not cite modern general subject-indexes that might have been useful and has no occasion to refer to the *Bibliotheca britannica.*

tinuing and developing bibliographical tradition that might have created an invaluable reference work. We see such a tradition in the history of bibliographies of incunabula. Johann Saubert listed those at Nuremburg in 1643, Philip Labbé those at Paris in 1653, and Cornelius à Beughem made a general list in 1689. The later history runs through Ludwig Hain's *Repertorium* (1826–1838) to the *Gesamtkatalog der Wiegendrucke* that was begun in 1925 and has now ceased publication. In every regard the history of subject-indexes offers a contrast to the history of bibliographies of incunabula. It began a century earlier; it shows marked confessional influences; it develops no generally accepted bibliographical procedure; it is strongly marked by nationalism; it chronicles works by men who knew little or nothing of cooperation; and it changes in character with the passage of time. Gesner's *Pandectae* looks chiefly to the classics, contemporary reference works, and books obtainable in northern Switzerland; modern subject-indexes emphasize the natural and physical sciences. Spach, Bolduanus, and Mareschal know nothing of one another. The *Bibliotheca materiarum* by the Catholic Molanus is an unintended complement to the *Partitiones* by the Protestant Gesner. The *Bibliotheca exotica* and Draud's *Bibliothecae* contain very little of what sixteenth-century compilers had assembled. We might continue in this fashion at great length. Had any compiler added references to his predecessors, he would have made his book indispensable. He would not have found it necessary to sacrifice one whit of his individual method and predilections. Such a book might have established a bibliographical tradition of the subject-index.

Compilers of subject-indexes do not ordinarily state the limitations within which they work and do not, I am afraid, always clearly perceive them. A demand for completeness is a demand for more than any man can satisfy, but we can properly ask him to recognize his deficiencies and then deal with them in a kindly manner. Compilers have been limited by their resources, their command of languages, and their decision to exclude certain kinds of materials. In pursuing an inquiry a reader must see clearly how important each of these limitations may be and must know how to deal with it.

At all times and in all countries bibliographers of subject matter are limited to books within their reach or at least known to them by titles. The full force of this limitation has never been perceived. An ingenious meditation on the reading and productivity of literary historians by Gerhard Eis, professor of German literature at Heidelberg, is instructive and can be readily generalized.[22] He was seated, he says, in the reading room of a library of moderate size when the thought occurred to him that he would like to know the contents of the books—perhaps 60,000 in number—around him. An estimate based on reading a book a day convinced him that this was entirely out of the question. If he had begun at 15 and should continue to read at this rate until he was 70, he would have 20,075 days for the task and would have read only one-third of the books. Deductions for military service, vacations, and illness would substantially reduce the figure. During a lifetime a fortunate literary historian, he thinks, can make the acquaintance of 10,000 volumes; a man of forty can know only half as many. These sobering thoughts might be turned into an argument for the improvement of our subject-indexes. Professor Eis makes a practical appli-

[22] "Von der Belesenheit und Fruchtbarkeit des Literarhistorikers," *Ruperto-Carola*, XXI, 119–123.

cation of his meditations. He quotes the following figures from a volume of criticism published in the early 1890s. In 1881 there were published more than 80 volumes of verse, more than 30 new editions, perhaps 20 volumes of translations, 10 anthologies,—in all, almost 150 volumes, and these include only part of what appeared in half a dozen journals devoted to verse. The figures of 1881 have long since been surpassed. What control of this flood can a literary historian have and when will he have time or strength to acquaint himself with verse in foreign languages, its influence in Germany, and with critical works?

In addition to the limitations imposed by time and human strength, the resources available to scholars set bounds they cannot exceed. The largest public or private libraries before 1700 were small according to modern standards and owned no considerable proportion of existing books. It is amazing what the diligence of Gesner, Spach, or Bolduanus in the sixteenth or early seventeenth centuries and of Lipenius, Marucelli, or Savonarola at the end of the seventeenth century accomplished with this handicap. Furthermore, the reference works and especially the lists made for the book trade were by no means satisfactory and were lacking in many countries. They were rarely known outside the countries in which they appeared. Finally, the lack of knowledge of languages has always been a handicap to the maker of a subject-index, and its significance has increased with the passage of time. In the Renaissance and the seventeenth century scholarly works were written in Latin, although both Italy and England showed a growing preference for the vernacular. From 1700 on the use of the native language grows rapidly. Under the circumstances we may expect references to English, Italian, and Spanish titles to be relatively inadequate in the earliest subject-indexes that were made in Switzerland and Germany, and we may expect them to be similarly inadequate in modern times for Dutch, Italian, Scandinavian, and less usual languages. Compilers of subject-indexes do not show themselves to be fully aware of such limitations. It was scarcely possible for makers of the earliest subject-indexes to overcome them and makers of modern ones are either unconscious of the limitations or not disposed to use the available means to discover materials in languages unfamiliar to them. The disappearance of Latin as an international means of communication, growing nationalism, the rising tide of books in the compiler's own language, and the desire of each man to make his book in his own way prevented the making of subject-indexes comprehensive and useful enough to establish themselves as indispensable reference aids.

The maker of a subject-index has undertaken an impossible task. Although he knows this, he does not face the fact and state clearly for himself or others what he can do, what its value is, and what means exist to remedy his unavoidable deficiencies. He usually thinks in more or less comprehensive terms. His book cannot help falling between two stools. When he lists relatively elementary books, as the admirable *Subject-Index of the London Library* does, he competes with the information offered by an encyclopedia. When he is more sophisticated, as Robert Watt was in the *Bibliotheca britannica,* he gives information useful only to a specialist and yet is necessarily incomplete. If he limits himself to currently useful books, his work quickly becomes obsolete. If he includes titles of all sorts and dates, he is damned for being "uncritical" and his unwieldy book finds few users. In naming these two subject-indexes I have intended to choose works that, within the limitations their makers accept, seem excellent. A compromise that will satisfy everyone is obviously out of the question. Although makers of subject-indexes have often aimed at being comprehensive (an intentional restriction to the best books or books in a particular language is most often found in recent subject-indexes), they have failed for many reasons to name all the pertinent titles. The quality of a subject-index is too easily and superficially tested by looking up a subject with which the inquirer is already familiar. We must be grateful for what a subject-index yields and must not complain loudly about its deficiencies.

The user of a subject-index has responsibilities as well as its compiler. He must be aware of the strength and weakness of the reference aid he is using and he must understand clearly what information he wants and what a subject-index can give him. He must be able to select what will serve his purpose, whether it is a general work, a work dealing with a particular period or country, a work concerned with details, or a historical survey. The compiler will rarely make descriptive or critical comment to guide his reader in making a choice. He should see that subject-indexes have peculiarities of their own and should be guided accordingly. They can be separated into two large classes, one including chiefly recent compilations of currently useful books and the other including more comprehensive compilations of all the titles available to their makers. Robert Watt, *Bibliotheca britannica* (1819–1824), the *Nouveau manuel* (1857), and Brunet's *Table méthodique* (1865) may be regarded as mountainpeaks on the watershed dividing subject-indexes listing books of all dates on subjects of all kinds from those listing modern books on modern subjects. The reader should know before opening a subject-index what he is likely to find in it. He should not hope to find much about the Gothic romance in the *Bibliotheca britannica* or much about mesmerism in the *Subject-Index of the London Library*. He should know that the latter will guide him to books for a "general reader" on subjects that interest a cultured and widely read Englishman: British life, politics, and significant figures in the widest national and international contexts, Africa (excluding Portuguese areas and including French areas bordering the Mediterranean), India and Indian religions, the United States, classical literature and the Renaissance, medicine in aspects having general interest, economics, anthropology, archaeology, travel, social welfare, and philosophy. He should know that the *Subject Index of works added to the Library of the British Museum since 1880* will range much farther and deeper. He should be aware that subject-indexes rarely cite "minor literature," that is to say, dissertations, German Programme, journal articles, treatises in academy publications, or privately printed books, however important they may be. He may be seeking information about Miracles of the Virgin Mary. From subject-indexes he will not obtain references to certain indispensable journal articles, fundamental monographs in the *Sitzungsberichte* of the Vienna academy, or G. F. Warner's invaluable edition for the Roxburghe Club of Jean Mielot, *Miracles de Nostre Dame*—all of which are essential for any serious study.[23]

[23] For references to these works see the bibliography in Evelyn Faye Wilson, *The "Stella Maris" of John of Garland* (Cambridge, Mass., 1946), pp. v–ix. The indispensable journal articles are not cited there. They are Albert Poncelet, "Index miraculorum B. V. Mariae quae latine sunt conscriptae," *Analecta Bollandiana*, XXI (1902), 241–360 and Sister Mary Vincentine Gripkey, "Mary Legends in Italian manuscripts in the major libraries of Italy," *Mediaeval studies*, XIV (1952), 9–47, XV (1953), 14–46.

The nature of a subject-index is obvious enough, but it does not appear that makers of them have considered carefully their function in scholarly economy. Nor have authors of guides to reference books. In a good *Introduction to reference books,* Chapter 10, "Bibliographies of older British books," [24] Arthur D. Roberts lists Robert Watt, *Bibliotheca britannica;* S. A. Allibone, *A critical dictionary of English literature* (1859–1891), and W. T. Lowndes, *Bibliographer's manual of English literature* (1857–1864) together and comments on the first:

In the subject index the headings are arranged alphabetically and, under each heading, works are arranged chronologically. Some works published abroad are also included in it, but they are not sufficiently numerous for us to regard *Watt* as a bibliography which is truly international in scope.

The criticisms are not altogether unfair, although the representation of foreign titles is more generous than one might guess. See Chemistry, Dress, Philosophy, Physic (i.e., Medicine). Yet this treatment of more than fifteen hundred closely printed quarto pages indexing thousands of titles is harsh. Published between 1819 and 1824, Watt's *Bibliotheca britannica* cannot offer information useful to a reader looking for recent writings about any subject. His book can only serve historical purposes. It will tell us more or less completely what was written about the Gothic language, Paris, or Taxation before 1819 and can do no more. An ordinary reader will call for recent books that Watt could not have named; he will not need to open the *Bibliotheca britannica.* Had makers of subject-indexes clearly perceived the situation, their books would have been generous with references to predecessors (these are almost always lacking), to encyclopedias (which are very

[24] 3d ed., London, [1956]). For the passage quoted see p. 130.

rarely cited, if at all, in subject-indexes made after the sixteenth century), and to a variety of other bibliographical tools.

Let those who would contribute to subject bibliography consider carefully before beginning their task just what information their readers want. We need not linger over modern subject-indexes for the sciences. Compilers of such works are fully aware that their readers want only the most recent information. The situation is different in historical and literary historical studies, where the reader will want a wider range of references. Is it justifiable for the maker of a general subject-index to reject as a matter of principle German dissertations, which often have as their chief merit a carefully made bibliography of a very small field, or journal articles, which are equally specialized contributions by one who has devoted serious efforts to a small subject? It is a counsel of perfection to call attention to such imperfections as these in the bibliographical record. No bibliographer can hope to remedy them. But, somewhere and somehow, he should make his reader realize that the record is likely to be deficient for the years before 1750, for publications in certain countries, and for publications of certain kinds. Neither the maker of a subject-index nor the writer of general guides to bibliography makes these imperfections clear, forces his reader to consider their possible significance for a particular task, and aids him to find and use means to cure them.

We shall probably not see another general subject-index to set beside those we have surveyed. While I write this, I would not be surprised to learn its author is already hard at work. W. P. Courtney essayed the task only sixty years ago and produced a book often cited by bibliographers. In the last ten years Werner Schuder and Gert A. Zischka endeavored, with certain limitations, to compile general subject-indexes. We need no more such works or, to speak more precisely, we need no more that deal with writings published since 1750, for there are many ways to get at them. Only a rare scholar will call for a reference work to fill the great gaps in our knowledge of the subject matter of older books. Most scholars will prefer to contend as best they can with the difficulties of assembling materials for their studies, whether they be the history of astronomy, medicine, music, or political economy. They will not usually be tempted to undertake a huge and difficult task intended to aid scholars in every field of study.

Anyone who undertakes the terrifying task of a general subject-index will do well to consider carefully the merits and demerits of earlier works of this kind before making a start. He should see clearly what place his book will fill. He might, for example, see that no one has made a "retrospective" subject-index and might therefore choose to re-edit and supplement the volumes for philosophy in Lipenius, *Bibliotheca realis.* In such a task he would not be duplicating the relatively adequate account of scholarship that we already have. He would not need to revise the volumes for theology, law, and medicine. He would have at his disposal the many large bibliographies of incunabula made during the last century and a half. Lipenius and the other older subject-indexes as well as the modern ones deal only superficially with books printed before 1500. He could use the excellent lists of English books printed before 1700 and the similar lists of books in foreign languages issued by the British Museum. He would be aware that books in certain languages are incompletely surveyed and would give special attention to them. With the use of rather few reference works he could produce a subject-index of unique usefulness.

If he is a still braver man, he might choose a convenient

large subject-index as a basis and cite briefly references under pertinent headings to other subject-indexes described in this study: Draud, Bolduanus, and Lipenius among those published before 1700; Watt, the *Nouveau manuel*, Brunet, Courtney, Peddie, and the subject-indexes of the London Library, the British Museum, and the Library of Congress; and the subject-indexes to the Danish and Portuguese and the Jesuit biobibliographical dictionaries. A blanket reference in the preface to these works will not be sufficient. They should be cited precisely with indications of the number of titles named by each one. When he has learned what subjects have been inadequately dealt with by bibliographers, he may venture to fill gaps. In a few years he will have produced an indispensable reference work—a subject-index to subject-indexes.

If he is an even braver man than those who might undertake the preceding tasks, let him attempt a selective compilation of the subject-catalogues of such great libraries as the New York Public Library, the Boston Public Library, Harvard University Library, and the Library of Congress in this country; the British Museum, the Bibliothèque nationale, and other judiciously chosen libraries. He will do well to exclude fields in which large subject-indexes are already available. When we remember what Robert Watt, C. T. Hagberg Wright, and Theodore Besterman have accomplished, we can expect him to finish his task in one lifetime. I fear that much of his work will duplicate what a conscientious specialist might easily gather for his own inquiry.

Since I have written with enthusiasm about subject-indexes, a warning about technical difficulties in using them, and specially the older examples, is in order. They will often disappoint a modern reader. Men with inadequate training and scanty resources were often tempted to make them. Those who were fully aware of the difficulties of the task have generally avoided it. The typographical arrangement is likely to be troublesome, and such necessary aids as tables of contents and indexes of names or subjects are often lacking. Cross-references will usually be scanty. Variation in terminology often make it hard to find the desired references. Philosophy, mathematics, and other disciplines include subjects that we now look for under other headings. Difficulties in bibliographical technique must be contended with: authors may be cited according to their Christian names, their names may appear in Latin translations (Lecoq may be cited as Gallus), titles may be quoted in translation, may be abbreviated, or may be entirely lacking, and the dates and places of publication may be lacking. Such variations from modern bibliographical style will annoy a reader today, but they are not defects that men of former centuries would necessarily have condemned. These men would have been more likely to note a failure to mention formats (folio, quarto, octavo) because this information was helpful in finding a book. Finally, the compilers have at all times relied too often on titles and secondary sources, citing books that they have not seen.

The approach to subject matter is often difficult and confusing, and our guides speak many tongues. Virgil was not thinking of subject-indexes when he wrote "Varium et mutabile semper" (*Aen.* 4. 569), but we can apply his words to Gesner's *Pandectae* of 1548 and Zischka's *Index* of 1959 and all the subject-indexes that lie between them.

Ave atque vale. After having had this study on my desk for a dozen years, I lay it aside with many different emotions. There is a feeling of relief at having finished a long and trying task. There are memories of kindnesses extended to me in my own university library in Berkeley and, looking eastward from it, in the Newberry Library and beyond it in the Royal Libraries in Copenhagen and Stockholm, the university libraries in Lund, Göttingen, and Tübingen, or the Biblioteca Angelica and the Bibliothèque Nationale. The list is long and others crowd my mind while I try to be brief. Librarians have warm hearts for strangers in search of obscure and little-used books. Without the help of the John Simon Guggenheim Memorial Foundation I could scarcely have visited so many libraries and found so many helpers. There is a bibliographer's pleasure in assembling information that may prove to be useful, a bibliophile's pleasure in finding rare books, and a scholar's pleasure in perceiving connections and developments and in making fresh evaluations and interpretations. Thomas Frognall Dibdin called bibliography a "hortus siccus," but I have found it a garden of an altogether different sort. I hope to have communicated something of all this to my reader.

BOOKS CITED BY AUTHORS' NAMES OR SHORT TITLES

Besterman, Theodore. The beginnings of systematic bibliography. 2d rev. ed., London, [1936]. Cited as Besterman, Beginnings.

———. A world bibliography of bibliographies. 3d and final ed., 4 vols., Geneva, [1955–1956]. Cited as Besterman, WBB or WBB according to columns. A fourth edition is now appearing.

Blum, Rudolf. "Vor- und Frühgeschichte der nationalen

Allgemeinbibliographie," Archiv für Geschichte des Buchwesens, II (1959), 233–303.

Brunet, Gustave. Dictionnaire de bibliologie catholique. Encyclopédie théologique, ed. Abbé Migne. 3d series, XLII. Paris, 1860. Cited as Brunet, Dictionnaire.

Brunet, Jacques-Charles. Manuel du libraire et de l'amateur de livres. 5th ed., 5 vols.; Paris, 1860–1865. Supplément by Paul Deschamps and Gustave Brunet, 2 vols., Paris, 1878, 1880. Cited as Brunet, Manuel; Deschamps and Brunet, Supplément.

Ebert, Friedrich Adolf. Allgemeines bibliographisches Lexikon. 2 vols., Leipzig, 1821, 1830. Cited as Ebert, Lexikon.

Kennedy, A. G. and D. B. Sands. A concise bibliography for students of English. 4th ed., Stanford, Cal. [1960].

Malclès, Louise-Noëlle. Les sources du travail bibliographique. 3 vols. (vol. II in 2 parts), Geneva, 1950–1958.

Morhof, D. G. Polyhistor litterarius, philosophicus et practicus, ed. J. A. Fabricius, 4th ed., 2 vols., Libeck, 1747. Cited according to volume, book, chapter, and section and also according to volume and page.

Ottino, Giuseppe and Giuseppe Fumagalli. Bibliotheca bibliographica italica. Graz, 1957 (a photographic reprint, with the supplements, of the first ed., Rome, 1889 ff.).

Petzholdt, Julius. Bibliotheca bibliographica. Leipzig, 1866.

Pollard, A. W. and G. R. Redgrave. A short-title catalogue of books printed in England . . . 1475–1640. London, 1926. Cited as STC.

Schneider, Georg. Handbuch der Bibliographie. 4th ed., Leipzig, 1930.

Saxius, Christophorus. Onomasticon litterarium. 2d ed.,
8 vols. Bonn, 1775–1803. Cited as Saxe.

STC. See Pollard and Redgrave.

Struve, B. G. Introductio in notitiam rei litterariae . . .
6th ed. by J. C. Fischer. Frankfurt a. M., 1754. Cited as
Struve-Fischer.

———. Bibliotheca historiae litterariae selecta, olim titulo
Introductionis in notitiam rei litterariae . . . , ed. J. F.
Jugler. 4 vols., Jena, 1754–1782. Cited as Struve-Jugler.

Taylor, Archer. Book-catalogues: their varieties and uses.
Chicago, 1957.

WBB. See Besterman.

Wing, Donald. Short-title catalogue of books printed in
England . . . 1641–1700. 3 vols., New York, 1945–1951.

Index I. Compilers of Subject-Indexes and Kindred Works[1]

[1] Subject-indexes of both general and limited scope are listed here according to their titles or the names of the compilers. So also are lost works and works never completed. Incidental comparisons and allusions are not indexed.

Index II. Typical Materials Cited in Subject-Indexes [1]

[1] Some headings cited in alphabetical groups as examples of methods in subject-indexes are not indexed here; see pp. 77, 117, 170, and 177.